BIAN 2nd edition - A framework for the financial

Other publications by Van Haren Publishing

Van Haren Publishing (VHP) specializes in titles on Best Practices, methods and standards within four domains:
- IT and IT Management
- Architecture (Enterprise and IT)
- Business Management and
- Project Management

Van Haren Publishing is also publishing on behalf of leading organizations and companies: ASLBiSL Foundation, BRMI, CA, Centre Henri Tudor, CATS CM, Gaming Works, IACCM, IAOP, IFDC, Innovation Value Institute, IPMA-NL, ITSqc, NAF, KNVI, PMI-NL, PON, The Open Group, The SOX Institute.

Topics are (per domain):

IT and IT Management	Enterprise Architecture	Business Management
ABC of ICT	ArchiMate®	BABOK® Guide
ASL®	GEA®	BiSL® and BiSL® Next
CMMI®	Novius Architectuur	BRMBOK™
COBIT®	Methode	BTF
e-CF	TOGAF®	CATS CM®
ISO/IEC 20000		DID®
ISO/IEC 27001/27002	**Project Management**	EFQM
ISPL	A4-Projectmanagement	eSCM
IT4IT®	DSDM/Atern	IACCM
IT-CMF™	ICB / NCB	ISA-95
IT Service CMM	ISO 21500	ISO 9000/9001
ITIL®	MINCE®	OPBOK
MOF	M_o_R®	SixSigma
MSF	MSP®	SOX
SABSA	P3O®	SqEME®
SAF	PMBOK® Guide	
SIAM™	Praxis®	
TRIM	PRINCE2®	
VeriSM™		

For the latest information on VHP publications, visit our website: www.vanharen.net.

BIAN 2nd Edition

A framework for the financial services industry

Colophon

Title:	BIAN 2nd Edition – A framework for the financial services industry
Author:	A publication of the BIAN Association
Contributing authors:	Martine Alaerts, Patrick Derde, Laleh Rafati, Guy Rackham
Reviewers:	Rajiv Dhir, Associate, Mundo Cognito Ltd
	David Gilmour, Associate, Mundo Cognito Ltd
	Cecil Jones ABD, CCP, PMP, MBA, Lean IT Professional, Vice President, JP Morgan Chase
	Wang Meng, Architect, Shanghai Pudong Development Bank
	Piyush Mittal, Client Partner, Global Banking and Financial Services, IBM
	Gerard Peters, Enterprise Architect Director, Financial Services Global BU, Capgemini
	Hans Tesselaar, Executive Director, Banking Industry Architecture Network
	René De Vleeschauwer, Partner, Envizion
	Roel de Vries, consultant, De Vries Consulting (chapter 2)
Text editor:	Steve Newton, Galatea
Publisher:	Van Haren Publishing, 's-Hertogenbosch, www.vanharen.net
Lay-out and DTP:	Coco Bookmedia, Amersfoort – NL
ISBN Hard copy:	978 94 018 0768 5
ISBN eBook:	978 94 018 0769 2
ISBN ePub:	978 94 018 0770 8
Edition:	Second edition, first impression, July 2021
Copyright:	© BIAN Association and Van Haren Publishing, 2021

Trademarks:
ArchiMate is a trademark of The Open Group.
FIBO as ontology is a joint effort of the EDM council and the Object Management Group.
IFX is a trademark of the Interative Financial eXchange (IFX) Forum.
ISO20022 is a trademark of the International Organization for Standardization.
SWAGGER API is a trademark of Smartbear Software Inc.
TOGAF is a trademark of The Open Group.

This document is provided "as is", and the BIAN Association and its members make no representations or warranties, expressed or implied, including but not limited to, warranties or merchantability, fitness for a particular purpose, non-infringement, or title; that the contents of this document are suitable for any purpose; or that the implementation of such contents will not infringe any patents, copyrights or other rights.

Neither the BIAN Association nor its members will be liable for any direct, indirect or special, incidental or consequential damages arising out of, or relating to, any use or distribution of this document unless such damages are caused by wilful misconduct or gross negligence. The foregoing disclaimer and limitation on liability do not apply to, invalidate, or limit representations and warranties made by the members to the BIAN Association and other members in certain written policies of the BIAN Association.

Foreword by the chairman of the BIAN Board

Why this book?

It's been over 10 years now since some influential players in the financial services industry joined forces to stop the ever-growing cost for IT integration. The Banking Industry Architecture Network was born.

So, after 10 years of hard work by all members in our community, we bundled all of the knowledge and insights into the first BIAN 2019 edition of this book. As BIAN is continuously evolving and improving, so the BIAN book is also evolving and improving. Hence this second edition.

There has never been a more exciting time to be part of the financial services industry. Whether you're a traditional player, a FinTech enterprise or a tech enabler, emerging technology and game-changing regulation is driving unique opportunities in the sector. Most banks embrace these new challenges by collaborating with rapidly emerging FinTechs, exploring the boundaries of their technological environments. It also gives the banks a unique opportunity to migrate away from their existing, and sometimes very outdated core systems, and move into a fully digital new world supported by industry standards.

This book covers all aspects of architecture for the financial services industry. It should support all those involved to help their organizations to enter a truly digital world.

Besides our original service-oriented view, the authors have also included our latest insights on enterprise architecture and provided you with guidance in the fast-evolving API arena.

I hope you will find what you need to perform your architecture role at its peak.

Enjoy reading!

Steve Van Wyk
Global Chief Information Officer at HSBC

Introduction by the Executive Director of BIAN

The Banking Industry Architecture Network (BIAN)

The Financial Services Industry Architecture Network (BIAN) is a global not-for-profit association of banks, solution providers, consultancies, integrators and academic partners with the shared aim of defining a semantic standard for the financial services industry covering almost all of the well know architectural layers[1].

Who is this book intended for?

This book is intended for those enterprise, business and solution architects in the financial services industry (FSI) who are interested in applying the BIAN industry standards in their organization. The authors of the book expect the readers to have knowledge of business and/or ICT[2] architectural principles and methodologies.

For those architects and organizations familiar with the TOGAF framework, we have added a chapter describing how one can apply the BIAN standards with this development framework.

How to use this book?

This book will provide you with an in-depth knowledge to understand the full construct of BIAN artifacts, how to apply them and how you can contribute to help the standards fulfill your organization's needs. We will start with a short introduction of the BIAN organization, its goals, the deliverables and the future state.

Due to the constant development and evaluation of the BIAN models, additions to this publication will be publicly available at the BIAN homepage (www.bian.org).

---
1 See Appendix A2.1 "Architecture layers and aspects".
2 Information and communication technology.

The Banking Industry Architecture Network

The Banking Industry Architecture Network (BIAN) was formed in 2008 by a group of banks and solution providers with the shared aim of solving the integration issues by defining a semantic service operation standard for the financial services industry. At a later stage other standard bodies joined, as did some academic partners. BIAN's expectation is that a standard definition of business functions, service interactions and Business Objects that describe the general construct of any bank, will be a significant benefit to the industry. When compared to a proliferation of proprietary designs, such an industry standard provides the following main benefits:
- It enables the more efficient and effective development and integration of software solutions for banks;
- It will significantly lower the overall integration costs;
- It improves the operational efficiency within and between banks, and provides the opportunity for greater solution and capability re-use within and among banks;
- It supports the current need for more industry integration and collaboration by the usage of open and standardized APIs;
- It supports the adoption of more flexible business service sourcing models and enhances the evolution and adoption of shared third-party business services both on-premise and in the cloud;
- It supports FinTechs and RegTechs to gain an easy insight in the complex FSI structure.

The BIAN Financial Industry Reference Architecture's development is iterative, relying on the active contribution of industry participants to build consensus and encourage adoption. BIAN coordinates the evolution of the BIAN Financial Industry Reference Architecture on behalf of its membership with regular version releases to the industry, and seeks feedback to help continually expand and refine its content.

The Banking Industry Architecture Network Service Domain Landscape

BIAN Service Definition Working Groups govern Service Domains[3]. Each Service Definition Working Group has an associated area of business expertise. The scope covered by individual Working Groups is defined in their charter so that collectively, Working Groups cover the whole landscape with no overlaps between them. The governance for Service Domains within an area of business expertise is assigned to a Working Group. The Working Group is then responsible for the initial specification and any subsequent updates to its assigned collection of Service Domains. This implies the content creation is driven by the BIAN members using their experts' expertise.

---

3 The core building block for the definition of business functions, service interactions and Business Objects that describe the general construct of any bank.

The Banking Industry Architecture Network and Open APIs
In 2018 BIAN launched their Open API Sandbox environment with a continuously increasing number of API descriptions. This open-for-all environment (www.bian.org/deliverables/bian-portal) is true open source, encouraging the industry to enhance the content provided by BIAN so it becomes easier to adopt. The BIAN API definitions are 1:1 aligned with all underlying models and we are capable today of generating the Swagger definitions and the microservices code directly out of our repository to ensure a world-class consistency.

We try, as far as possible, to align with the ISO 20022 definitions in order to increase the overall usability.

Just recently we enhanced the portal with new features and content so it is a real source of information for all who undertaking an 'Open Banking' journey.

The Banking Industry Architecture Network and Open Data

Driven by the growing importance of data as the lifeblood of effective decision-making, BIAN started developing the BIAN Information Architecture or "BIAN BOM", (which stands for the BIAN Business Object Model).

The objective is to develop a standard Open Financial Services Conceptual Data Model. Where possible, BIAN aligns with existing standards such as ISO 20022 and FIBO.

BIAN applies a specific methodology to create Service Domain Business Object Model diagrams. All the identified Business Objects and the relationships between each other are consistent within and between the Service Domain Landscape.

Hans Tesselaar
Executive Director
Banking Industry Architecture Network

About this second edition

The content of this second edition is a fully revised version of the first edition of BIAN, that was published in 2019 (BIAN Edition 2019).

The theory and principles of the BIAN Framework and its application in practice, are now treated in two separate parts of the book.

The most recent additions to the BIAN standards are the Semantic API descriptions and the Business Object Model (BOM). These are treated in more detail. The application of the BIAN Framework in different contexts is treated more extensively and has been illustrated with lots of (semi-)real-life examples.

Following topics have been added: the newly developed "BIAN adoption journey" and the Business Capability Model.

Contents

FOREWORD BY THE CHAIRMAN OF THE BIAN BOARD.............................V

INTRODUCTION BY THE EXECUTIVE DIRECTOR OF BIAN VII

ABOUT THIS SECOND EDITION...XI

PART I
INTRODUCING BIAN AND ITS REFERENCE ARCHITECTURE FOR THE FINANCIAL INDUSTRY   1

1 INTRODUCING BIAN, THE ORGANIZATION AND ITS REFERENCE ARCHITECTURE FOR THE FINANCIAL INDUSTRY....................3

    1.1   The Banking Industry Architecture Network, mission and vision 3
           1.1.1   The Banking Industry Architecture Network..................... 4
           1.1.2   BIAN: vision, mission and Service Landscape 4
           1.1.3   BIAN's Reference Architecture for the Financial Industry 5
    1.2   Principles of The Reference Architecture for the Financial Service Industry.. 6
           1.2.1   Challenges for the financial industry 6
           1.2.2   Agile… the silver bullet?..................................... 8
           1.2.3   BIAN and agile architecture principles 9
           1.2.4   BIAN is changing enterprise architecture thinking 14
    1.3   Positioning the BIAN standard 17
    1.4   BIAN, the organization 19
           1.4.1   How the BIAN Architecture evolves 19
           1.4.2   The BIAN Framework, a toolbox 21

	1.4.3	BIAN Open Digital Repository	23
	1.4.4	BIAN certification	24
	1.4.5	BIAN adoption journey	25
1.5	Test yourself questions		26

2 EXPLAINING THE BIAN ARCHITECTURE 29

2.1	Notation of the BIAN Architecture Model		30
2.2	The BIAN Metamodel		31
	2.2.1	Role of the BIAN Metamodel	31
	2.2.2	Overview of the BIAN Metamodel	32
2.3	The Service Landscape		36
	2.3.1	Business Area level	39
	2.3.2	Business Domain level	39
	2.3.3	Service Domain level	40
	2.3.4	Service Landscape diagram	40
2.4	BIAN Service Domain		40
	2.4.1	Functional Pattern	41
	2.4.2	Generic Artifact	41
	2.4.3	Asset Type	44
	2.4.4	Service Domain representations	45
2.5	BIAN Control Record and Service Domain Information Profile		46
	2.5.1	Control Record	47
	2.5.2	Behavior Qualifier	48
	2.5.3	Behavior Qualifier Type	49
	2.5.4	Service Domain Control Record Diagram	51
2.6	BIAN Business Object Model		52
	2.6.1	Business Object versus Business Concept	53
	2.6.2	BOM content pattern	55
	2.6.3	BOM structure pattern	56
	2.6.4	The Service Domain BOM Diagram	59
	2.6.5	BOM abstraction levels	59
	2.6.6	BOM - ISO 20022 mapping	59
2.7	BIAN Service Operation and Semantic API		61
	2.7.1	Nature of the Service Operation: Action Term	62
	2.7.2	Subject of the Service Operation	64
	2.7.3	Semantic API	65
	2.7.4	Swagger File	68
2.8	The Service Domain Overview Diagram		68

	2.9	BIAN Business Scenarios and Wireframes 70
		2.9.1 Business Scenario 70
		2.9.2 Wireframe 72
		2.9.3 Service Connection 72
	2.10	BIAN Business Capability 73
	2.11	Test yourself questions 76

PART II
APPLYING BIAN   79

3 INTRODUCTION TO PART II, APPLYING BIAN 81

4 WHAT BIAN CAN DO: GENERAL ABILITIES 85

- 4.1 BIAN as Frame of Reference 85
  - 4.1.1 Common vocabulary 87
  - 4.1.2 Common Frame of Reference 87
  - 4.1.3 Adding features 88
  - 4.1.4 Organizing and exploiting documentation 89
  - 4.1.5 Building blocks for a reference architecture 90
- 4.2 Tailoring BIAN 91
  - 4.2.1 Detailing specifications and models 91
  - 4.2.2 An organization-specific Frame of Reference 92
- 4.3 BIAN can be introduced gradually 95
- 4.4 Test yourself questions 98

5 BIAN FOR A HOLISTIC ENTERPRISE VIEW 99

- 5.1 Defining and architecting Business Capabilities 102
  - 5.1.1 Business Capabilities for strategy 102
  - 5.1.2 Service Domains for architecture 103
- 5.2 Assembling an enterprise blueprint 105
- 5.3 Enterprise blueprint as/or a Frame of Reference 108
  - 5.3.1 Defining and documenting strategy direction and requirements .. 109
  - 5.3.2 Charting and evaluating the "operations" landscape down the stack 110
  - 5.3.3 A uniform and stable base for performance management 112
  - 5.3.4 BIAN for investment and change portfolio management 113
- 5.4 Testimonial 118
- 5.5 Test yourself questions 119

6 BIAN FOR THE BUSINESS LAYER ... 121

- 6.1 BIAN for business architecture ... 122
  - 6.1.1 A Frame of Reference for the business landscape ... 122
  - 6.1.2 Elaborating the organogram ... 122
  - 6.1.3 Charting and assessing the business landscape ... 122
  - 6.1.4 Governing the business architecture ... 125
  - 6.1.5 Building blocks and principles for a reference business architecture ... 129
- 6.2 BIAN for business investment and change portfolio ... 131
  - 6.2.1 Supporting mergers and acquisitions ... 131
  - 6.2.2 Business change portfolio ... 132
- 6.3 BIAN for business design ... 133
  - 6.3.1 BIAN for business process management ... 133
  - 6.3.2 BIAN for business requirements ... 135
- 6.4 Test yourself Questions ... 139

7 BIAN FOR THE APPLICATION LAYER ... 141

- 7.1 BIAN for application architecture ... 142
  - 7.1.1 A Frame of Reference for the application landscape ... 143
  - 7.1.2 Charting and assessing the application landscape's coverage ... 143
  - 7.1.3 Utilities vs Service Domains ... 146
  - 7.1.4 Governing the application architecture ... 146
  - 7.1.5 Building blocks and principles for a reference application architecture ... 148
  - 7.1.6 Assessing and improving the application landscape ... 151
- 7.2 Linking the technology landscape to Service Domains ... 157
- 7.3 BIAN for application investment and change portfolio ... 158
- 7.4 BIAN for application systems ... 159
  - 7.4.1 End-to-end solution architecture ... 159
  - 7.4.2 Creating "the system" ... 161
- 7.5 BIAN and application architecture styles ... 165
- 7.6 Test yourself questions ... 168

8 BIAN FOR INFORMATION AND DATA ... 171

- 8.1 Tailoring the BIAN BOM ... 173
- 8.2 The BIAN BOM for information and data architecture ... 175
  - 8.2.1 Frame of Reference for the information and data landscape ... 175
  - 8.2.2 Evaluating and improving the data landscape ... 176
  - 8.2.3 In aid of the BI environment ... 179
  - 8.2.4 BOM for information classification ... 179
  - 8.2.5 Linking to data technology ... 180

8.3	Business cases for the information and data investment and change portfolio	180
8.4	BIAN for information and data on system level	180
8.5	Test yourself questions	182

9 BIAN FOR INTEROPERABILITY ... 183

9.1	BIAN as organizing Frame of Reference for the application service portfolio	184
	9.1.1 The Service Domain / Service Operation Frame of Reference	184
	9.1.2 Organizing the application service catalog	185
9.2	BIAN supporting application service landscape management	187
	9.2.1 Steering the use of application services	187
	9.2.2 Evaluating and improving the application service landscape	188
	9.2.3 Changing and migrating the application (service) landscape	190
9.3	BIAN for future-proof APIs	192
	9.3.1 Delimit service centers and services	193
	9.3.2 Elaborate API specifications	194
9.4	Testimonial	197
9.5	Test yourself questions	198

PART III
BIAN AND OTHER STANDARDS   199

10 BIAN AND TOGAF ... 201

10.1	A short introduction to TOGAF	201
10.2	BIAN and the ADM phases	206
	10.2.1 Preliminary phase	206
	10.2.2 Phase A: Architecture vision	207
	10.2.3 Phase B: Business architecture	208
	10.2.4 Phase C: Information systems srchitecture	208
	10.2.5 Phase D: Technology architecture	209
	10.2.6 Phase E: Opportunities and solutions	209
	10.2.7 Phase F: Migration planning	210
	10.2.8 Phase G: Implementation governance	210
	10.2.9 Phase H: Architecture change management	210
	10.2.10 Requirements management	210
10.3	Test yourself questions	210

11 ALIGNMENT WITH OTHER STANDARD BODIES 213

    11.1   ISO 20022 213
    11.2   OMG & EDM Council 214
    11.3   The Business Architecture Guild® 214
    11.4   Test yourself questions 214

APPENDICES   215

APPENDIX 1:   BIAN ADOPTION JOURNEY 217

APPENDIX 2:   TERMINOLOGY AND CONCEPTS 223

    A2.1   Architecture layers and aspects 223
    A2.2   Zooming levels for architecture 225
    A2.3   Terms and abbreviations 226

APPENDIX 3   FEEDBACK TO THE TEST YOURSELF QUESTIONS 231

    Feedback Section 2.11 232
    Feedback Section 4.4 233
    Feedback Section 6.4 234
    Feedback Section 7.6 235
    Feedback Section 8.5 236
    Feedback Section 9.5 236
    Feedback Section 10.3 237
    Feedback Section 11.4 238

APPENDIX 4   LITERATURE AND SOURCES 239

INDEX 241

Figures

Figure 1-1	Darwin applies to the financial ecosystem too	8
Figure 1-2	Service orientation - layered view	11
Figure 1-3	A BIAN Service Domain is a component for an agile architecture	12
Figure 1-4	Comparing enterprise architecture and city planning	14
Figure 1-5	A well-designed city plan can support any journey	15
Figure 1-6	Migrating to a well architected application landscape	17
Figure 1-7	BIAN as "common language" between other standards and regulations	18
Figure 1-8	BIAN validation process	20
Figure 1-9	BIAN's toolbox to create an agile banking architecture	22
Figure 1-10	Landing page of the BIAN Digital Repository (version 9)	23
Figure 1-11	The BIAN adoption journey, overview	25
Figure 2-1	The role of the BIAN Metamodel	31
Figure 2-2	BIAN Metamodel, overview	32
Figure 2-3	BIAN Service Landscape, Matrix view	37
Figure 2-4	BIAN Service Landscape, Value Chain view	38
Figure 2-5	Three elements defining the structure of the BIAN Service Landscape	39
Figure 2-6	BIAN Metamodel, Service Landscape view	39
Figure 2-7	BIAN Metamodel, Service Domain view	41
Figure 2-8	Functional Pattern - Generic Artifact Mapping	44
Figure 2-9	The Current Account Service Domain, its Asset Type, Functional Pattern and Generic Artifact	45
Figure 2-10	BIAN Metamodel, Control Record Model view	47
Figure 2-11	"Party Reference Data Directory Entry" Control Record	48
Figure 2-12	Party Reference Data Directory Entry Control Record and its Behavior Qualifiers	49
Figure 2-13	Break down of a Control Record into Behavior Qualifiers and Sub-qualifiers	51
Figure 2-14	Party Reference Data Directory Control Record Diagram	52
Figure 2-15	Metamodel for the Control Record Diagram	52
Figure 2-16	BIAN Metamodel, Business Object view	54
Figure 2-17	BIAN BOM content pattern	55

Figure 2-18	Applying the BIAN BOM in payments.	56
Figure 2-19	BIAN BOM structure pattern	57
Figure 2-20	Payment Order BOM Diagram	58
Figure 2-21	Example of abstraction levels in the BIAN BOM	60
Figure 2-22	The scope of the ISO 20022 Business Model	60
Figure 2-23	BIAN Metamodel, Service Operation view	61
Figure 2-24	Action Terms per Functional Pattern	62
Figure 2-25	Current Account Service Operations work on different levels of the information profile.	65
Figure 2-26	Current Account Semantic API and its Endpoints	66
Figure 2-27	BIAN Semantic API Endpoint format	68
Figure 2-28	Service Domain Overview Diagram for Current Account	69
Figure 2-29	BIAN Metamodel, Business Scenario and Wireframe view	70
Figure 2-30	An example of a BIAN Business Scenario Diagram	71
Figure 2-31	An example of a BIAN Wireframe Diagram	72
Figure 2-32	An example of a BIAN Service Connection, related to its Service Operation	73
Figure 2-33	Customer Management Business Capability Decomposition view	75
Figure 2-34	BIAN Metamodel, Business Capability view	75
Figure 2-35	Business Capability Model, top level.	74
Figure 3-1	M5 Banking Group's "Group Synergy" strategy	83
Figure 4-1	BIAN as a common Frame of Reference	88
Figure 4-2	Using BIAN as Frame of Reference to find and compare candidate solutions.	90
Figure 4-3	M5 Banking Group's generalization of the loan product fulfilment Service Domains.	94
Figure 4-4	M5 Banking Group's very own Standing Order Service Domain is split off from the Current Account Service Domains.	95
Figure 4-5	The first components of Mfour Bank's "new" application platform (late 1970's) mapped on the BIAN Service Landscape	97
Figure 5-1	Different disciplines in search of a common language and Frame of Reference	100
Figure 5-2	The common Frame of Reference provided by BIAN, enables a holistic enterprise view	101
Figure 5-3	Business Capabilities are served by several Service Domains that can serve several Business Capabilities.	103
Figure 5-4	Service Domains are the linking pin between strategic business capabilities and the architecture that realizes them	104
Figure 5-5	Three steps in developing an enterprise blueprint	106
Figure 5-6	Assigning the responsibility for Service Domains in the ArchiMate language.	108
Figure 5-7	The "bank on a page" for a line of business is its view on the common Frame of Reference	109

Figure 5-8	Examples of performance measures	113
Figure 5-9	Using the enterprise blueprint as a common Frame of Reference for change management,	115
Figure 5-10	M5 Group's strategy: assessments lead to requirements, both attributed to Service Domains	116
Figure 5-11	Blueprint of M5 Banking Group's "Group Services" entity, with assigned responsibilities.	117
Figure 6-1	The responsibilities of an accounting department and a loan sales process clarified.	123
Figure 6-2	Business pain-points visualized on the "bank on a page" of a BIAN member	124
Figure 6-3	Maturity rating per Service Domain, represented on the "bank on a page" of a BIAN member	127
Figure 6-4	Strategic requirements per Service Domain presented as a heat map on the "bank on a page" of M5 Banking Group	128
Figure 6-5	Service Domains cooperate in patterns, enabling a secure, controlled delivery of financial services	130
Figure 6-6	Process steps expressed as Service Domains facilitate the selection of business partners	134
Figure 6-7	The requirements for Service Domains and for their interactions are specified	135
Figure 6-8	Business Scenarios are consolidated into a Wireframe, a holistic view on the requirements,	138
Figure 7-1	Mapping Service Domains on application components reveals the variety of business functionality they support – and identifies duplications	143
Figure 7-2	A potential Service Domain duplication issue is mitigated by the data integration architecture	145
Figure 7-3	The "bank on a page" of a BIAN member being used to communicate an aspect of the application architecture strategy to management	148
Figure 7-4	Conceptual reference architecture pattern for secure customer access	150
Figure 7-5	Mzero Bank's monolithic Loan application is decomposed step-by-step	156
Figure 7-6	Wireframe for the end-to-end embedding of a payment solution	160
Figure 7-7	Mapping of the "Reuse" candidates and a vendor offer ("Buy") on the Service Domains required for the new Group Payment application	163
Figure 7-8	Requirement coverage comparison of candidate Group Payment systems for one Service Domain	163
Figure 7-9	A software product, as a cluster of three Service Domains, internally remains "uncluttered"	165
Figure 8-1	Information realization view	176

Figure 8-2	Labelling of data stores with BOM Business Objects reveals problems.	178
Figure 8-3	Data Integration ensures the duplicated Party information remains consistent.	178
Figure 8-4	High level information model for the Payment Group Service of the M5 Banking Group	181
Figure 9-1	The Service Domain / Service Operation Frame of Reference facilitates the search in M5 Banking Group's application service catalog.	186
Figure 9-2	API coverage heatmap on the BIAN-Service Landscape,	189
Figure 9-3	Testimonial: delimiting and prioritizing the development of future-proof APIs	190
Figure 9-4	Business Scenarios provide business context and information content to the service exchanges	194
Figure 9-5	Mapping of Mfour Bank's party information services on BIAN's Semantic API Endpoints.	196
Figure 9-6	A bank's BIAN-based API development and governance toolbox.	196
Figure 10-1	The phases of the TOGAF ADM	202
Figure 10-2	TOGAF's "zooming" levels imply an iterative approach to elaborating architectures	204
Figure 10-3	The Enterprise Continuum according to TOGAF and the position of the BIAN Reference Architecture for the financial industry	204
Figure 10-4	The Enterprise Repository according to TOGAF	205
Figure 10-5	BIAN's contribution to the enterprise architecture toolbox	207
Figure A1-1	Stage 1 of a BIAN adoption roadmap: Evaluate BIAN	218
Figure A1-2	Stage 2 of a BIAN adoption roadmap: Build pilot case	219
Figure A1-3	Stage 3 of a BIAN adoption roadmap: Pilot BIAN	220
Figure A1-4	Stage 4 of a BIAN adoption roadmap: Adopt BIAN.	220
Figure A1-5	Stage 5 of a BIAN adoption roadmap: Evolve your Architecture Practice.	221
Figure A2-1	A bank consists of three different layers.	223
Figure A2-2	Viewpoints on a bank: Architecture layers and aspects.	224
Figure A2-3	Zooming levels: divide and conquer a wide scope and a great complexity	226

PART I

INTRODUCING BIAN AND ITS REFERENCE ARCHITECTURE FOR THE FINANCIAL INDUSTRY

What to expect

This part of the book aims to create an understanding of the BIAN Framework.
This entails two objectives:
Firstly, the reader should understand the philosophy upon which BIAN's Reference Architecture for the Financial Industry is based and the "constructs" (techniques and organization) used to create its elemental, mutually exclusive, collectively exhaustive building blocks.
Secondly, the reader will obtain an overview of what BIAN has to offer to facilitate the adoption of this Architecture. BIAN's framework is a "toolbox" that supports financial institutions in their journey towards an agile architecture. BIAN's Reference Architecture for the Financial Industry is the core of this framework.

Readers in a management position as well as business and application architects, need to understand the unique characteristics of the BIAN Reference Architecture and the toolbox supporting its adoption, that distinguish BIAN from other standards.

Business and application architects need a solid understanding of the principles that the Architecture is based on and of the type of "building blocks" that make up this Architecture.

1 Introducing BIAN, the organization and its Reference Architecture for the Financial Industry

This chapter introduces the BIAN organization and its Reference Architecture for the Financial Industry and how BIAN supports financial institutions in the adoption and application of its framework.

BIAN provides the financial industry with a "Reference Architecture" as a means to realize its mission and vision (Section 1.1).

To survive in these challenging times, where technology and regulations drive a drastic change in the financial ecosystem, banks need agile systems that can provide the required business agility. BIAN's Reference Architecture is based on agile principles and supports a financial institution in the elaboration of, and migration to, an architecture that provides that necessary agility (Section 1.2).

The characteristics of the BIAN Reference Architecture provide it with a unique position compared to other standards (Section 1.3). BIAN aligns with all relevant standards. It has the ambition to provide a "common language" between different banking standards and regulations.

The BIAN organization (Section 1.4) provides a framework consisting of its Reference Architecture as well as publications, training and a certification program that support individuals and organizations to adopt its Reference Architecture. This framework evolves and keeps in touch with the reality of the financial industry through co-creation by its members, coordinated by BIAN.

■ 1.1 THE BANKING INDUSTRY ARCHITECTURE NETWORK, MISSION AND VISION

The BIAN organization was created to support financial institutions in their journey to an agile banking architecture on both an enterprise and solution level.

BIAN, the "Banking Industry Architecture Network", offers a Banking Reference Architecture Framework that is an enabler to become an adaptive financial institution, conformant to the principles of an agile enterprise architecture.

1.1.1 The Banking Industry Architecture Network

The Banking Industry Architecture Network (BIAN) is a global, not-for profit association of banks, solution providers, consultancy companies, integrators and academic partners with the shared aim of defining a semantic standard for the banking industry covering almost all the well-known architectural layers.

The Banking Industry Architecture Network was formed in 2008 by a group of banks and solution providers with the shared aim of defining a semantic Service Operation standard for the financial services industry. At a later stage other standards bodies, like ISO and FDX joined, along with some academic partners.

The BIAN Association strives to enhance the flexibility and agility of financial services systems by improving the integration of these with an architecture that is based on services.

1.1.2 BIAN: vision, mission and Service Landscape

BIAN's **vision** and expectation is that a standard definition of business functions, service interactions and business objects that describe the general construct of any bank will be of significant benefit to the industry.

The central objectives for ICT in the banking industry are to provide flexibility, to lower the ICT and operational costs of the bank and to help banks mitigate the risks and seize the opportunities associated with technology innovation.

BIAN's **mission** is to provide the world with the best banking architecture framework and banking standard. BIAN provides a trusted roadmap for constant innovation.

The goal of the BIAN Association is to develop the most important content, concepts and methods in interoperability, supporting the aim of lower integration costs in the financial services industry and facilitating business innovation and agility by:
- Providing an architecture framework with all of the necessary elements, tools and methodologies for a sustainable operational model through the adoption of, and alignment with, available market standards;
- Focusing on the definition of semantic services and/or API-definitions to improve the semantic integration of the financial services landscapes;
- Enabling the financial services industry to develop and run a loosely coupled environment successfully;
- Gaining acceptance from the members of the BIAN Association and the industry of the way the requirements will be implemented by both financial institutions and

solution suppliers, resulting in the defined services becoming the de-facto-standard in the financial services industry.

1.1.3 BIAN's Reference Architecture for the Financial Industry

BIAN's Reference Architecture is a collection of architecture artifacts that makes up its industry standard. The main fundamental building block within the BIAN Reference Architecture is the "**Service Domain**".

The BIAN Service Domains define financial services-specific semantic services. The Service Domains are the cornerstone upon which to achieve agile flexibility.

BIAN's **Service Landscape** is the term used to refer to the collection of Service Domains that are defining the functional capacity building blocks within the banking industry.

The value of BIAN is the standardization of those functional services based on a well drafted architecture with elements carefully chosen from industry best practices.

It is the ambition of the BIAN Association to achieve a consensus on the service definition among leading banks and providers in the financial services industry, which in due time should lead to standardized services.

When compared to an increasing number of proprietary designs, a dedicated industry standard, like BIAN, provides the following main benefits:
- Created by industry experts from around the globe;
- Regular updates following the market developments and industry needs;
- It enables a more efficient and effective development and integration of software solutions within the bank and between banks;
- It significantly lowers the overall integration costs;
- It improves the operational efficiency within and between banks and provides the opportunity for greater solution and capability re-use within and among banks;
- It supports the current need for more industry integration and collaboration through the usage of (open) APIs;
- It supports the adoption of more flexible business service sourcing models and enhances the evolution and adoption of shared third-party business services;
- It supports FinTechs and RegTechs to gain an easy insight in the complex financial services industry structure.

Banks can use BIAN to define their bank-specific agile architecture, supporting the interoperability of information and information services between participants of the financial industry eco-system. BIAN can also be used to optimize the interoperability of information and information services within the organization.

1.2 PRINCIPLES OF THE REFERENCE ARCHITECTURE FOR THE FINANCIAL SERVICE INDUSTRY

The financial industry, with banks, real credit institutions, pension and property management companies, is one of the most digitalized industries in the world. Digitalization is evolving and changing fast and so is the financial ecosystem. Financial institutions are in need of support for agile digital transformation in an open finance ecosystem. It is BIAN's vision and mission to provide such support.

1.2.1 Challenges for the financial industry

Financial industry in movement
The industry as a whole is facing one of the most challenging evolutions in history. Change is happening faster than ever. Disruptive technology is changing the lives of consumers in small but extraordinary ways. Today, virtual assistants schedule appointments, while smartwatches monitor our sleep patterns and voice command technology turns off our house lights.

Banking needs to fully participate in this evolution. Advancements in technology have increased demand for accessible and convenient solutions that meet a consumer's banking needs. On top of that, the industry is aware of a new disruption that is brewing – one that will once again transform the industry over the coming years.

It is not only technology that is changing the scene. New regulations are changing the playing field dramatically. They force financial institutions to disclose financial information to Third Party Providers (TPPs), providing access to financial services to new players and facilitating the competition of FinTechs and RegTechs in the financial playing field. Regulations impose security requirements to protect person-related data. After the worldwide financial crisis in 2008, regulators are requesting comprehensive financial and risk reporting, including data lineage requirements.

Besides the drivers mentioned above the unforeseen disruption caused by COVID-19 extremely impacted the behavior of all parties involved in our industry. We are moving from "Cash" to "Cashless" and from "Face2Face" to "Virtual". This all sets additional demands on technology and therefore on Architecture.

Boosted by COVID-19, regulations, RegTechs and FinTechs, the interoperability of financial data and services via "Open Linked Data" and "Open Banking APIs" is rapidly becoming an indispensable requirement for creating innovative financial services. It facilitates all types of customer journeys, from buying bread to buying a house, from commuting to and from work to planning to travel for leisure or business. In every journey where financial and trusted services are needed and trust is required, banks are seeking to be the preferred partner.

To remain the preferred partner in this changing financial ecosystem, financial institutions need to be information-driven, having the right data, of the right quality, at the right time at the right place, in the possession of the right party. Information that comes from a trusted source of truth. Next Best Offer, context specific offers, risk profiles... based on data that is unique to the financial sector, help financial institutions make informed decisions and remain the trusted partner that helps customers make informed decisions.

Financial information requirements and financial services are changing at a very high speed. The financial ecosystem is continuously changing, at an ever-increasing pace. This requires an adaptive and agile banking business. Adaptability to new regulations, service requirements, new market players and stakeholders drives the speed and dynamics of the financial world.

The financial industry services and data must become more transparent, secure and open. The financial services need to be tailored and deeply integrated into consumer's lives, seamlessly, with information created on the spot by Artificial Intelligence Systems and offered at the right time at the right place to the right person.

Financial institutions partner with other ecosystem players, offering services that will extend beyond banking. The financial industry will provide services in a hyper networked service-oriented "Open API economy", where multiple ecosystem players participate in collaboratively fulfilling the financial needs of the customer.

In this changing ecosystem, financial institutions want to remain "trusted custodians of financial services and customer assets[4]".

Legacy complexity
Financial institutions were among the first to automate their businesses and are now among the most digitalized service providers. They have pervasive but often complex legacy ICT platforms, with lots of duplication of functionality and data. Monolithic systems, stovepipe systems, are connected through point-to-point connections with numerous interface adapters. These legacy systems are a barrier to reacting in a timely and cost-effective manner to market and ecosystem changes. Their complexity results in inflexible/unresponsive systems, inflated enhancement, increasing maintenance and operational costs, and an inability to rapidly leverage advanced solutions, technologies, approaches and business models.

To survive in an industry with high investments in digitalization and low margins, financial institutions are searching to lower the integration and interoperability costs, while being able to respond very quickly to change.

---
4   Which could expand to include digital identities.

1.2.2 Agile... the silver bullet?

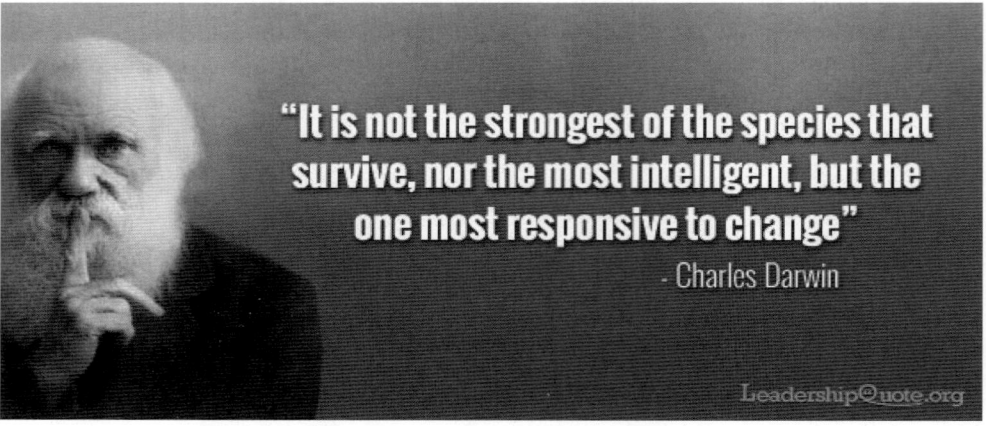

Figure 1-1 Darwin[5] applies to the financial ecosystem too

The traditional way of realizing big transformation projects, changing the "current state" through a big "waterfall" project to a new "future state", is no longer viable. The current state is constantly changing and the future state is a moving target. Big change programs are too slow in delivering outcomes. Continuous improvement, transformation and change capabilities at all levels of the organization are required.

Additionally, the traditional enterprise architecture approach that focuses on technical solution architecture is no longer sufficient to meet the needs of today's financial institutions. Today's enterprise architects are responsible for designing intelligence into the business and operating models, identifying ways to help their organization use data, analytics and artificial intelligence to plan, track and manage digital business investments.

Financial institutions are finding better and more rapid ways of developing software by co-creation. In-house development is combined with outsourced development and third-party software solutions.

BIAN offers a Reference Architecture for the Financial Industry that enables gradual transformation of legacy platforms, rapid response to changing demands and cooperation with partners.

BIAN offers an architecture that provides agility. However, agile is not equal to "doing Scrum".

---

5   The quote in this figure is often, but without real evidence, attributed to Charles Darwin.

> *"**Agility** is a **persistent behavior** or ability of an entity that exhibits **flexibility** to accommodate expected or unexpected **changes** rapidly, follows the **shortest time span**, and uses **economical, simple, and quality instruments** in a **dynamic environment**"*[6]

This high-level definition applies to at least three main areas of agility:
- **System agility**: being agile in the organization's operations (business and ICT operations);
- **Process agility**: being agile in the development and change processes;
- **Business agility**: having agility as a strategic focus, based on the financial institution's process and system agility.

In order to be adaptive in rapidly changing circumstances, financial institutions need an agile banking architecture on an enterprise level. BIAN supports financial institutions in system agility, through an agile enterprise architecture. Together with a bank's process agility, this enables the required business agility.

1.2.3 BIAN and agile architecture principles

BIAN's Reference Architecture for the Financial Industry is developed according to agile principles.

Separation of concerns
Complex systems can be unraveled by defining sets of responsibilities that are elemental and non-overlapping. The responsibility areas are layered[7] and capability[8] based. The capabilities are "components", concentrating functionality in specific places.

This ensures that the impact of changes remains as local as possible. Also, a limited number of people need to be involved in decisions about changes.

Loose coupling
The "components" identified by "separating concerns" are "loosely coupled" if they have a low number of dependency relations between them. Each component will fulfill its responsibilities by offering services, with minimal dependency on the services of other components. There is a high internal coherence of functionality and data, which facilitates analysis and understanding of the component as such.

Changes are kept within the component and propagation of the changes throughout the system is avoided.

---
6   Qumer & Henderson-Sellers, 2008.
7   Layering refers to the separation of strategy, business, application, data and technology responsibilities. Each of the layers takes care of its own goals and security.
8   An ability that an organization, person, or system possesses (TOGAF version 9.2).

Reusability
Components are "reusable" if they can be used in multiple situations and are independent of the status in an end-to-end process. Reusability is fostered if elements can easily be lifted out of their context and plugged in elsewhere. The design of the components is done with the objective of independency and reuse. This is a strategic choice. It requires the use of common standards for connections between components, such as a common vocabulary, common data, common service definitions and common documentation structures.

Encapsulation
A component is "encapsulated" if each component has its own internal data structure and process definitions to realize the offered services. The services of the components are made available to the environment by means of clearly defined interfaces which hide the internal complexity from the ease of use for the requester of the services.

Interoperability
Components exchange information and functionality services as if there are no boundaries between the components. An information system, a business function or other element, is connected to the rest of the architecture landscape by using clearly defined interfaces based on standards[9] and designed by a contract specifying the service level arrangements.

New or changed business processes can thus be assembled as an orchestration of such components.

Service orientation
Components deliver services to each other. Business functions offer and consume internal and/or external business services. In a digitalized world, business services are supported by applications which offer and consume internal and/or external application services (Figure 1-2)[10]. Direct access to the data is not allowed but needs to be requested through a service.

The advantage is that when someone needs information, there is no need for knowledge of the internal structure of the data and the internal process realizing the service. Changes to this internal structure can be hidden from the user of the service.

---

9   Examples of such standards are: for payments, the ISO 20022 standard; for financial product definitions, the ISO/TC 68; for accounting, IAS; for Party related information GDPR; for financial data access authorization, PSD2; for security, ISO 27001.
10 "Internal" services are exchanged within the same layer, e.g. A2A (application to application). "External" services support the "higher" layer – or, in the business layer's case, people (e.g. the customer).

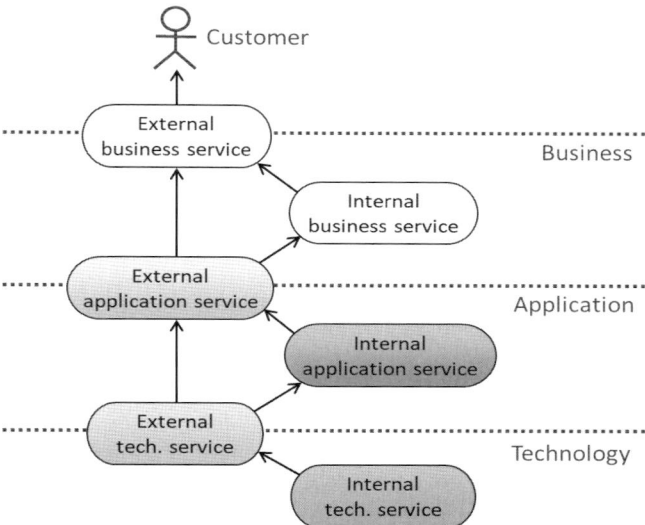

Figure 1-2 Service orientation - layered view

BIAN's Reference Architecture provides building blocks for an agile architecture

The BIAN Reference Architecture for the Financial Industry conforms to all of the agile principles described above. In this section, we provide an overview of the most important building blocks of the BIAN architecture and how and why they result in an agile architecture. Chapter 2 elaborates on the concepts and constructs of the BIAN architecture.

The Service Domain, the core concept of the BIAN architecture, conforms to all criteria of a building block for an agile architecture (Figure 1-3).

BIAN provides a Mutually Exclusive, Collectively Exhaustive (MECE) collection of Service Domains, elemental capability building blocks that together cover all banking functionality. To ensure an adequate separation of concerns BIAN uses a pattern that addresses the elemental nature and MECE nature of these building blocks.

Each Service Domain is "encapsulated" by a series of services (called Service Operations) that offer the Service Domains functionality and provide information to the other Service Domains and the environment (other organizations (B2B) or customers (B2C)). Any functionality can be realized as an orchestration of Service Domains exchanging Service Operations. Service Domains and Service Operations can be reused in an unlimited number of orchestrations.

Service Operations are defined on a fairly elemental level. They are described on a level of detail that provides clarity about their service offering (in the "Semantic API"). Service Operations are distinguished and detailed through the application of a pattern, ensuring their elemental and MECE character.

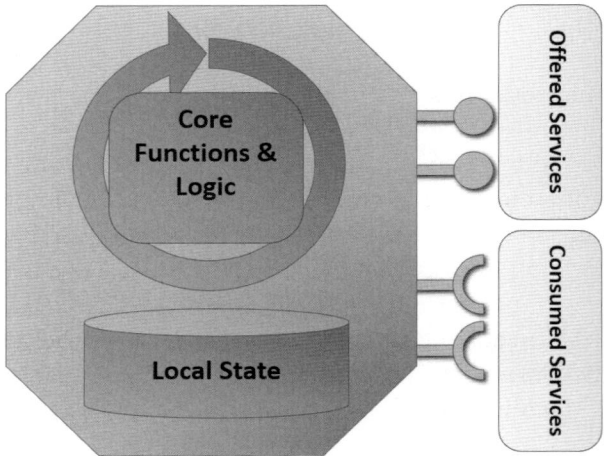

Figure 1-3 A BIAN Service Domain is a component for an agile architecture

Service Domains and Service Operations[11] -as all BIAN deliverables- are defined on a semantic level, i.e. they describe *what* the elemental *business* responsibility encompasses, not *how* and *with what* this is implemented. BIAN chooses to remain implementation and technology agnostic, as this ensures its applicability in any environment and stability over time.

The required "building blocks" of functionality and information are common between financial institutions and remain fairly stable over time. How they are combined is unique to every institution. The means through which they are realized, tends to change at an increasingly rapid pace.

(Groups of) Service Domains and their Service Operations can be used to orchestrate business processes and delimit application components and their application services. Application components that have been designed this way, will be replaceable by other components that have been designed according to the same delimitation. The impact[12] of the change will be limited to the area's close to the service interactions.

Each Service Domain is responsible for its own information, but this information is defined as a view on the "information building blocks" that BIAN defines. These "Business Objects" are modeled in the BIAN Business Object Model (BIAN BOM). The BIAN BOM is a consolidation of the information needs of all Service Domains. The application of a specific pattern-based approach ensures that the structure of the BIAN BOM, as well as the terminology and definitions, are independent of the context(s) in which the information is used. These patterns also ensure the consistency of the BIAN BOM.

---

11 BIAN uses the "REST" style to describe the detail of Service Operations. Nevertheless, this is meant to be a "semantic" definition. Even though Swagger Files can be generated, there is no prescription as to the technology that needs to be used to implement BIAN-based application services.
12 Functional impact that is, not technology impact.

BIAN's Reference Architecture enables simplicity
The final agile principle is "simplicity" – as opposed to "complexity". Using the BIAN Reference Architecture enables (a migration towards) simplicity.

Complexity between systems is created by many point-to-point connections between them. Complexity within a system is created by concentrating too much functionality in it[13]. When scoping the responsibility of components, the balance between controlling complexity inside systems and the need for interoperability between them is a challenge.

BIAN uses patterns to ensure an adequate delimitation of components, providing "elemental building blocks". A bank does not need to align to this elemental level when defining its systems, but the BIAN "building block box" will support the optimization of functionality concentration.

These BIAN-based systems will provide BIAN-based services that should be reusable in many contexts[14], providing an ordered business and application service landscape.

Before a change can be designed and implemented in business operations and/or application platforms, it is necessary to create insight into the complexity of the "as-is" situation. Changes in complex environments are very risky because of the numerous dependencies. Local changes may have many unforeseen side-effects, sometimes in unexpected places. Extensive testing is needed.

Business Capabilities and the structure of application systems are often not aligned with each other. For example, a monolithic system that needs to serve both a commercial front-office and an administrative back-office. As a consequence, they are subject to quite different flexibility requirements, such as rapidly – and even iteratively- creating new product offerings versus stability.

Complex systems also complicate the decision-making processes. Many people and/or organizational units have something to say about the system. This has a negative impact on the time to market of a change.

The BIAN Service Landscape and the BIAN BOM can be used as a "Frame of Reference" to identify and trace the functionality, services and information as they are implemented on both a business and application level. This provides insight in the "as-is" situation and enables a systematic, step by step unraveling towards the desired state. A desired state that will correspond to the "simplicity" principle. A desired state that enables (for example) a back-office, with a need for stability, and customer-facing channels, with a

---

13 It is known that 25% more functionality doubles the complexity of a system (analysis by Cynthia Rettig, Rettig C. 2007).
14 Abstraction being made of "non-functional" requirements, as described in Chapter 8.

need for flexibility, to evolve at their own pace and according to their own risk profile. A desired state that limits the impact of changes to where they are required.

1.2.4 BIAN is changing enterprise architecture thinking

The nature of the BIAN architecture helps financial institutions moving from process thinking to loosely coupled component and service-oriented thinking.

Enhancing the application landscape via a sound definition of business architecture is a well-established approach in the financial industry. It seems, however, that tremendous architecture efforts often failed to solve the problem of an over-complex, non-responsive application portfolio.

The BIAN Association was set up to address this issue by developing a common industry standard that defines functional partitions and Service Operations, and that can be used by any financial organization, resulting in an agile architecture that can produce the benefits enumerated in Sub-section 1.1.2.

The objective of the BIAN Association raises a key question: "Why should the BIAN model and approach be more successful than others in addressing application portfolio and interoperability complexity?".

At the core of the proposition of the BIAN Association is the adoption of a capability-oriented approach to architecting the business and ICT systems that support the financial organization. This approach is fundamentally different from the prevailing "process–centric" designs. To highlight this critical difference, a comparison can be made between the architectural disciplines applied to the highly tangible problem of designing the layout of a city, with the much less tangible design of a commercial enterprise such as a financial institution (Figure 1-4).

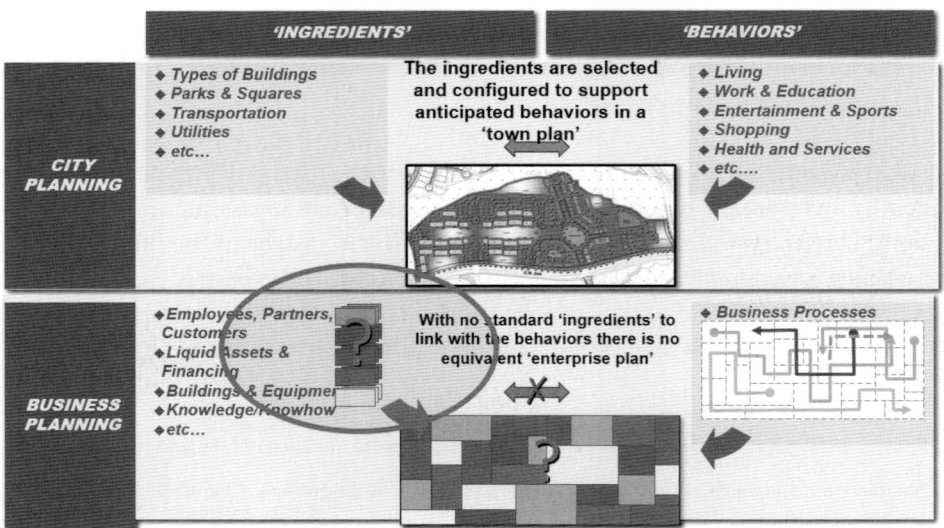

Figure 1-4 Comparing enterprise architecture and city planning

1 Introducing BIAN, the organization and its Reference Architecture for the Financial Industry

Any architecture and design combine two perspectives: the "ingredients" that are used and the "behaviors" that the architecture is intended to support.

The ingredients relate to static or persistent things that are deployed, whilst the behaviors refer to more dynamic patterns of desired responses to anticipated events or triggers. An architect develops an overall design based on an understanding of how the ingredients need to be configured to support the intended behaviors.

In the case of the town planner, this "architecture design" is a town plan. The "ingredients" seen in the town plan are, for example, the buildings of different purpose (such as homes, shops, theatres), open space (parks), communication infrastructure and utilities (such as water, electricity...) that need to be in place to support the anticipated behaviors of the town's inhabitants (such as living, shopping, working, recreation of different types...).

The "ingredients" for every town are the same, but the anticipated behavior of its in habitants can be different. Hence, the town plan will be different based on the local circumstances. The town plan is a static view of the actual (as-is) or desired (to-be) layout of the city. This town plan can support any desired journey through the city in an efficient and effective way (Figure 1-5).

The "utility and infrastructure ingredients" of a city provide standardized "connection interfaces". The to-be town plan and these standards enable an architect designing a new building to profit from the available infrastructure and utilities, while bringing the actual town plan one step closer to the desired state.

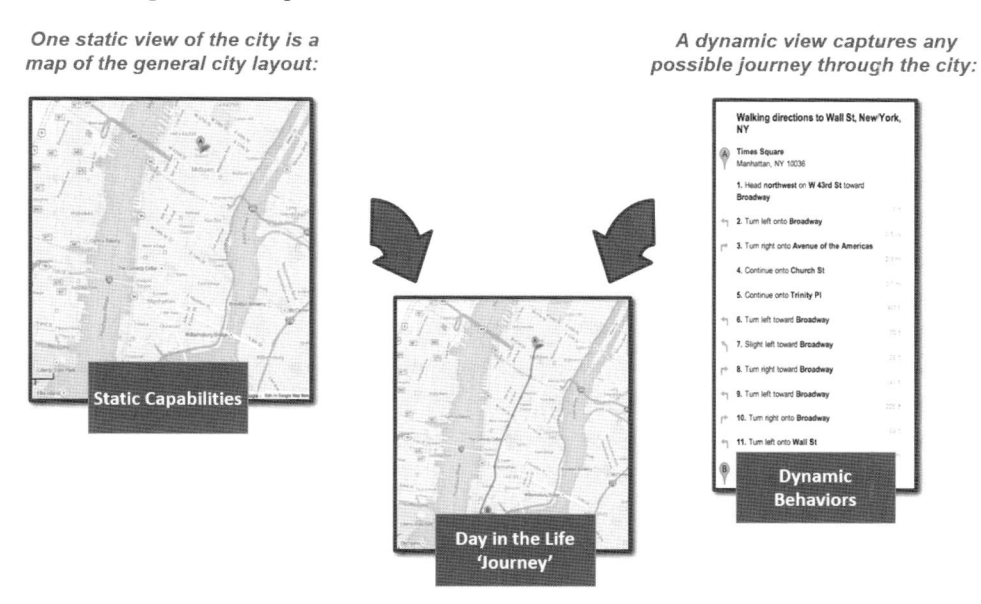

One static view of the city is a map of the general city layout:

A dynamic view captures any possible journey through the city:

Figure 1-5 A well-designed city plan can support any journey

Comparing city planning and building design, as practiced by the town planner and architect, with the job of an enterprise and solution architect in a bank reveals an important shortfall in the arsenal of tools for banking architects.

The "ingredients" that make up the bank are not tangible things like buildings and roads, they are the far less tangible capabilities that a bank must establish. The behaviors that are modelled as journeys through the town are the business processes that the bank supports. Banking architects have extensive experience in modeling processes. The key issue for the business and application architect, is defining the generic capability building blocks that they should select and configure to create the equivalent of the town plan for the bank. These capabilities can, in different combinations and sequences, then support those more familiar processes.

The result of building without a governing town plan is a shanty-town – buildings and roads are put up as and when they are needed, sewage, water and electricity supply is deficient and, over time, chaos is inevitable.

Without a town plan for the business, systems are built to meet the immediate needs of the processes as they are today, which will eventually lead to the same inevitable chaos in terms of overlapping and redundant applications and lack of functionality.

The problem of application complexity goes much further than the obvious problem of redundancy in the overlapping applications. It is greatly exacerbated when the applications need to interact with each other. Every application has its own specific scope and boundary, and every point-to-point connection is unique. As the application portfolio grows to several hundred overlapping systems it is no surprise that adding or enhancing any system becomes an exercise in tracing highly complex dependencies.

The functional partitions of the BIAN standard define discrete non-overlapping capabilities. The BIAN Service Landscape seeks to identify all possible "elemental" business functions that might make up any bank. A blueprint for a bank, assembled using the BIAN partitions, creates the same organizing blueprint as the town plan – eliminating overlaps and defining standard connections.

By adopting the BIAN standard, banking architects are provided with a list of "ingredients" and standard connections, that will enable them to progressively rationalize the bank's application portfolios, eliminating the redundancy and the associated operational complexity (Figure 1-6).

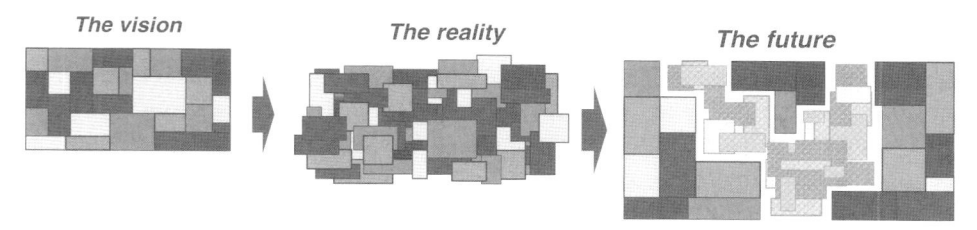

Figure 1-6: Migrating to a well architected application landscape

Part II of this book (Chapters 4 through to 9) covers the ability of the BIAN architecture to support the elaboration of, and migration to, an agile, service-oriented architecture (SOA) in detail. It illustrates how banks can adopt a service-based approach incrementally, targeting those areas where existing complexity is constraining the business most, or where more flexible and responsive systems are most needed to exploit new business opportunities.

■ 1.3   POSITIONING THE BIAN STANDARD

BIAN provides a world leading Reference Architecture for the Financial Industry. It provides a definition of business functions, service interactions and business objects[15] that describe the general construct of any bank. These deliverables are positioned to be a world leading standard, that can act as a "connecting hub" between other standards for the financial industry as well as regulations for that industry.

BIAN is concerned with **content.**

It uses two **notation** standards to document its deliverables: the ArchiMate® and UML standards. How this is done, is explained in Section 2.1. BIAN does not provide a **methodology** to use its deliverables in the elaboration and maintenance of an architecture. The BIAN Association and The Open Group published several papers on how to use the BIAN deliverables in the TOGAF framework. As the joint application of both standards is synergetic, this provides an extra impulse for the adoption of the BIAN deliverables. A summary of the role BIAN deliverables can play in the TOGAF® Architecture Development Methodology can be found in Chapter 10.

BIAN is **semantic**. It describes *what* needs to happen/needs to be known and not *how* and *with what* this should be implemented. This provides stability and universality to the standard. What needs to be done/known is common to every bank, while every bank or third-party provider can decide how and with what this is achieved. How and with

---
15   BIAN provides other deliverables to support a financial institution in its journey to an agile architecture. These are however not positioned as standards. They are archetypical examples, that can be used for inspiration.

what evolve more rapidly than ever thanks to the revolution in available technology. The semantic nature of the BIAN standard allows it to be used to guide and direct B2B (Business to Business) and A2A (Application to Application) service interactions.

BIAN is **exhaustive**. It covers all domains of banking activity. It covers business functionality as well as information and interoperability. BIAN acts on both a high abstraction (**architecture**) level and a more detailed (**design**) level.

Most standards for the financial industry cover only a selection of domains. Regulations that apply to the financial industry often also apply to specific areas. Each standard and each regulation uses its own concepts and terminology.

In the landscape of financial services standards and regulatory bodies, BIAN has a unique position. Not only does it cover all aspects of the financial industry, BIAN applies a specific approach to identifying, defining and naming banking concepts independent of the context (explained in Section 2.6). This allows the "BIAN vocabulary" to be used as a "common language", to connect and understand the meaning of terms and definitions used in diverse standards and regulations. Thus, BIAN facilitates conformance to standards and regulations. Figure 1-7 illustrates the many regulations and standards that are involved in the financial ecosystem.

The BIAN Association has a strong working relationship with many other standard bodies. Sections 11.1 and 11.2 describe the working relationship with ISO 220020, OMG and EDM Council and the Business Architecture Guild. BIAN does not want to reinvent the wheel. For each Service Domain, alignment with the standards that fit best for that Service Domain is sought.

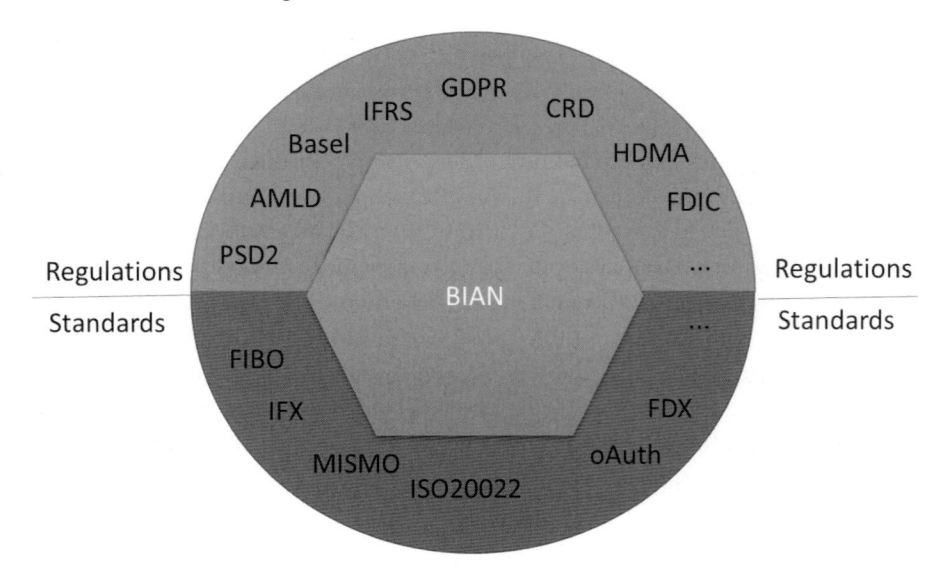

Figure 1-7: BIAN as "common language" between other standards and regulations

In the period 2018 to 2021, the BIAN Association was placing a strong emphasis on the standardization of API specifications, in parallel with expanding and detailing the "logical data model". The priority is to enrich the BIAN Service Landscape with maximum content detail, so it will be used as the reference model in the financial services industry and become a de facto standard. This is seen as the horizontal expansion of the BIAN content work.

Focusing on the semantics of services and attribute definitions is perceived as an important element to solve the integration issues of financial services software and to ensure cross-vendor standardization. Therefore, a financial services business vocabulary is elaborated as part of the BIAN Business Object Model.

■ 1.4 BIAN, THE ORGANIZATION

1.4.1 How the BIAN Architecture evolves

BIAN is a result of co-creation
The development of the BIAN architecture is iterative, relying on the active contribution of industry participants to build consensus and encourage adoption.

BIAN brings together the best minds in banking architecture to collaborate and share, in an open way, the best expertise across our global ecosystem of leading banks. Banks, technology providers, FinTechs, RegTechs, academics and consultants cooperate to define a revolutionary framework that standardizes and simplifies the overall banking architecture.

BIAN creates a best practice architecture that the world's banks can 100% rely upon.

The BIAN Association coordinates the evolution of the BIAN Architecture on behalf of its members, with regular new version releases. It seeks feedback to help continually expand and refine its content.

The latest list of BIAN members can be viewed at https://bian.org/members/bian-members/

BIAN Working Groups govern specific areas of expertise. Service Definition Working Groups for example, each cover a group of Service Domains. The scope covered by individual Working Groups is defined in their charter so that, collectively, Working Groups cover the whole landscape with no overlaps between them.

The following options are in place to collect and process feedback:

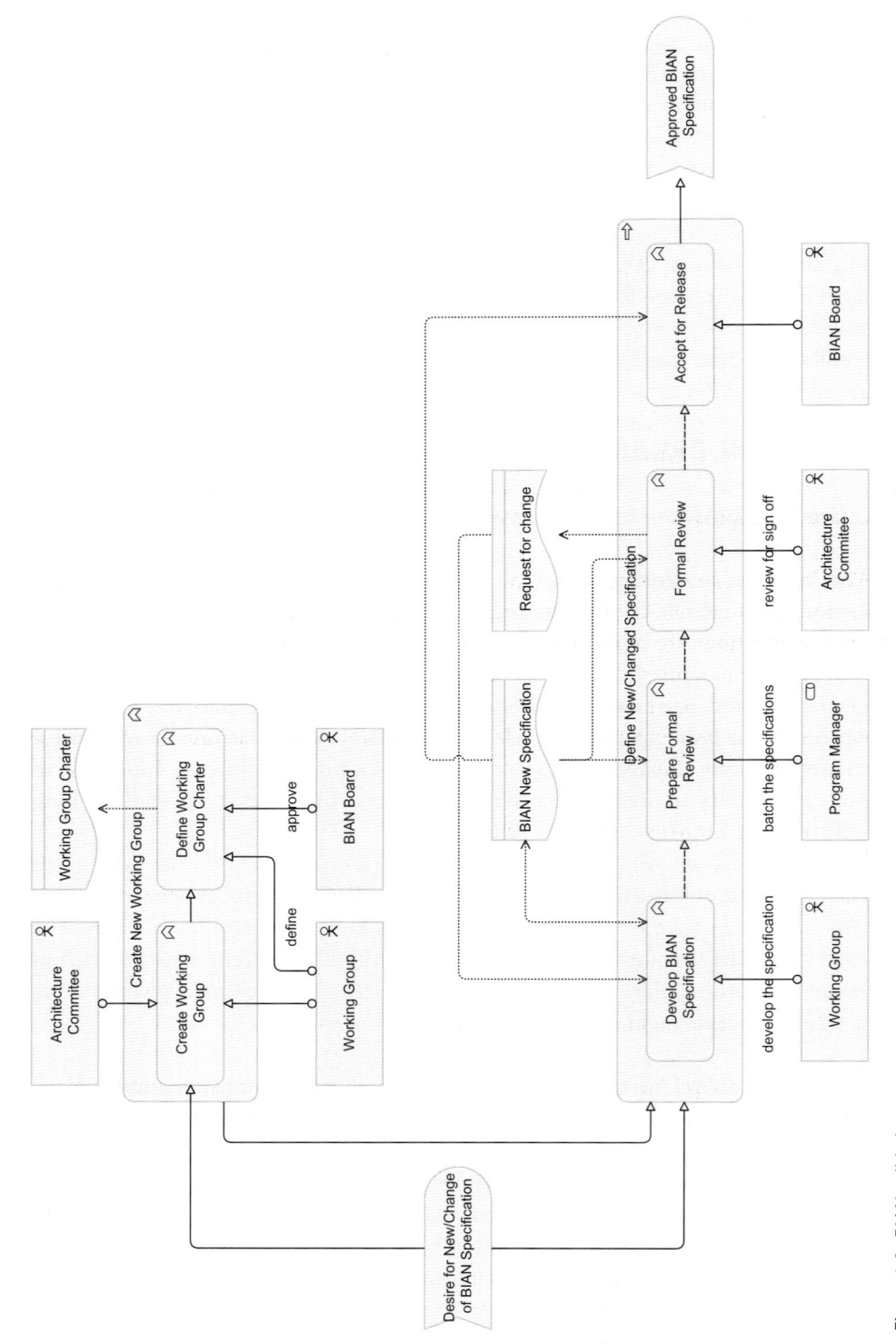

Figure 1-8: BIAN validation process

BIAN members are encouraged to provide feedback to the Architecture Committee, Architecture Framework & Foundation Working Group, by using the BIAN Wiki, or via their representatives.

Non-members are invited to post their suggestions by using the BIAN website.

BIAN validation and approval procedure
The development of the BIAN architecture is iterative. The validation and approval procedure is described in Figure 1-8.

A request for a new or updated BIAN specification is sent to the Architecture Committee. If there is an active Working Group responsible for that area of expertise, this Working Group will take in the request. If not, a new Working Group is established. A Working Group should have at least two banks as participants. The Working Group writes a Working Group Charter in which its responsibility and desired outcome is articulated. This Charter is approved by the BIAN Board.

The Working Group defines and presents a new or updated specification. The updates can be batched together by the Program Manager for a formal review. The new/updated specifications are submitted for comment to the Architecture Committee. This committee either accepts the proposal or requests changes/clarifications. Once these have been made and agreement is reached, the Architecture Committee signs off and the changes are included in the next release. The BIAN Board has review and release authority over the releases.

1.4.2 The BIAN Framework, a toolbox
The Reference Architecture for the Financial Services Industry is the core value proposition of BIAN. But the BIAN Framework is more than that: it offers an entire "toolbox" that supports an architect (vendor, FinTech…) in understanding and applying the BIAN Reference Architecture.

Figure 1-9 depicts the toolbox that is the BIAN Framework.

BIAN's Reference Architecture is described in a collection of architecture artifacts that make up its industry standard. BIAN's toolbox contains a **Digital Repository** (Subsection 1.4.3) that contains the elements of the BIAN Reference Architecture:
- The Service Domain Landscape (or "Service Landscape") that provides access to the collection of Service Domains - Service Domains being the functional capacity building blocks for the financial industry and the core element of the BIAN standards:
- A collection of archetypical Business Scenarios, depicting how an orchestration of the Service Domains, interacting through Service Operations, can realize any functionality required by the financial industry;

- An API Portal, providing access to BIAN's Semantic API definitions, that have the ambition to be(come) standards;
- A collection of logical data model diagrams, views on the BIAN BOM (which is a "Canonical" Data Model for the financial industry);
- A collection of archetypical Business Capabilities.

BIAN has become the reference standard for an open, service-oriented banking architecture. It is founded on well documented analysis and design patterns defined in the "**BIAN Metamodel**".

White papers and **implementation guidelines,** available on the BIAN website, facilitate the usage of BIAN by architects and vendors. Members using BIAN actively for different purposes share their experience in **webinars**, also available as part of the BIAN toolbox. This "**BIAN book**" gives an overview of this information.

BIAN has developed a **training** and a **certification** approach for architects and is working on a certification approach for products and organizations (Sub-section 1.4.4).

BIAN published an "archetypical" approach for the **adoption** of the BIAN Framework in a financial institution (Sub-section 1.4.5).

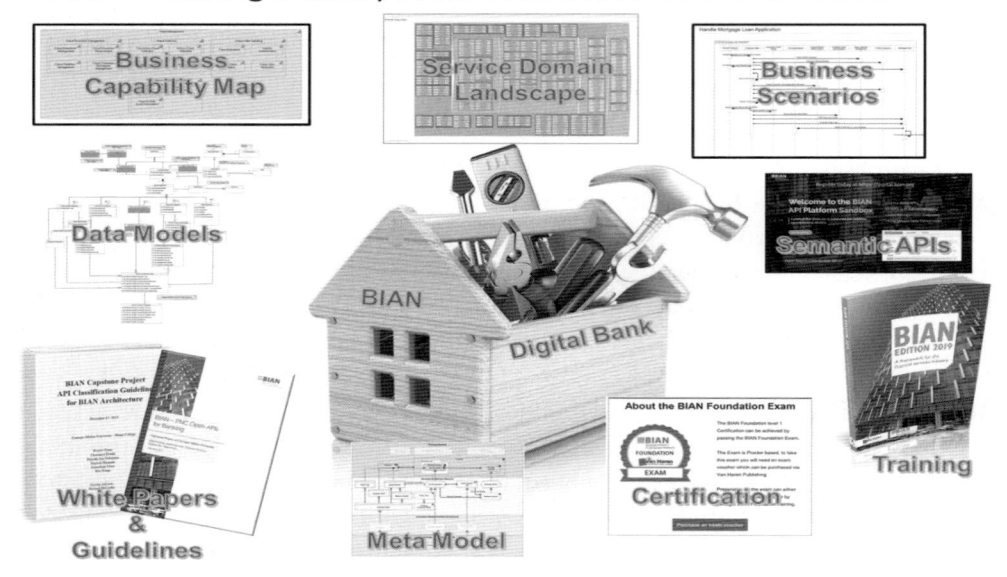

Figure 1-9 BIAN's toolbox to create an agile banking architecture

1.4.3 BIAN Open Digital Repository

The BIAN Reference Architecture is made available via two main information portals.

Most of the BIAN model elements, artifacts and diagrams are published in the "Digital Repository". At the time of writing, the repository can be accessed via https://bian.org/servicelandscape-9-0/.

The landing page is shown in Figure 1-10.

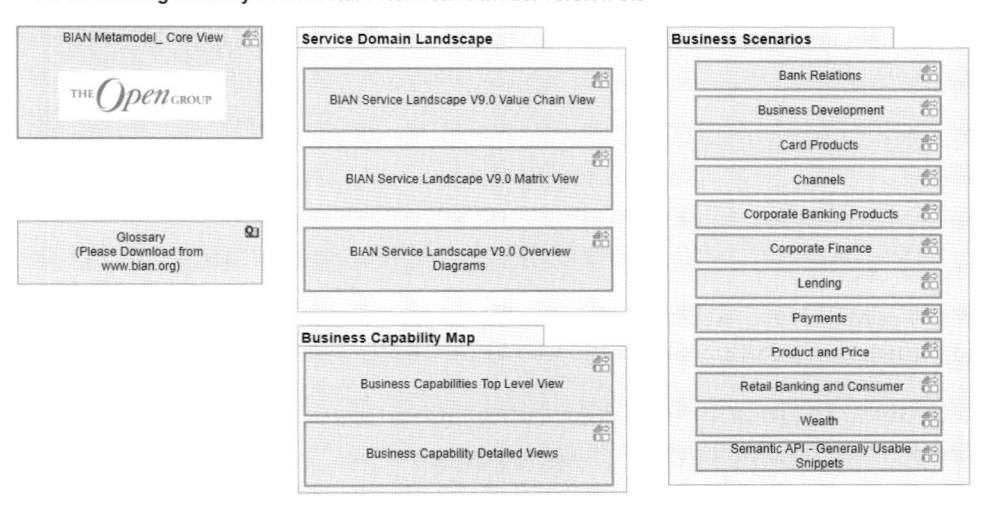

Figure 1-10: Landing page of the BIAN Digital Repository (version 9)

The BIAN Semantic APIs are published on the BIAN API Portal. At the time of writing of this book, it can be accessed via https://portal.bian.org

The "BIAN Metamodel" box on the landing page of the Digital Repository shows the BIAN Metamodel. As explained in Section 2.2, the Metamodel defines how the BIAN Architecture is modeled and how it is managed and stored in the Digital Repository. It also defines the navigation paths that are implemented in the Digital Repository and between the Digital Repository and the API Portal.

Clicking on the other boxes provides access to diagrams, containing model elements that allow navigation to further diagrams, or to model elements and their descriptions. In Chapter 2, we explain that the BIAN model elements and diagrams are represented in either the ArchiMate or the UML language. The model elements themselves, however, are documented only once, both languages refer to the same concept. The Repository enables the navigation between all representations.

A video explaining and illustrating the navigation is available on the BIAN website.

1.4.4 BIAN certification

BIAN members and the broader community who are using the BIAN standard, often enquire about the definition and implementation of some measure of alignment to the standard and for a certification. Currently, compliance measurement/certification focuses on two aspects:

Certification for architects
This certification is intended for business and application architects in the financial services industry, on both an enterprise and solution level, who are interested in applying the BIAN Industry Standard in their organization. It is also intended for those architects who are interested in contributing to the continuous improvement of the BIAN standard.

Certification for architects provides proof of their knowledge and insight of the BIAN Framework and of the way it can be applied in an organization, to improve the agility of its architecture. For both the organization employing the architect and the architect as a person, it is a hallmark of professionalism.

A certification approach has been launched where training is based on the "BIAN Semantic API Practitioner's Guide" and this book. Testing is through multiple choice questionnaires. As the training and tests are refined, it is possible that two levels of certification will be defined. The first level would test the expertise needed to correctly interpret the standard in different deployment scenarios. The highest level would also cover the complete theory and principles behind the standard.

Certification for products
This certification is intended for those solution providers in the financial services industry who are interested in applying the BIAN Industry Standard in their solution offering(s).

Certification of products is a hallmark of their ability to provide the buyer with the benefits of a BIAN-based architecture, such as:
- improved industry integration and collaboration through the usage of (open) APIs;
- enhanced adoption of shared third party business services and application software and services;
- improved operational efficiency within and between banks;

These will significantly lower the integration risks and costs for the buyers and enable them to adopt a more flexible business and ICT service sourcing model.

The basis for certification will reflect how the product aligns to the Service Domain partitions and supports their service interfaces. This approach is still under development.

1.4.5 BIAN adoption journey

BIAN provides a typical adoption roadmap that can be used as guidance in the adoption journey of BIAN within a financial institution. This journey is animated on the BIAN website. An overview is given in figure 1-11.

The journey starts when business and/or ICT professionals in the organization believe that a Financial Services Reference Model can help in the creation of an organization-specific banking architecture and improve the architecture practice. This should enable the organization to respond to the rapidly changing financial ecosystem, including new technologies, pressing regulations, RegTechs, FinTechs and non-financial companies entering the financial market, Open Banking APIs, etc. The journey starts when these people believe that BIAN might be helpful in supporting the definition of a banking architecture that is able to respond to the current and future requirements and strategic decisions.

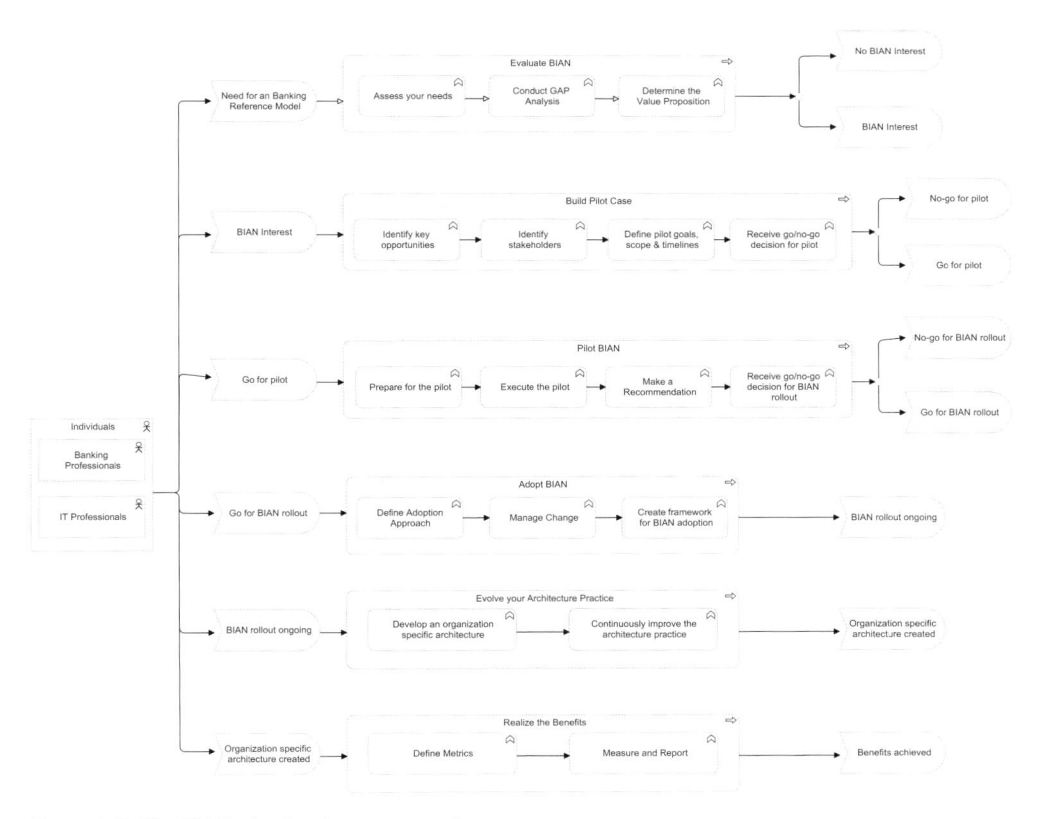

Figure 1-11: The BIAN adoption journey, overview

In the first stage of the adoption journey, BIAN is evaluated and compared with other frameworks. As interest is growing, stage 2 is entered: a BIAN pilot is prepared. At the point when the pilot's scope and goals are well defined and key stakeholders are committed and involved, the pilot can be executed (stage 3 of the adoption journey).

During the pilot, expectations will be confirmed - or not. A decision to rollout BIAN (or not) is prepared. If the adoption of BIAN is actually confirmed, the necessary is done to introduce BIAN in the organization (stage 4). From now on, BIAN will be used as a means to support the creation and evolution of an organization-specific banking architecture and architecture practice. The architecture will be realized and deployed (stage 5). The new architecture is monitored by assessing the key indicators that enable the follow-up of the realization of the BIAN value proposition. A continuous improvement cycle keeps the process running (stage 6).

The journey to adopt a Banking Reference Architecture is described in more detail in Appendix 1.

■ 1.5 TEST YOURSELF QUESTIONS

1. **What is not part of the BIAN Framework?**
   A. A digital repository with the model elements and artifacts of BIAN's Reference Architecture for the Financial Industry.
   B. Guidelines on what modeling language and what tool to use when applying the BIAN Reference Architecture in your bank.
   C. Trainings and certification.
   D. An API portal with Semantic API descriptions.

2. **The goal of the BIAN Association is to develop the most important content, concepts and methods in interoperability, supporting the aim of lower integration costs in the financial services industry and facilitating business innovation and agility.**
   Which statement does not express how BIAN seeks to achieve this?
   A. By providing an architecture framework with all of the necessary elements, tools and methodologies for a sustainable operational model through the adoption of, and alignment to, available market standards.
   B. By focusing on the definition of semantic services and/or API-definitions to improve the semantic integration of the financial services landscapes.
   C. By enabling the financial services industry to develop and run a loosely coupled environment successfully.
   D. By imposing and enforcing standards on how requirements should be implemented by both financial institutions and solution suppliers.

3. **What statements describe the BIAN approach?**
   A. BIAN's Reference Architecture wants to enable banks to migrate to an agile architecture by applying a proven process-driven approach.
   B. BIAN's Reference Architecture includes the latest technology developments.

C. BIAN's Reference Architecture for the Financial Industry is developed according to agile principles.
D. BIAN's Reference Architecture wants to provide the financial industry with the "ingredients" that can be combined with the "behaviors" to result in an "enterprise plan", comparable to how town planners make a "town plan".

2 Explaining the BIAN Architecture

This chapter explains the concepts through which BIAN's Reference Architecture for the Financial Industry captures the reality of the financial services industry. It only describes the concepts, not the way they can serve a bank in achieving an architecture. Part II (Chapters 4 through to 9) elaborates on "applying BIAN".

The BIAN Metamodel (Section 2.2) provides an overview of these concepts and how they relate to each other. The Metamodel has a central role in documenting and exploiting the Reference Architecture offered by BIAN.

The Service Landscape (Section 2.3) is a structure facilitating an overview of, and access to, the collection of Service Domains, the core concept in the BIAN Architecture.

The Service Domain, a "service center" that provides a unique, elemental capability building block for a financial institution, is described in Section 2.4. A Service Domain is carefully delimited, in view of a "MECE[16]" coverage of a financial institution's functionality, through the application of a pattern combining an asset and a use.

A Service Domain is a self-contained service center that takes responsibility for its part of the information required by a financial institution. This "Service Domain Information Profile", with "Control Record" as its main constituent, is described in Section 2.5.

The services offered by a Service Domain – the Service Operations- are described in more detail in the Service Domain's Semantic API and its Endpoints. BIAN also offers a "Swagger File" translation of the Semantic API. This is described in Section 2.7.

The BIAN Business Object Model (BIAN BOM) offers a usage-independent view on the information required by a financial institution. The pattern, used to elaborate the BIAN BOM, is explained in Section 2.6.

---
16 Mutually Exclusive, Collectively Exhaustive.

The Service Domain Overview Diagram (Section 2.8) gives an overview of all these model elements, from the point of view of the Service Domain.

Orchestrations of the elemental service centers represented by the Service Domains, can provide any functionality required by a financial institution. BIAN provides Business Scenarios and Wireframes that represent archetypical functionality. These artifacts are described in Section 2.9.

BIAN also provides archetypical Business Capabilities (Section 2.10).

■ 2.1 NOTATION OF THE BIAN ARCHITECTURE MODEL

BIAN uses two standard notation languages to describe the artifacts maintained in the BIAN repository and published on the BIAN portal (https://www.bian.org/).

The usage of these languages coincides with the two levels of abstraction BIAN provides deliverables on: the "architecture" level and the "design" level. The architecture level focuses on the fundamental concepts and the relationships between them. It creates an understanding of the coherence between the different aspects and provides a structure to manage the evolution of systems. It supports strategy and portfolio management. Deliverables on this level are documented using the ArchiMate 3.1 language[17].

The design level adds details to architecture model elements, to support the business process modelers and software/application designers. On this level, UML 2.1[18] is used.

This chapter explains what language(s) and language elements are used to express a building block of the BIAN architecture, for every type of diagram on which it is used. It will be clear that one building block (e.g. a Service Domain) can be represented in different notation languages. However, these are just representations, the concept itself is managed only once. The Digital Repository enables the BIAN user to navigate between the different representations (see also Sub-section 1.4.3).

The fact that BIAN uses ArchiMate and UML to document its deliverables does not imply that banks should use these languages to document their architecture and designs.

---

17 Detailed information of the ArchiMate 3.1 specification can be found at https://www.opengroup.org/archimate-home
18 Detailed information of the UML specification can be found at the website of The Object Management Group OMG https://www.uml.org/

2.2 THE BIAN METAMODEL

This section gives an overview of the concepts BIAN uses to document its Financial Services Industry Reference Architecture. These concepts are formalized in the BIAN Metamodel.

2.2.1 Role of the BIAN Metamodel

A model is an abstract representation of reality. A metamodel defines the constructs and rules for creating such models. An architecture model consists of a set of building blocks and their relationships. The metamodel defines the types of building blocks and the possible relationships between them. The architecture model can be managed in an architecture repository, according to the metamodel. According to the metamodel, the architecture model can then be exploited, to produce "architectural artifacts" that can provide information for stakeholders.

The BIAN Framework uses a standard metamodel that defines the types of building blocks BIAN uses to capture the reality of a financial institution in an architecture model. It also describes what artifacts BIAN produces to support financial institutions. The role of the BIAN Metamodel is illustrated in Figure 2-1.

The reality of the financial world is captured in the BIAN Architecture Model according to the Metamodel. BIAN's Architecture Model is managed in the BIAN Architecture Repository, available on "www.bian.org". BIAN provides a series of architecture artifacts, based on the model elements in its repository. The repository can also be queried to provide "custom-made" artifacts.

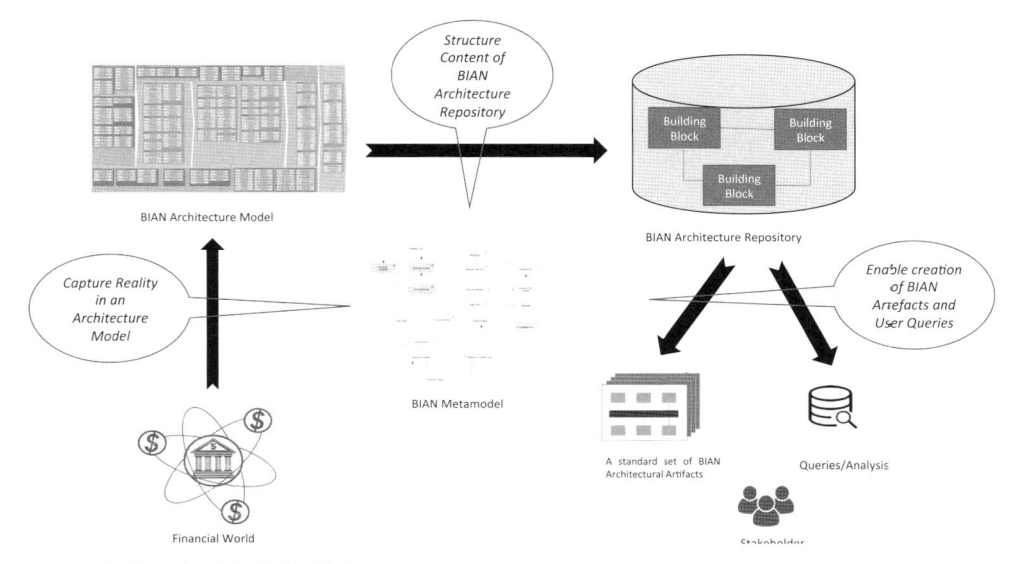

Figure 2-1 The role of the BIAN Metamodel

2.2.2 Overview of the BIAN Metamodel

Figure 2-2 depicts the BIAN Metamodel in the ArchiMate Language.

The **Service Domain** is the central concept in BIAN's Reference Architecture for the Financial Services Industry. A Service Domain is an elemental business capability; it is a conceptual, MECE building block for the functionality of any financial institution. All functionality required by a financial institution can be realized by an orchestration of Service Domains, exchanging **Service Operations.**

The BIAN Service Landscape provides an overview of all the functionality required for a financial institution. It represents the collection of BIAN Service Domains, for overview reasons grouped in **Business Domains**, in their turn grouped in **Business Areas.**

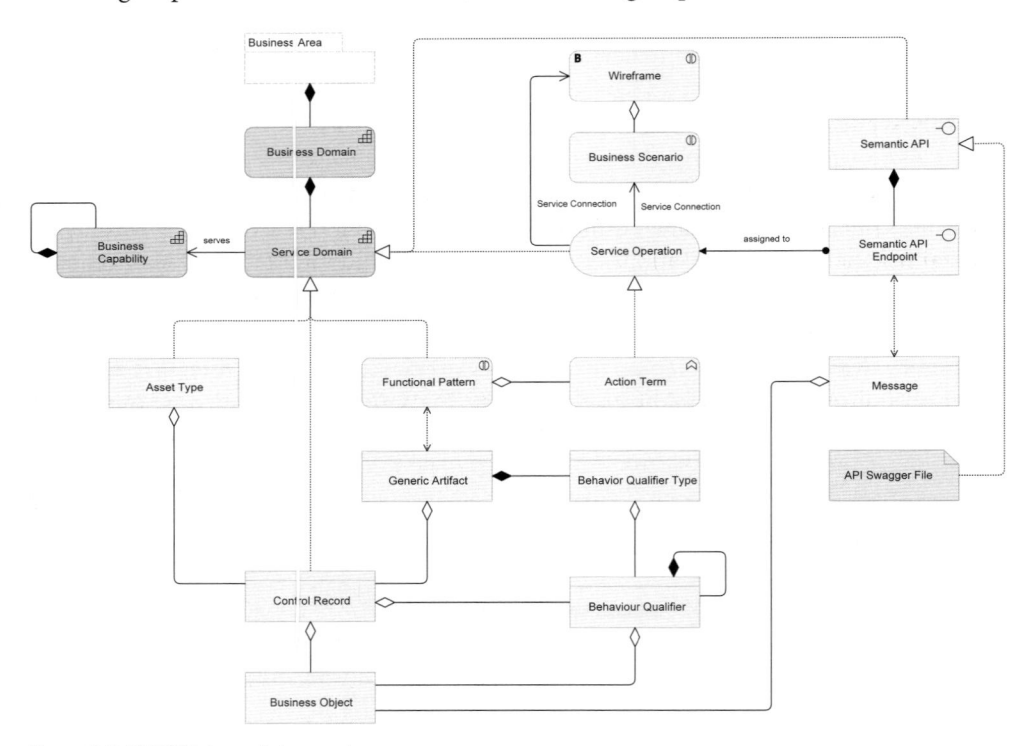

Figure 2-2 BIAN Metamodel, overview

BIAN's Service Domains are pattern-based.

The role of each Service Domain in the financial institution is to execute a **Functional Pattern** on an **Asset Type**. A Functional Pattern is composed of a set of **Action Terms**. Executing the Actions that compose this Functional Pattern on this Asset Type is the unique responsibility of this Service Domain in the ecosystem of the financial institution.

The Service Domain's **Control Record** is the information involved in the fulfillment of the Service Domain's role. It combines information related to the Asset Type and the **Generic Artifact**– which is the information created by the execution of the Service Domain's Functional Pattern.

Each Service Domain provides a set of services, called Service Operations. BIAN's Service Operations are conceptualized as follows. The Service Domain's Functional Pattern consists of a set of Action Terms. Each Action Term generates a set of Service Operations. BIAN is detailing and clarifying the Service Operations in the **Service Domain Semantic API**. This Semantic API consists of a series of **Semantic API Endpoints**, each describing the functionality and payload of one elemental Service Operation. The input and output information exchanged in a Semantic API Endpoint is contained in its **Message.**

BIAN provides **API Swagger Files**, that contain the Semantic API description in a machine-readable format.

A Control Record can be further subdivided in **Behavior Qualifiers** – according to the **Behavior Qualifier Types** that subdivide the Generic Artifact. This subdivision helps in detailing the Service Operations. The Semantic API Endpoint and its Message relate to the Control Record or to a specific Behavior Qualifier. This clarifies what the Action Term acts upon/provides information about.

The BIAN Business Object Model (BIAN BOM) is the counterpart of the Service Landscape. It depicts the information required to run a financial institution, just as the Service Landscape depicts the functionality. The BIAN BOM consists of **Business Objects**, that are the MECE building blocks for a financial institution's information and their relationships.

Asset Type, Generic Artifact, and its Behavior Qualifier Type, as well as the Control Record and its Behavior Qualifiers, are views on these Business Objects. As such, the Message of the Semantic API Endpoint is also a view on the BIAN Business Objects.

BIAN offers "architecture artifacts", composed of Service Domains interacting through Service Operations. A **Business Scenario** represents an orchestration of Service Domains (interacting through their Service Operations), in response to an event. A **Wireframe** is a set of pathways between Service Domains, mediated by Service Operations.

BIAN elaborates a set of **Business Capabilities**, that can be used as inspiration for a bank's strategic Business Capabilities. A Business Capability can be composed of other Business Capabilities. BIAN's Service Domains can be capability building blocks for several Business Capabilities.

Table 2-1 gives an overview of the model elements of the BIAN Metamodel. The Semantic Definition and the notation in the ArchiMate Language are depicted.

Table 2-1 BIAN Metamodel elements definitions and ArchiMate notations

Element	Semantic definition	ArchiMate modeling notation
Action Term	A fundamental unit of behavior that characterizes the purpose of a Service Operation.	Action Term
API Swagger File	A machine-readable format (according to Swagger[19] ™) of a semantic API description.	API Swagger File
Asset Type	Something tangible or intangible the bank has ownership and/or influence over, that can create value for the bank.	Asset Type
Behavior Qualifier	A set of business information that qualifies (i.e., refines) the Control Record of a Service Domain.	Behavior Qualifier
Behavior Qualifier Type	A type of information that refines the Generic Artifact and specifies a classification of Behavior Qualifiers.	Behavior Qualifier Type
Business Area	A grouping of Business Domains used for a structured presentation of the Service Landscape.	Business Area
Business Capability	A particular ability that a business may possess or exchange to achieve a specific purpose.	Business Capability
Business Domain	A grouping of Service Domains used for a structured presentation of the Service Landscape.	Business Domain

---

[19] Swagger™ allows you to describe the structure of your APIs so that machines can read them. It enforces adherence to the Open API Specification.

Element	Semantic definition	ArchiMate modeling notation
Business Object	Something that exists in reality, concrete or abstract, and participates and/or influences the nature of the business.	Business Object
Business Scenario	A linked sequence of interactions between Service Domains in response to a business event.	Business Scenario
Control Record	A set of business information that reflects all information needed to support the fulfillment of the role of a Service Domain on instances of an Asset Type.	Control Record
Functional Pattern	A behavior or mechanism that can be applied to some asset in the execution of commercial business.	Functional Pattern
Generic Artifact	The general type of artifact produced and/or managed by any Service Domain that conforms to the Functional Pattern.	Generic Artifact
Message	The input and output parameters exchanged through a Semantic API Endpoint.	Message
Semantic API	The collection of the Semantic API Endpoints of one Service Domain.	Semantic API
Semantic API Endpoint	An access point where one Service Operation offered by one Service Domain is made available to the environment.	Semantic API Endpoint
Service Domain	An elemental or atomic functional building block that can be service enabled as a discrete and unique business responsibility.	Service Domain

Element	Semantic definition	ArchiMate modeling notation
Service Operation	A business service that is exposed by a Service Domain.	Service Operation
Wireframe	An interaction representing the available Service Connections for a selection of Service Domains.	Wireframe

■ 2.3 THE SERVICE LANDSCAPE

The BIAN Service Landscape is a representation that organizes the BIAN Service Domains. The Service Domains are grouped into Business Domains, which are subsequently grouped into Business Areas. This creates an access path that facilitates finding and accessing Service Domains.

The Service Landscape is not intended to represent a design blueprint for any bank. Such blueprints and the techniques for assembling them are covered in Section 5.2. In fact, BIAN has been using several representations, grouping the Service Domains according to different criteria. The "Matrix" representation of the BIAN Service Landscape is shown in Figure 2-3.

Figure 2-4 shows an alternative representation of the BIAN Service Landscape: The Value Chain view.

There are three elements that determine the structure of the BIAN Service Landscape: Business Area, Business Domain and Service Domain, as pointed out in Figure 2-5.

BIAN does not define specific Business Areas and Business Domains as canonical standards, as it is not possible to force a particular hierarchical decomposition of business functions on all banks. The BIAN Service Domains, on the other hand, are canonical standards. They can fit into an arbitrary number of Business Area - Business Domain hierarchies.

The Metamodel view on the elements of the Service Landscape is represented in Figure 2-6.

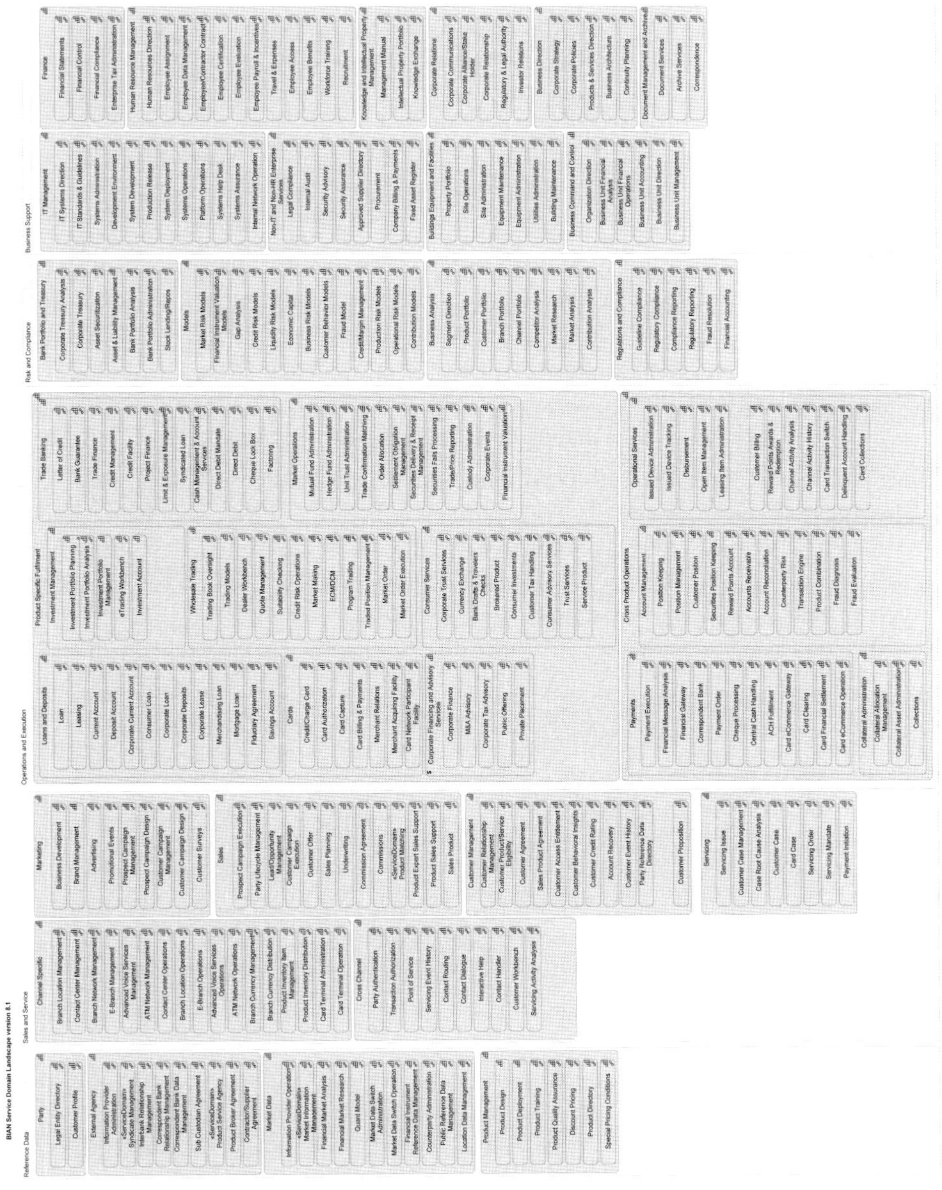

2 Explaining the BIAN Architecture

Figure 2-3 BIAN Service Landscape, Matrix view

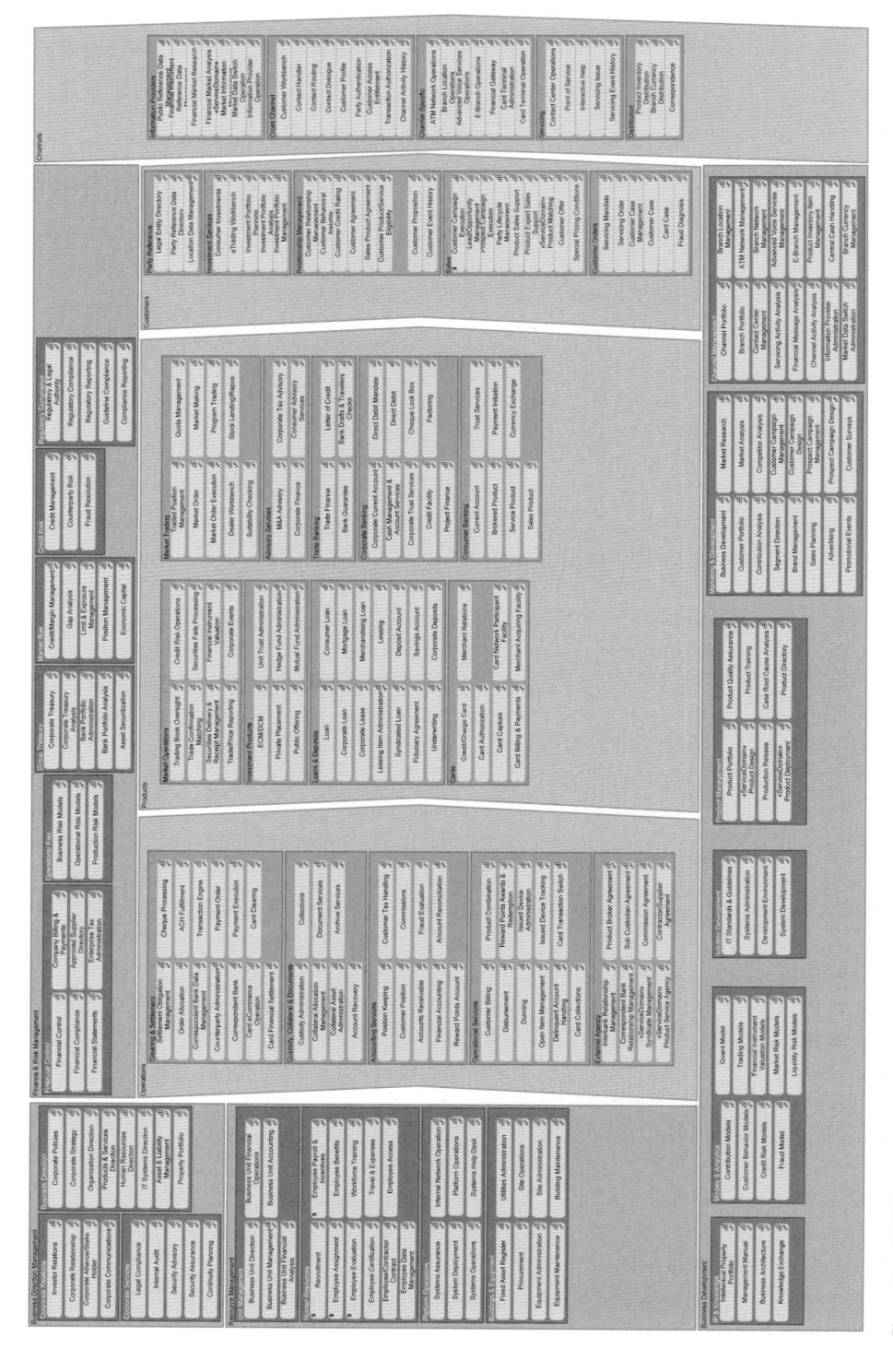

Figure 2-4 BIAN Service Landscape, Value Chain view

2 Explaining the BIAN Architecture

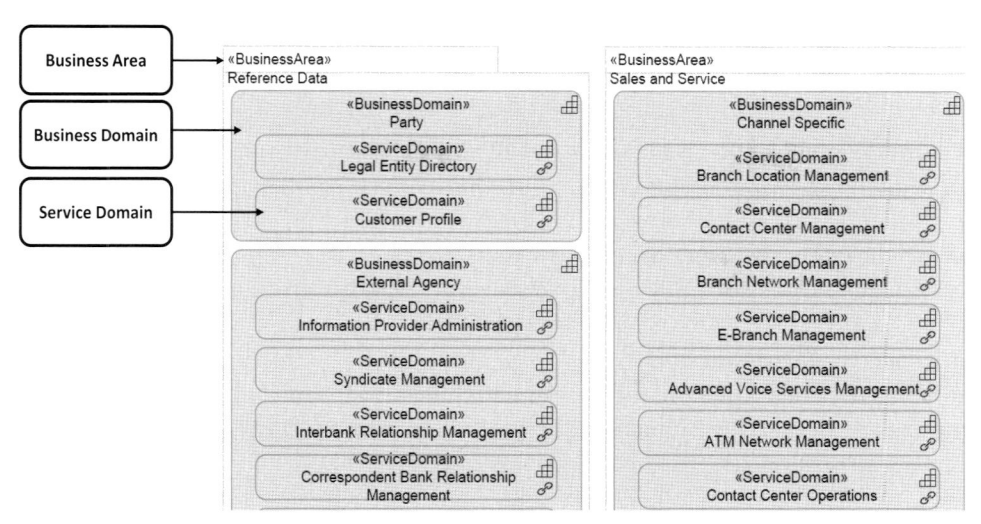

Figure 2-5 Three elements defining the structure of the BIAN Service Landscape

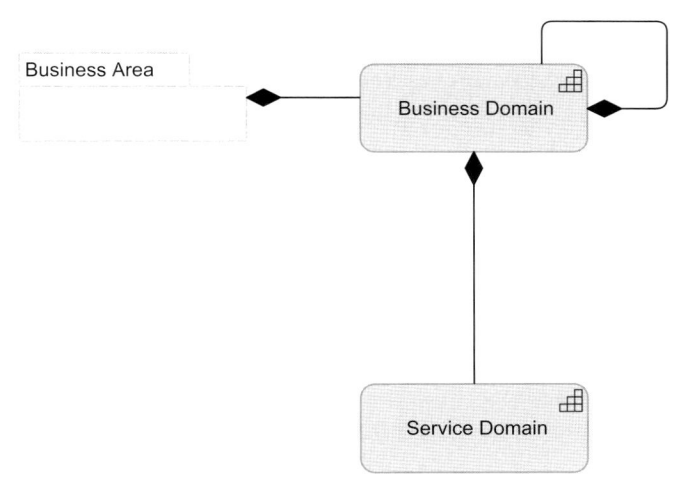

Figure 2-6 BIAN Metamodel, Service Landscape view

2.3.1 Business Area level
A Business Area is a broad set of capabilities and responsibilities and is positioned at the highest level of the BIAN Service Landscape hierarchy. It is a grouping of Business Domains into larger units, as these are frequently found in banks to show their high-level business functions. Here, the objective is to make the great number of Service Domains better accessible.

The ArchiMate representation of a Business Area is a grouping.

2.3.2 Business Domain level
A Business Domain is a clustering of Service Domains within the Service Landscape along lines that are often used in banks to denote their high-level capabilities. Business

Domains in BIAN are not prescriptive; the main objective of their use is to provide a roadmap into the large number of individual Service Domains.

A Business Domain belongs to exactly one BIAN Business Area and may be decomposed in more detailed Business Domains.

The ArchiMate representation of a Business Domain is a "capability", as Business Domains can be considered to be coarse grained Business Capabilities.

2.3.3 Service Domain level

The BIAN Service Domain is the elemental building block of the BIAN Service Landscape. The Service Domain is a core concept in the BIAN architecture. It is described in Section 2.4.

2.3.4 Service Landscape diagram

The Service Landscape is represented as an ArchiMate capability map.

BIAN currently provides two Service Landscape representations: the Matrix view and the Value Chain view.

■ 2.4 BIAN SERVICE DOMAIN

The **Service Domain** is a core concept in the BIAN architecture. A BIAN Service Domain represents the smallest functional partition that can be service-enabled as a discrete and unique business responsibility. All BIAN Service Domains taken together make up a "peer set" with each performing its own specific business function or purpose. Together, interacting through their Service Operations, they can cover all of the functionality required by a bank.

As a Service Domain is elemental or atomic in scope, the capability cannot be further decomposed into more detailed capabilities. Service Domains are mutually-exclusive and collectively-exhaustive. There is no functional redundancy between the Service Domains.

A Service Domain offers its services (Service Operations) to other Service Domains. This allows Service Domains to fulfil their role by delegating the execution of functionality to other Service Domains. The interaction between the Service Domains realizes the business activities that make up a bank.

A Service Domain is constructed according to a pattern, as represented in Figure 2-7. A **Service Domain** fulfills its role by executing a **Functional Pattern** on instances of an **Asset Type**. Each Service Domain combines a single primary Functional Pattern (e.g.

manage, design, operate) with an Asset Type (e.g., a piece of equipment, a customer relationship). A **Generic Artifact** is the information central to the execution of the Functional Pattern.

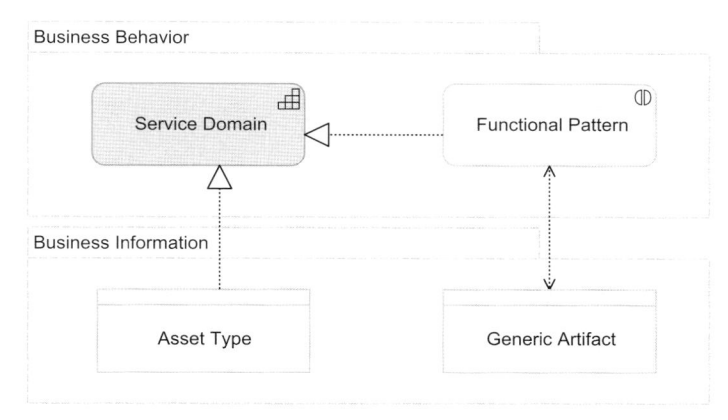

Figure 2-7 BIAN Metamodel, Service Domain view

BIAN has defined standard Functional Patterns and associated Generic Artifacts and a hierarchical classification of the Asset Types that may make up any bank.

2.4.1 Functional Pattern

A Functional Pattern (FP) is a behavior or mechanism that can be applied to instances of some asset in the execution of commercial business. The business role or purpose of a Service Domain is characterized by its Functional Pattern.

BIAN has identified 19 Functional Patterns that can be applied to Asset instances in order to model all aspects of banking. Table 2-2 contains the descriptions of the Functional Patterns defined by BIAN.

A Functional Pattern is a combination of Action Terms. The business service center implemented by a Service Domain can be accessed through Service Operation calls. A Service Domain's Service Operations are characterized by the Action Terms that are associated with its Functional Pattern. This is covered in Section 2.7. Figure 2-24, depicted in that section, gives an overview of the Action Terms associated with each Functional Pattern.

2.4.2 Generic Artifact

A Generic Artifact is the general type of artifact produced and/or managed by a Functional Pattern.

The Generic Artifact is used to make the functioning of a Service Domain more tangible. Each time the Service Domain performs its role of applying a behavior to an Asset instance, its activity and progress is steered and tracked using an instance of its associated Generic Artifact. There is one Generic Artifact defined for each Functional Pattern. For example, the Generic Artifact associated with the Functional Pattern "manage" is a "management plan".

Figure 2-8 shows the Generic Artifacts associated with each Functional Pattern. Table 2-3 contains descriptions of the Generic Artifacts.

Table 2-2 BIAN Functional Pattern descriptions

FP Group	FP Name	FP Description
CREATE	Direct	Define the policies, goals & objectives and strategies for an organizational entity or unit. Example: Direct a division of the enterprise.
	Manage	Oversee the working of a business unit, assign work, manage against a plan and troubleshoot issues. Example: Manage the day-to-day activities at a bank branch location.
	Administer	Handle and assign the day-to-day activities, capture time, costs and income for an operational unit. Example: Administer the time reporting and billing for the specialist sales support team.
	Design	Create and maintain a design for a procedure, product/service model or other such entity. Example: Create and maintain product designs and analytical models.
	Develop	To build or enhance something, typically an IT production system. Includes development, assessment and deployment activities. Example: Build, enhance, test and deploy a major enhancement to a production product processing system.
INITIATE	Process	Complete work tasks following a defined procedure in support of general office activities and product and service delivery. Example: Process the evaluation and completion of customer offers.
	Operate	Operate equipment and/or a largely automated facility. Example: Operate the bank's internal intranet facility.
	Maintain	Provide a maintenance service and repair devices/equipment as necessary. Example: Establish a maintenance and repair program covering the PC technology used in the central offices.
	Fulfill	Fulfill any scheduled and ad-hoc obligations under a service arrangement, most typically for a financial product or facility. Example: Perform the scheduled (e.g., statements, standing orders) and ad-hoc/requested (e.g. balance inquiries, fund transfers) fulfillment tasks for a customer current account facility.
	Transact	Execute a well-bounded financial transaction/task, typically involving largely automated/structured fulfillment processing. Example: Execute a payment transaction.
	Advise	Provide specialist advice and/or support as an ongoing service or for a specific task/event. Example: Handle the provision of specialist advice/expertise.

2 Explaining the BIAN Architecture

FP Group	FP Name	FP Description
	Monitor	Monitor and define the status/rating of some entity. Examples: Monitor the status and key indicators of a customer to influence online interactions and track the status of issued cards for security and access control.
	Track	Maintain a log of transactions or activity, typically a financial account/journal or a log of activity to support behavioral analysis. Examples: Maintain a financial journal of transactions processed for a product or service and maintain a log of customer events and activity for subsequent analysis.
REGISTER	Catalog	Capture and maintain reference information about some type of entity. Example: Maintain party reference information.
	Enroll	Maintain a membership for some group or related collection of parties. Example: Administer the membership status of a syndicate of investors.
EVALUATE	Agree terms	Maintain the terms and conditions that apply to a commercial relationship. Example: Define and maintain the terms governing the contractual relationship with a customer.
	Assess	To test or assess an entity, possibly against some formal qualification or certification requirement. Examples: Perform regulatory tests on a proposed financial transaction and check that a new offer conforms to an existing contractual agreement.
	Analyze	Analyze the performance or behavior of some on-going activity or entity. Examples: Provide behavioral insights and analysis into customer behavior and analyze financial market activity in order to identify opportunities, define pricing and evaluate risks.
PROVIDE	Allocate	Maintain an inventory or holding of some resource and make assignments/allocations as requested. Example: Track the inventory and administer the distribution of central cash holdings throughout the branch & ATM network.

Table 2-3 BIAN Generic Artifact (GA) descriptions

GA name	GA description
Maintenance arrangement	An arrangement to maintain something. Maintaining is the set of activities as an ongoing support to safeguard something.
Development project	A discrete or bounded effort with a defined remit and intended purpose/outcome.
Procedure	The performance of a supporting office activity within the enterprise (not product/service fulfillment specific).
Administrative plan	The plan that defines the clerical support for an operational unit/function of an enterprise.
Agreement	A set of promises that contractual parties agreed on as a unit of contract.
Arrangement	An engagement between two or more parties to do something or not to do something, to give something or not to give something.
Allocation	A service to track the availability and allocate business resources (staff and/or facilities) on request.
Management plan	The management and oversight while running an operational unit of an enterprise.

GA name	GA description
Operating session	The operation of a technical/automated facility employed/provided by an enterprise.
Analysis	A service to apply specific types of analysis against a set of provided data related to an item or activity.
Membership	A registry of entities that qualify for membership to a group with a recognized business purpose or categorization.
Log	A mechanism to track and record specific events and, if necessary, maintain associated derived/accumulated values.
Specification	A specification of a product or service offering, covering all aspects required for its use.
Transaction	The execution of a financial transaction.
Strategy	The purpose and mission for the enterprise including its competitive positioning and basis for competing in the market.
Assessment	A formal evaluation or test of a subject against a predefined set of properties or performance criteria.
Directory entry	A registry of items recording key reference information and properties relating to each item.
State	A mechanism to track and report on the state or dynamic property of some item or activity.
Advice	Provide specialist consultancy/support.

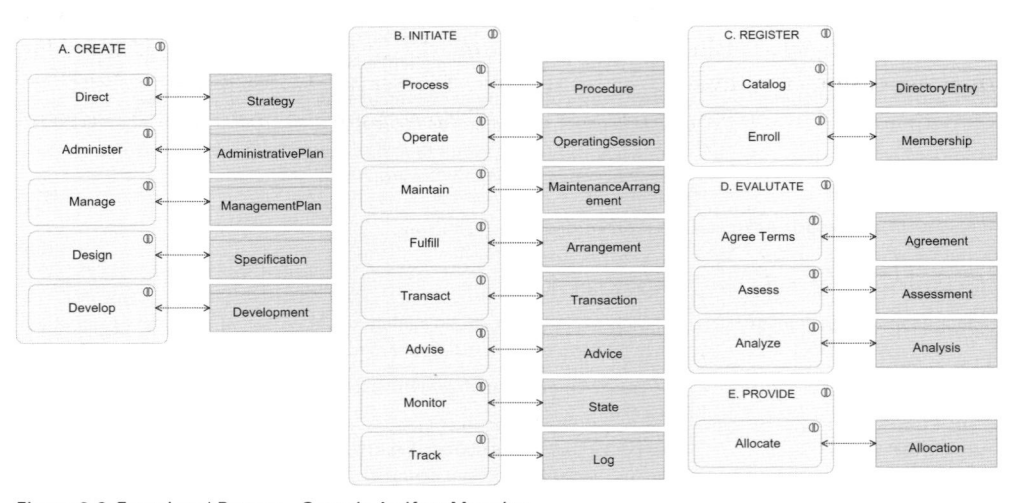

Figure 2-8 Functional Pattern - Generic Artifact Mapping

2.4.3 Asset Type

A Service Domain is responsible for applying its Functional Pattern on each instance of its Asset Type.

An Asset Type refers to something tangible or intangible that the bank has ownership and/or influence over and has one or more inherent uses or purposes for, that create commercial value.

BIAN has defined the likely Asset Types found in any bank. Some Asset Types are obvious - for example a machine or building. Some are intangible but easily identified such as knowhow, knowledge, relationships, reputation. Some are less obvious - most common is the "capacity to perform" type which applies to many BIAN Service Domains. For example, in the case of product fulfillment and support activities like party authentication, the asset is the bank's ability to perform these activities.

BIAN has defined a hierarchical Asset Type classification, up to a certain level of granularity. The Asset Type is defined at the level of granularity (referred to as the "threshold of decomposition", where in combination with the applied Functional Pattern, the associated Service Domain's responsibility is elemental or uniquely assignable. In other words, the bank either requires the functionality in its entirety or not at all, it does not perform some sub-partition of the functionality.

For example, as illustrated in Figure 2-9, the role of the "Current Account Service Domain" can be formulated as "to fulfill" (refers to Functional Pattern) "the arrangements" (refers to Generic Artifact) of the instances of "current account" (refers to Asset Type).

A Service Domain is responsible for implementing its Functional Pattern on each instance of its associated Asset Type for its full lifecycle. So, for example, the Service Domain that "manages" the "customer relationship" is responsible for doing so for every customer relationship, from the first time the customer is identified, to the last time the customer is involved with the bank. The Service Domain that "fulfills" the "arrangements" of the "current accounts", will do so from the opening of the account till its closing.

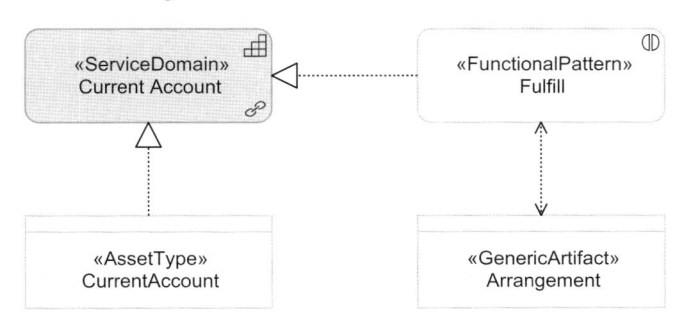

Figure 2-9 The Current Account Service Domain, its Asset Type, Functional Pattern and Generic Artifact

2.4.4 Service Domain representations

The Service Domain is *the* central concept in the BIAN architecture, and plays a prominent role in practically all applications of the BIAN Framework, as described in Part II.

It is also used in different contexts within the BIAN Architecture itself. The modeling language used to represent it and the symbol used within that language depend on the viewpoint of the BIAN Architecture in which it appears.

In the Metamodel, a Service Domain is represented as an ArchiMate capability. It appears as such in the Service Landscape diagrams (Section 2.3), in its relationships to the BIAN Business Capabilities (Section 2.10), in the Wireframes (Sub-section 2.9.2) and in the Service Domain Overview Diagram (Section 2.8).

Service Domains are also represented as UML classes. In the Business Scenarios they appear as lifelines on the UML Sequence Diagram (Sub-section 2.9.1).

The BIAN repository links these different representations to the same Service Domain concept.

■ 2.5   BIAN CONTROL RECORD AND SERVICE DOMAIN INFORMATION PROFILE

The Control Record describes the main business information governed by the Service Domain.

As shown in the BIAN Metamodel view represented in Figure 2-10, a Service Domain fulfills its role and responsibility by the execution of a Functional Pattern on an Asset Type. The **Control Record** is the result of the execution of this role. Each time a Service Domain fulfills its role, a Control Record instance is created or adapted.

The complete collection of business information governed by a Service Domain when implemented as a stand-alone service center, is described by the **Service Domain Information Profile**. The Service Domain Information Profile consists of information on two levels:

- Information at the level of service domain ("**SD Information**") used for the control and management of the Service Domain as a service center. This includes its specification, set-up, any externally referenced information retrieved from other service centers and also service analysis and reporting information.
- Information at the level of the Service Domain's role execution. This is covered by the **Control Record** instances. The Control Record can be further decomposed into **Behavior Qualifiers** according to a **Behavior Qualifier Type**.

The Control Record structure is based on a "pattern", as explained in the following sections.

2 Explaining the BIAN Architecture

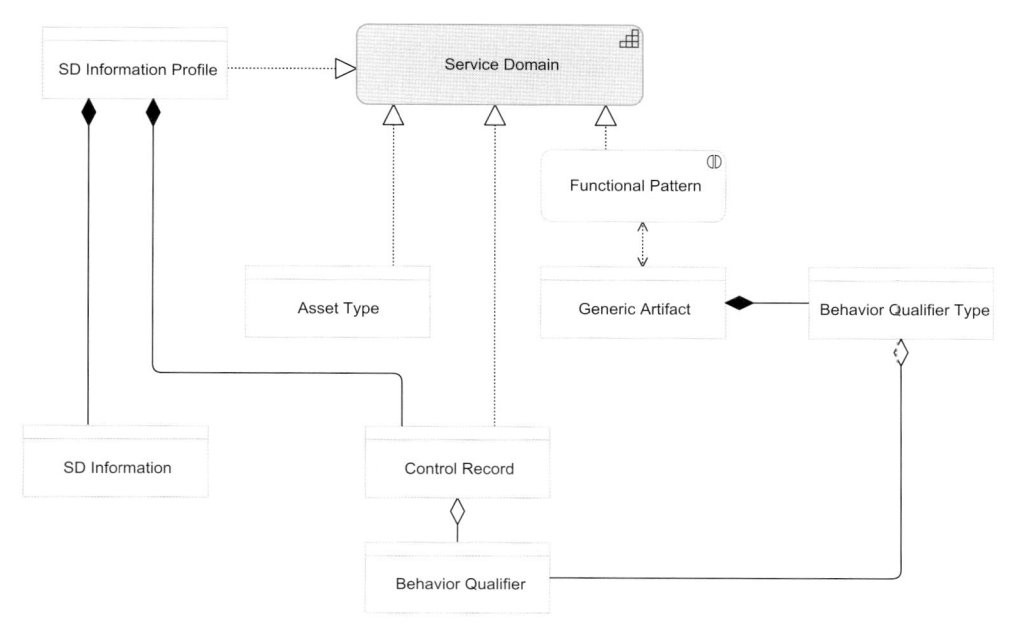

Figure 2-10 BIAN Metamodel, Control Record Model view

2.5.1 Control Record

A Control Record represents a set of business information that reflects all information created during the fulfillment of the role of a Service Domain on instances of an Asset Type.

A Service Domain fulfills its role and responsibility by the execution of a Functional Pattern on an instance of an Asset Type. Hence, the Control Record represents the information about the **Asset Type** combined with the information that is central to the execution of the Functional Pattern, the **Generic Artifact**. Therefore, the following naming convention is used for the Control Record of a Service Domain: the concatenation of the Asset Type and the Generic Artifact.

The Service Domain is responsible for executing the Functional Pattern and managing the Control Record accordingly, during the entire lifespan of the Asset instance.

For example, Figure 2-11 shows the Control Record for the "Party Reference Data Directory" Service Domain. The Service Domain's role is fulfilled by the execution of its Functional Pattern "Catalog" on its Asset Type "Party Reference Data". The Generic Artifact of "Catalog" is "Directory Entry". Hence, the Control Record is named "Party Reference Data Directory Entry". The Control Record of this Service Domain represents the directory of reference data about "party". For each party, there is one Party Reference Data Directory Entry. This directory entry is created by the Service Domain and managed (updated) during the full lifecycle of this information: as long as the party and its Party Reference Data are relevant for the bank.

```
                    ┌─────────────────────────────┐
                    │      «ServiceDomain»        │
                    │  Party Reference Data Directory │
                    └─────────────────────────────┘
                         △       △       △
                         ┊       ┊       ┊
                         ┊       ┊       ┌─────────────────┐
                         ┊       ┊       │     Catalog     │
                         ┊       ┊       └─────────────────┘
                         ┊       ┊                ↕
┌──────────────────────┐ ┊       ┊       ┌─────────────────┐
│     «AssetType»      │ ┊       ┊       │ «GenericArtifact»│
│  PartyReferenceData  │ ┊       ┊       │  DirectoryEntry  │
└──────────────────────┘ ┊       ┊       └─────────────────┘
                         ┊
              ┌────────────────────────────────────┐
              │         «ControlRecord»            │
              │ PartyReferenceDataDirectoryEntry   │
              └────────────────────────────────────┘
```

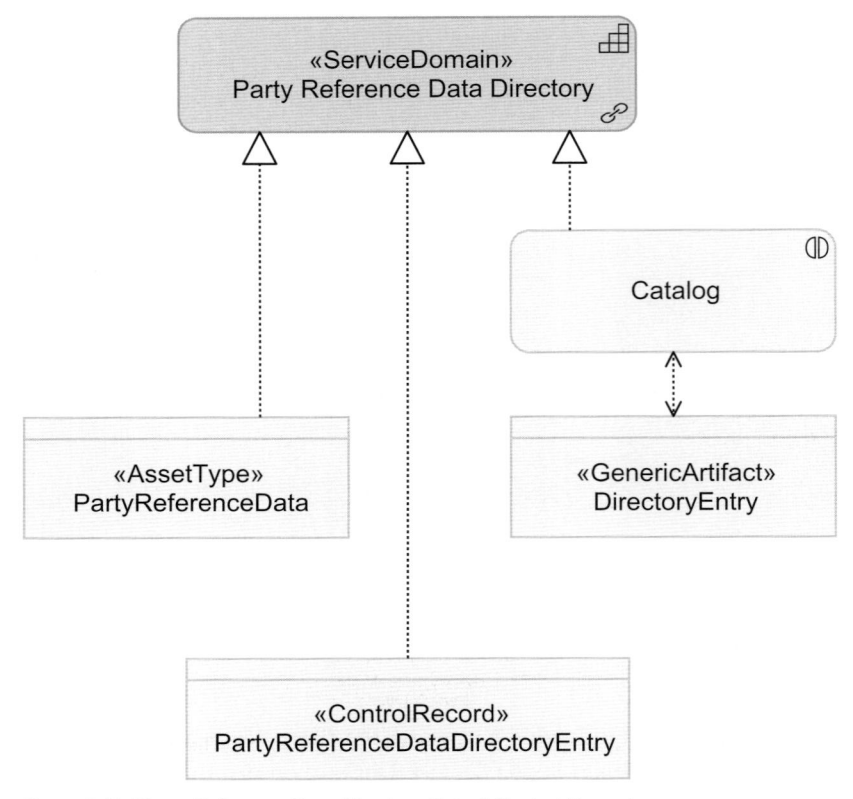

Figure 2-11 "Party Reference Data Directory Entry" Control Record

A Service Domain can be responsible for one Control Record instance, e.g. a business plan, or for multiple instances, e.g. the reference data of many parties. A Control Record can be short-lived, e.g. a customer interaction, or long-lived, e.g. party reference data.

2.5.2 Behavior Qualifier

The work performed by the Service Domain will be captured in the Control Record and its constituent elements called Behavior Qualifiers. A **Behavior Qualifier** is a set of business information that qualifies (i.e. refines) the Control Record of a Service Domain.

A Control Record is decomposed into its constituent elements according to a Behavior Qualifier Type as explained in the next section.

Figure 2-12 shows the "Party Reference Data Directory Entry" Control Record, decomposed into four Behavior Qualifiers. The Behavior Qualifier "References" represents properties which are general party reference details. "Associations" represents properties about the party's links and associations to other parties of interest. "Demographics" represents demographic, employment, and educational background properties for the party. "Bank Relations" represents information about any bank-to-party links.

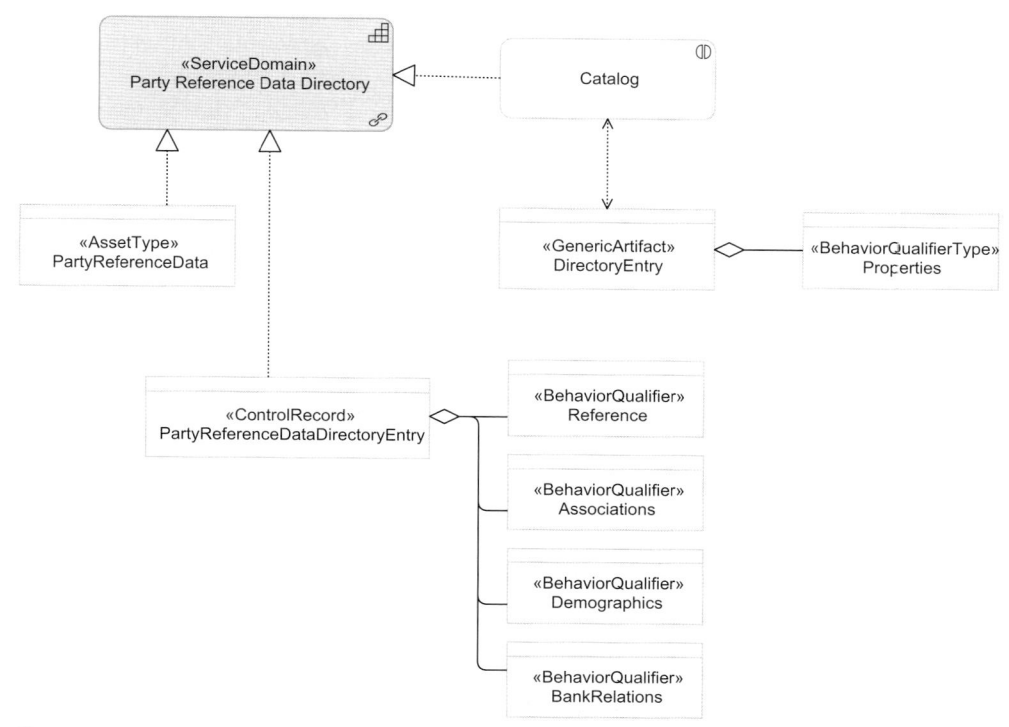

Figure 2-12 Party Reference Data Directory Entry Control Record and its Behavior Qualifiers

2.5.3 Behavior Qualifier Type

A **Behavior Qualifier Type** is a type of information that refines the Generic Artifact.

A Behavior Qualifier Type is a classification of Behavior Qualifiers. For example, the Behavior Qualifier Type for the Generic Artifact "Directory Entry" is "Property".

Figure 2-12 shows the properties of a party according to which the Party Reference Data are decomposed.

The Functional Pattern represents the "conceptual behavior" of the Service Domain. The information central to the execution of this Functional Pattern is the "Generic Artifact". The "Behavior Qualifier Type" is a decomposition of this Generic Artifact. Hence, the Behavior Qualifier Type qualifies (refines) the conceptual behavior of a Service Domain. This partitioning results in the partitioning of the Control Record into its constituent Behavior Qualifiers.

For example, for a Control Record representing a procedure (Generic Artifact for Functional Pattern Process), the Behavior Qualifier Type is "worksteps". A Behavior Qualifier will be a specific Control Record partition, in line with the associated Behavior Qualifier Type. For example, a work-step in a billing process could be "to issue an invoice".

In the example in Figure 2-12, the "Catalog" behavior (or Functional Pattern) creates a "Directory Entry" (Generic Artifact), with Behavior Qualifier Type "properties". The behavior of "cataloguing" is partitioned by cataloguing each one of the "properties" of the party.

Another example is a Service Domain that "fulfills" (Functional Pattern) an "arrangement" (Generic Artifact). Each "feature" (Behavior Qualifier Type) of the arrangement, such as "interest arrangement" or "fee arrangement" (Behavior Qualifier) will be fulfilled by the Service Domain.

The Behavior Qualifier types used to break down the BIAN Functional Patterns and their Generic Artifacts, are shown in Table 2-4.

Table 2-4 Functional Pattern, Generic Artifacts and Behavior Qualifier types

Functional Pattern	Generic Artifact	Behavior Qualifier Type	Example
DIRECT	Strategy	Goals	Increase market share
MANAGE	Management Plan	Duties	Relationship development, Troubleshooting
ADMINISTER	Administrative Plan	Routines	Time-sheet recording
DESIGN	Specification	Aspects	Business requirements
DEVELOP	Development	Deliverables	Functional module specification
PROCESS	Procedure	Worksteps	Invoice generation
OPERATE	Operating Session	Functions	Message capture/routing
MAINTAIN	Maintenance Arrangement	Tasks	Preventive maintenance task
FULFILL	Arrangement	Features	Current account standing order
TRANSACT	Transaction	Tasks/Steps	FX pricing, market trade, clearing & settlement
ADVISE	Advice	Topics	Tax advice, Corporate finance
MONITOR	State	Measures	Composite position, Customer alert
TRACK	Log Record	Events	Customer life event, Servicing event
CATALOG	Directory Entry	Properties	Product pricing rules, Customer reference details
ENROLL	Membership	Clauses	Qualification/membership purpose
AGREE TERMS	Agreement	Terms & Conditions	Required disclosures,
ASSESS	Assessment	Tests	Password verification
ANALYSE	Analysis	Algorithms	Average balance calculation, Propensity to buy
ALLOCATE	Allocation	Criteria	Staff assignment, Facility allocation

Though a single general Behavior Qualifier type is associated with each Functional Pattern, the actual Behavior Qualifiers defined for a Service Domain will be particular/specific to the Service Domain. For example, a Service Domain with the Functional Pattern "process" has the associated Behavior Qualifier type "work-steps". The actual work-steps defined for each Service Domain with the Functional Pattern "process" will reflect its own specific business role. The work-steps that make up the processing for the Customer Billing Service Domain, for example, reflect how it processes a customer bill, i.e. the customer invoice generation; invoice transmission/dispatch; payment tracking; and payment processing work-steps. Processing other Asset Types will result in different work-steps.

Currently BIAN only breaks down Service Domain Control Records to a first level of Behavior Qualifiers. For some Service Domains with extensive information or functional content, architects may find it necessary to define additional levels of "sub-qualifiers" that break the Control Record down even further. This will, amongst other things, be necessary to define suitably focused Service Operations. One example of possible sub-qualifiers is shown in Figure 2-13 for the Party Reference Data Directory Service Domain with its Functional Pattern "catalog", Generic Artifact "directory entry" and Behavior Qualifier Type "properties".

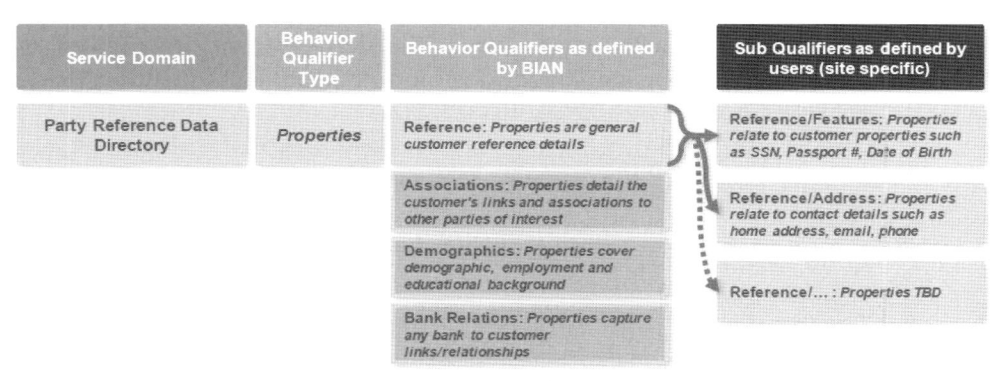

Service Domain	Behavior Qualifier Type	Behavior Qualifiers as defined by BIAN	Sub Qualifiers as defined by users (site specific)
Party Reference Data Directory	Properties	Reference: Properties are general customer reference details	Reference/Features: Properties relate to customer properties such as SSN, Passport #, Date of Birth
		Associations: Properties detail the customer's links and associations to other parties of interest	Reference/Address: Properties relate to contact details such as home address, email, phone
		Demographics: Properties cover demographic, employment and educational background	Reference/...: Properties TBD
		Bank Relations: Properties capture any bank to customer links/relationships	

Figure 2-13 Break down of a Control Record into Behavior Qualifiers and Sub-qualifiers

Currently, BIAN goes to only one level of decomposition as this seems sufficient to define unambiguous business service exchanges. In implementation, additional levels of decomposition can be added, but these are likely to be site-specific. For the further decomposing of Behavior Qualifiers to "Sub"-behavior Qualifiers, it is important that the Behavior Qualifier Type is applied consistently, and the sub-qualifiers define a MECE decomposition of their parent Behavior Qualifier.

2.5.4 Service Domain Control Record Diagram
In the BIAN Repository a **Control Record Diagram** has been created for each Service Domain. It is represented as a UML Class Diagram.

Figure 2-14 shows the Control Record Diagram for the "Party Reference Data Directory" Service Domain. The Control Record Model, depicted in the diagram, is a hierarchic model that assigns the attributes which BIAN defines on the level of Control Record and Behavior Qualifier. It is not BIAN's ambition to define all attributes managed by a Service Domain. The attributes should clarify the responsibility of a Service Domain while remaining sufficiently generic to be relevant for all banks.

This Control Record Diagram only represents the Control Record and Behavior Qualifier "attribute sets" as UML classes, not the Service Domain Information. There is no diagram representing the Service Domain Information Profile (Figure 2-15).

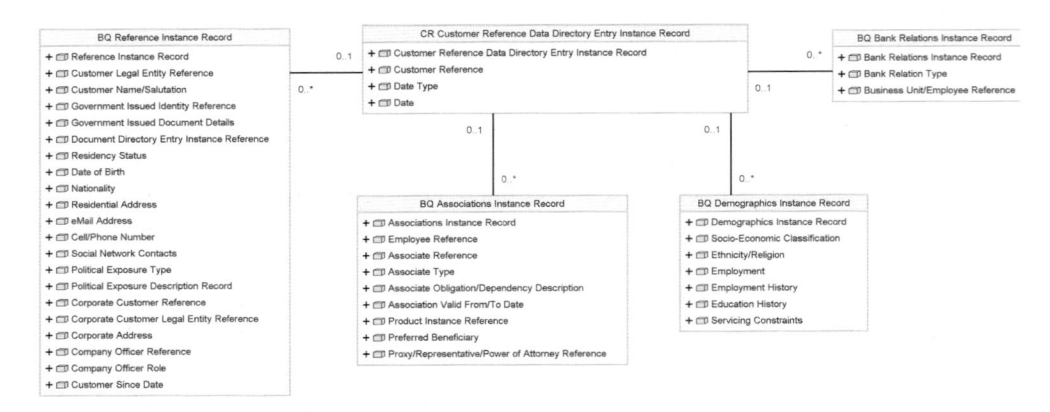

Figure 2-14 Party Reference Data Directory Control Record Diagram

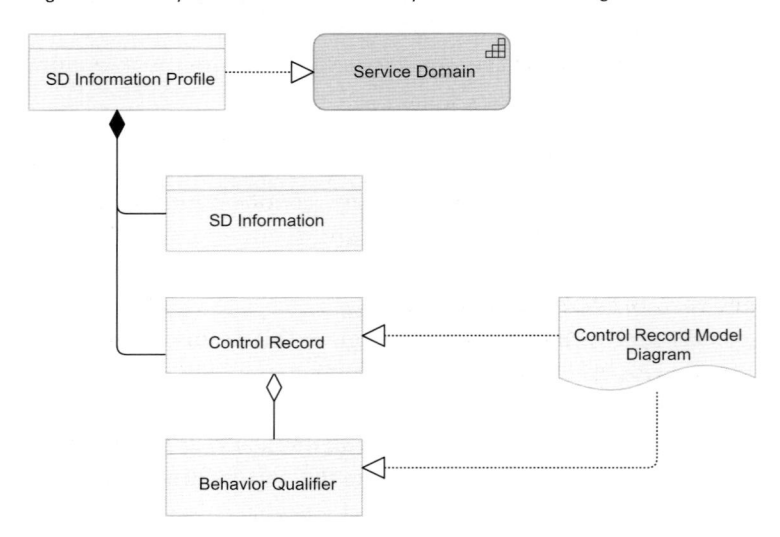

Figure 2-15 Metamodel for the Control Record Diagram

■ 2.6 BIAN BUSINESS OBJECT MODEL

BIAN is developing a **Business Object Model** (BOM) for the financial industry, called the "BIAN BOM".

The existing banking data models and standards such as ISO 20022, IFX, and SWIFT™ are focused on defining the *messages* exchanged in Application Program Interfaces (APIs). These messages are *views* on the core *Business Objects* in banking (such as bank products and services, bank agreements and arrangements). They do not represent a model of the Business Objects themselves. BIAN applies a Business Object Modeling approach to identify all **Business Objects** that are relevant for the financial industry and to model their relationships. The BIAN BOM provides the financial sector with a reference model for information architecture that can be customized to individual needs.

The BIAN BOM is elaborated by modeling the information needs of every BIAN Service Domain, as expressed in its Control Record, according to the "Business Object Modeling approach". The resulting individual Service Domain Business Object Models (Service Domain BOMs) are consolidated into the BIAN BOM. The "Business Object Modeling approach" (or "BOM approach") used to define the Service Domain BOMs and to consolidate them in the BIAN BOM, ensures the consistency of the BIAN BOM.

Figure 2-16 shows the information view on the BIAN Metamodel. Business Objects represent the banking objects, as modelled in the BIAN BOM, independent of any context. The Control Record, Behavior Qualifier, Asset Type and Generic Artifact are "information objects" representing views on these Business Objects from the viewpoint of "business behavior", performed by a Service Domain.

The BOM approach applies a way of thinking, supported by two abstract reference models that are used as patterns for the actual BOM. In the following sections, a summary of the way of thinking and the content and structure patterns is given.

2.6.1 Business Object versus Business Concept

Two key notions in the BOM approach's way of thinking are "business concept" and "business object". Being able to make the distinction is key.

A "concept" is whatever can be thought of. A business concept is a concept that is of importance to the business, i.e. something the business wants to be informed about. A business object relates to something tangible or intangible that exists in reality.

To fulfill the information requirements of the business, business concepts need to be identified. Each business concept should be defined unambiguously by means of a business definition, to avoid misunderstandings between involved parties. The business glossary represents the collection of business concepts, the terms used to reference them and their definition.

To inform businesses concerning the concepts in which they are interested, data needs to be captured and managed. Business concepts, however, are not the building blocks for the information architecture required to steer an effective data architecture.

The building block of the business information architecture is the Business Object. It is a mutually exclusive, collectively exhaustive unit of information. Business Objects relate to each other, and thus constitute the BOM.

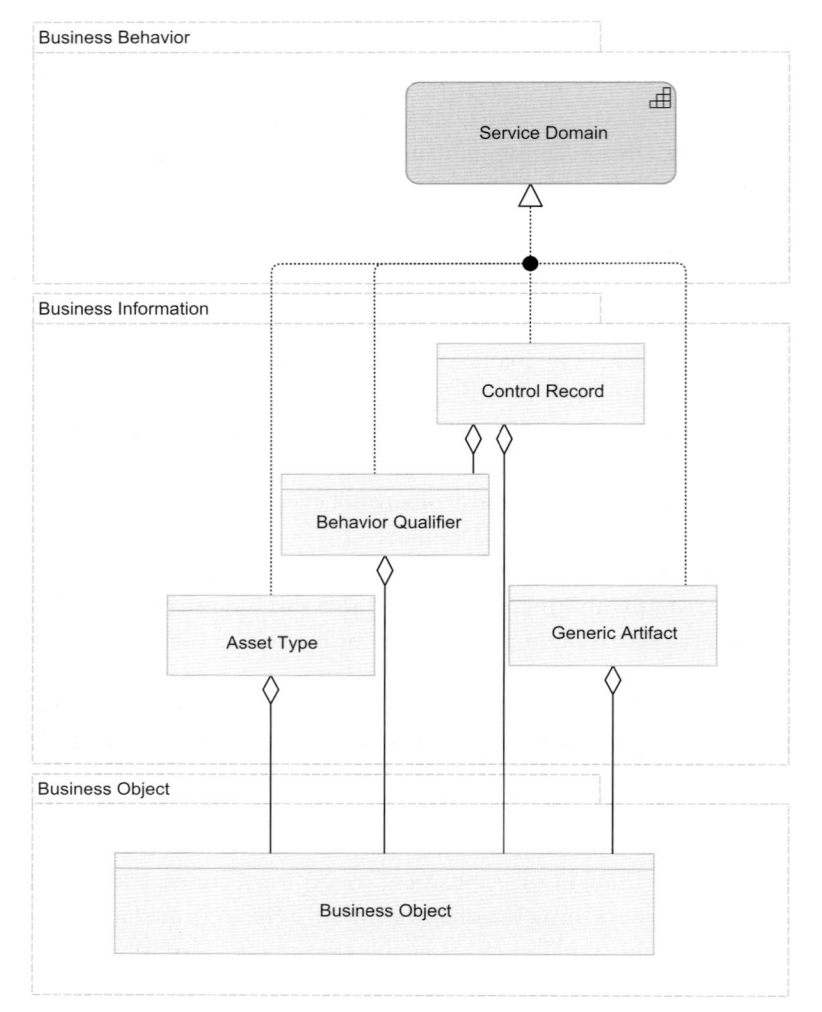

Figure 2-16 BIAN Metamodel, Business Object view

The content and structure patterns of the BOM approach are used to produce unambiguous definitions for business concepts and to distinguish Business Objects from business concepts.

For example, "customer" is clearly a business concept. Any organization will be interested in the parties it serves. However, it is not a business object. A "customer" is a role of a "party". "Party" is a business object. A customer is "a party that buys products from the bank". The same party can have a "supplier" ("a party that supplies items or services to the bank") and "co-worker" ("a party that has an employment agreement with the bank") role.

2.6.2 BOM content pattern

The BOM content pattern, shown in Figure 2-17, is an abstract information model, valid for any business. It contains the Business Objects and their relationships, that make up any business, on a high abstraction level. This model can be made more specific for a particular business context.

The content pattern consists of following Business Objects:

Businesses distinguish themselves from others by the **product**s and **services** which they offer on the market. The sale of a product is concluded in an **agreement** with the **party.**

An agreement (a formal or informal common understanding between two or more parties) is expressed in a set of **arrangements,** where one party engages him/herself against another party "to give, to do, or not to do something".

The fulfillment of one or more arrangements of an agreement can be triggered by giving an **instruction** to do or to give something. Instructions trigger the **transactions** needed to fulfill the arrangements.

The results of these transactions (such as movements in value or amounts of assets, rights and obligations) can be registered through **account entries** on a measuring state called an **account**.

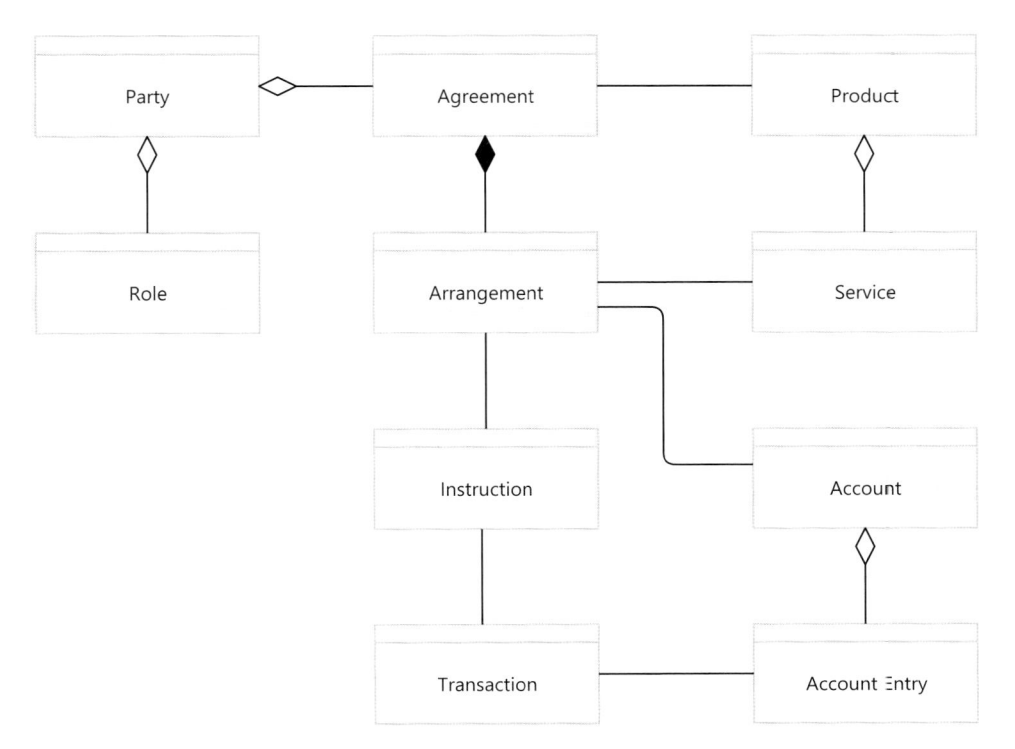

Figure 2-17 BIAN BOM content pattern

Figure 2-18 shows an example of the application of the content pattern. A current account product is sold, resulting in a current account agreement with one or more parties. This agreement consists of (among other) an arrangement concerning the ability to transfer funds (credit transfer service arrangement) and concerning the payment of fees (pricing arrangement). A payment order instruction triggers the necessary payment transactions. This is registered through a current account booking on the account that manages the balance of the current account agreement.

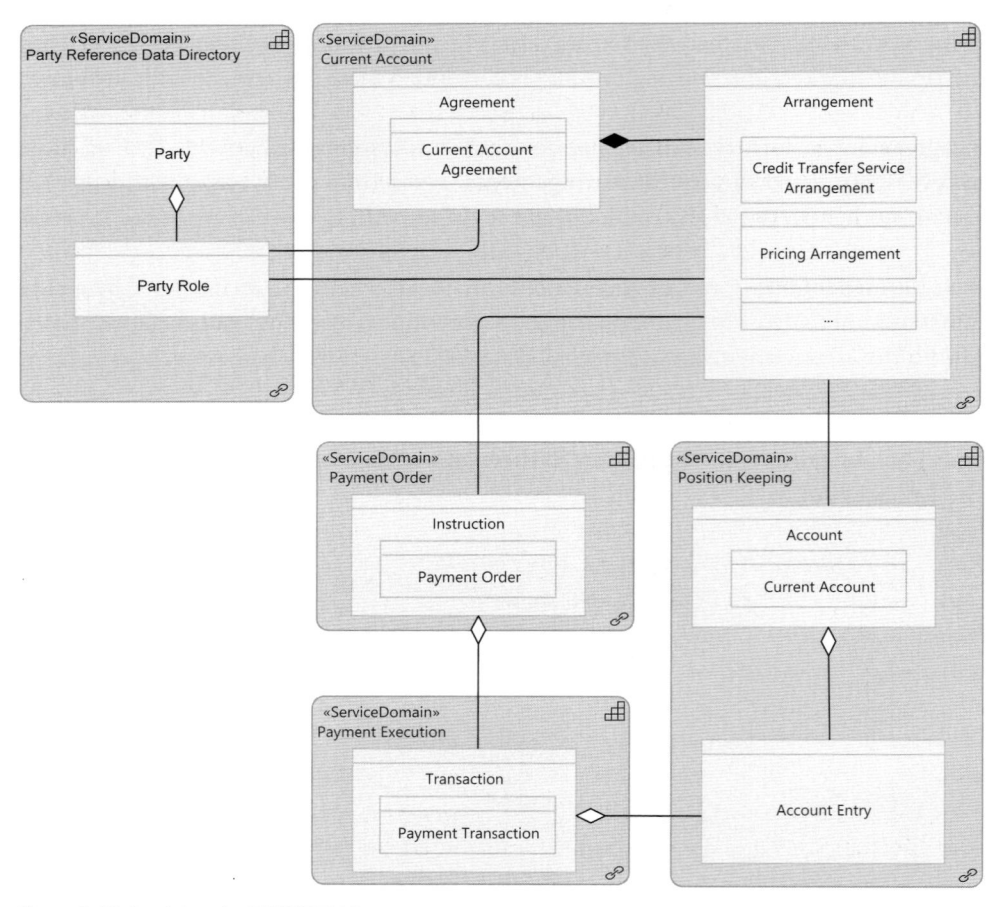

Figure 2-18 Applying the BIAN BOM in payments

2.6.3 BOM structure pattern

The **BOM structure pattern,** depicted in Figure 2-19, enriches the content pattern.

A Business Object can be classified in different ways (it can belong to different "Business Object Types") For example, a party can be an individual (human being) or an organization. It can be a man or a woman.

In applying the BOM approach, we discerned that these concepts are "types" (classifications) of the Business Object "party".

A Business Object is described by Business Object descriptors (such as gender, date of birth...) that are of a certain Business Object descriptor type (e.g., describing, identifying)[20].

Business Objects have Business Object relationships to each other, relationships of a Business Object relationship type.

For example, applying the BOM approach, we discerned that the business concept "spouse" is defined as "the relationship between two parties (Business Object) that is the result of a marital agreement (Business Object)". The "customer" in our example above, is "a party" (**Business Object**) that buys (the relationship) products (Business Object) from the bank (a specific instance of the Business Object "party").

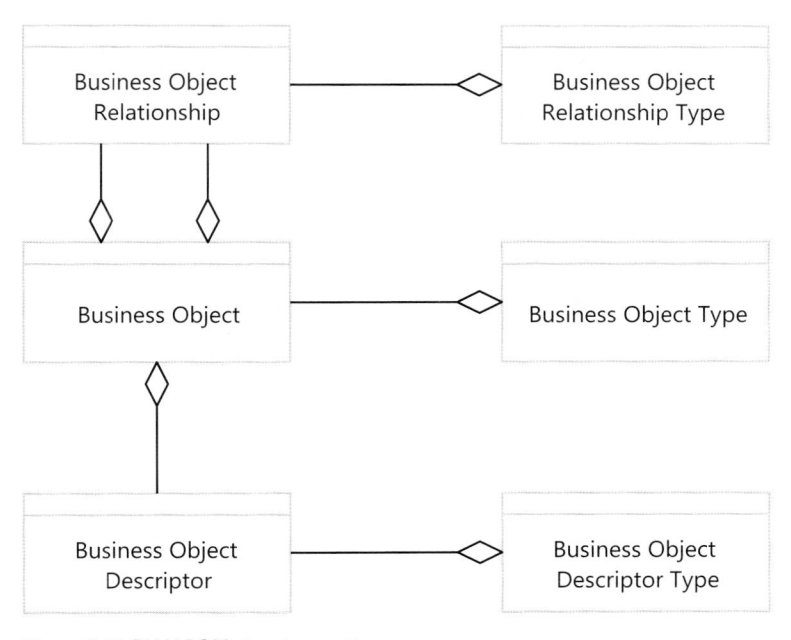

Figure 2-19 BIAN BOM structure pattern

---

20 The classification of parties into "man" or "woman", is based on the Business Object Descriptor "gender". "Gender" is a business concept but not a "Business Object", it is a "Business Object descriptor".
The classification of a party as "man" or "woman" is called a "taxonomical classification". A classification based on a functional perspective; it is called a "functional classification". For example, a party can be classified according to its role in an agreement, e.g., buyer or seller. Again, "buyer" and "seller" are business concepts, but not Business Objects.

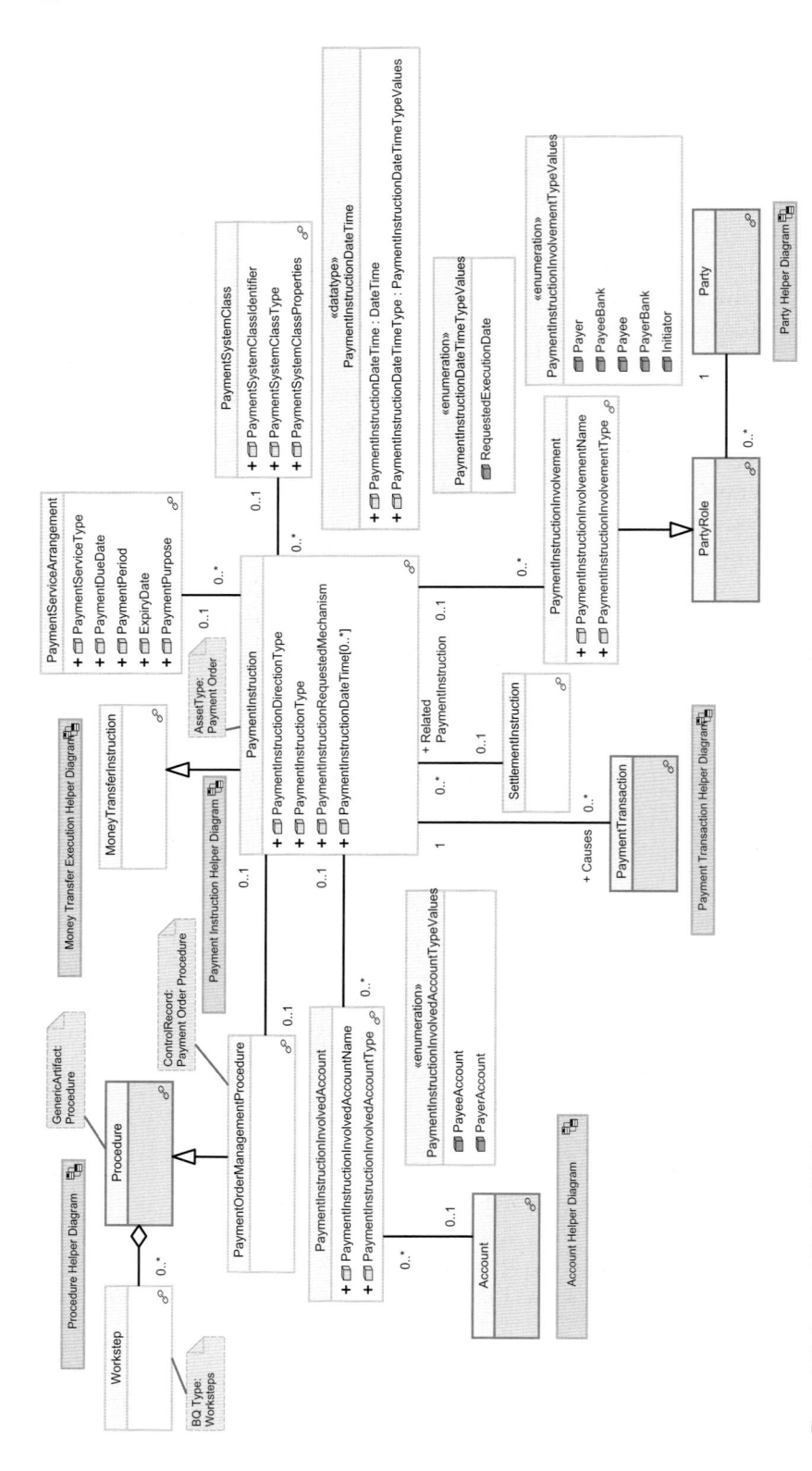

Figure 2-20 Payment Order BOM Diagram

2.6.4 The Service Domain BOM Diagram

For each Service Domain, a BOM Diagram has been created, that represent the Business Objects that support the functionality of the Service Domain and their relationships. This diagram is a BIAN artifact defined at the level of design.

A Service Domain BOM Diagram, as illustrated in Figure 2-20, is represented as a UML Class Diagram, that shows the attributed entities (in white color) managed and maintained by the Service Domain. In the diagram, the entities colored in red are managed and maintained by other Service Domains but referenced in this Service Domain. For example, in the BOM diagram for the Payment Order Service Domain (Figure 2-20), "Party" and "PartyRole" are two Business Objects colored in red. These are managed by the Party Reference Data Directory Service Domain, but there is a reference to them in the Payment Order BOM. These red Business Objects are the "sticking edges" that link Service Domain views on the BIAN BOM together.

2.6.5 BOM abstraction levels

The Business Objects of the content pattern are present as the highest abstraction[21] level of the BIAN BOM. They can appear as such in a Service Domain BOM or as a generalization of the Business Objects that play a role in a Service Domain.

Figure 2-21 shows a view on the Current Account Service Domain BOM, with several levels of abstraction. The Current Account Agreement is a specialization of the content pattern object "Agreement". The Current Account Arrangement is a specialization of "Arrangement". It is specialized in turn into the different types of arrangements relevant for a Current Account Agreement (such as "Interests Arrangement" and "Fees Arrangement").

2.6.6 BOM - ISO 20022 mapping

The ISO 20022 Business Model is a part of the ISO 20022 standard, an ISO standard for electronic data interchange between financial institutions. The ISO 20022 Business Model is used to derive the data elements used in ISO 20022 message definitions (the ISO 20022 message concepts), thereby ensuring a common understanding across all messages used to support the various business domains.

As shown in Figure 2-22, the ISO 20022 Business Model is part of the ISO 20022 Data Dictionary which includes detailed information about every business concept.

BIAN has developed a mapping between the Business Objects and attributes of the BIAN BOM and the business components and elements of the ISO 20022 Business Model. This is called the "ISO 20022 Light Mapping".

---

21 Abstraction in the sense of "generalization", not "detailing".

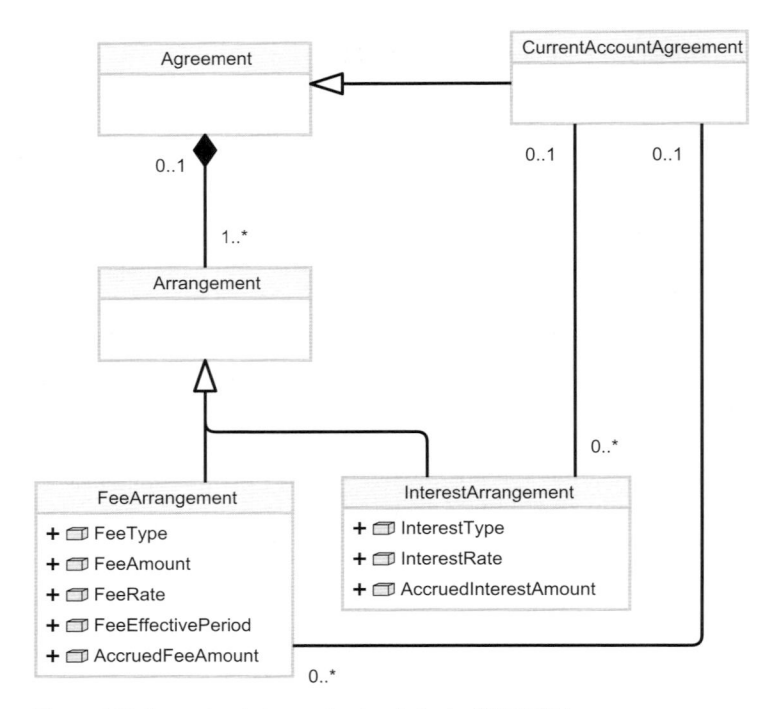

Figure 2-21 Example of abstraction levels in the BIAN BOM

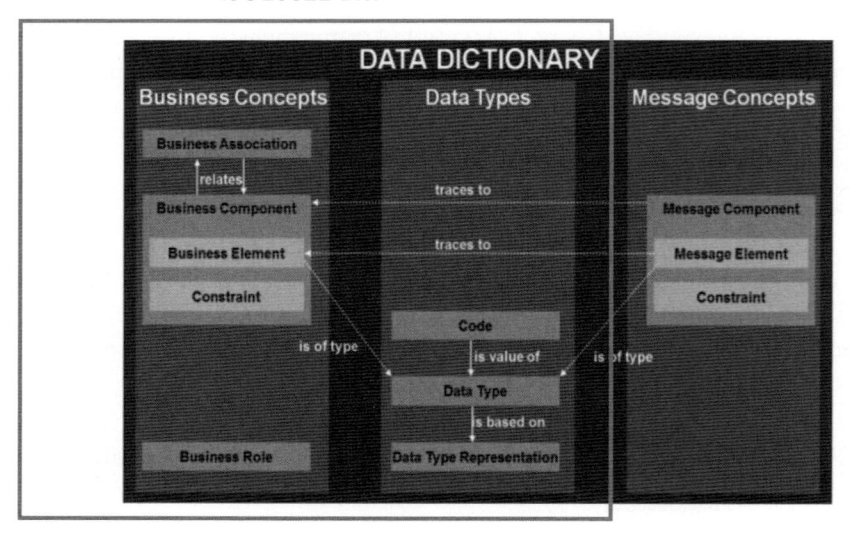

Figure 2-22 The scope of the ISO 20022 Business Model

The ISO 20022 Light Mapping is only defined for Service Domains that are relevant to the ISO 20022 business domains: Payment, Securities, Trade Service and Forex.

These mappings are published as tables in Excel files on the BIAN Wiki page.

■ 2.7 BIAN SERVICE OPERATION AND SEMANTIC API

BIAN specifies **Service Operations** and **Semantic API** definitions to support the challenges of interoperability within a bank and in the open finance ecosystem.

Service Operations are defined (refined) according to a "pattern", explained in the following sections.

As shown in the view on the Metamodel represented in Figure 2-23, every **Service Domain** offers a collection of **Service Operations.** The purpose of an offered service is characterized by an **Action Term** which is a fundamental unit of behavior. A Service Operation offered by a Service Domain is made available to the environment through an access point called a **Semantic API Endpoint.** The collection of the Semantic API Endpoints of one Service Domain is represented by its **Semantic API**.

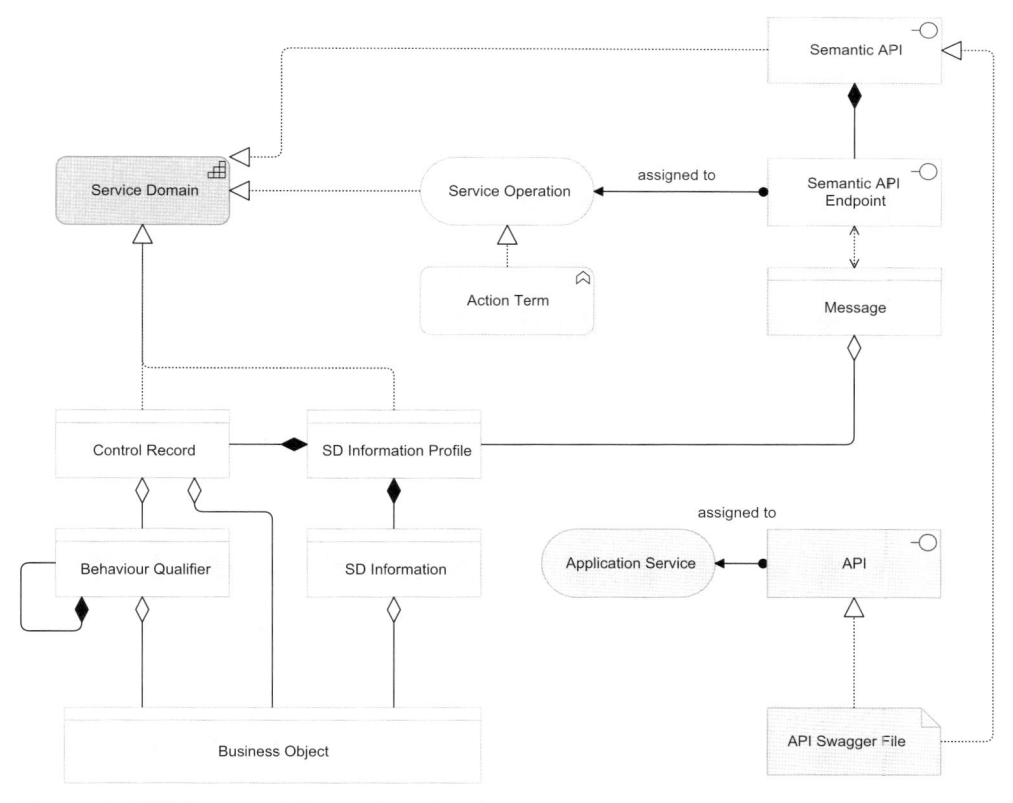

Figure 2-23 BIAN Metamodel, Service Operation view

The **Message**, containing the information exchanged in a Service Operation, as described in its Semantic API Endpoint, refers to the **Information Profile** of the Service Domain, or any of its constituent parts. This information content can also be expressed as a view on the Business Objects, as defined in the BIAN BOM. The Service Operation and its

Semantic API can be used to define and design **Application Services** and **APIs** (not part of the BIAN Framework). A machine-readable **Swagger File** can be generated from the Semantic API. The Semantic API Swaggers can be extended to create Application APIs and microservices.

2.7.1 Nature of the Service Operation: Action Term

An Action Term is a fundamental unit of behavior that characterizes the purpose of a Service Operation.

BIAN has identified a standard set of actions that characterize the different types of Service Operations. Each Service Operation executes exactly one Action Term. The collection of Action Terms is intended to cover all the main types of service exchange any Service Domain might support.

Figure 2-24 shows the Actions Terms as they apply for different Functional Patterns. A Service Domain with a certain Functional Pattern, will have Service Operations corresponding to these Action Terms.

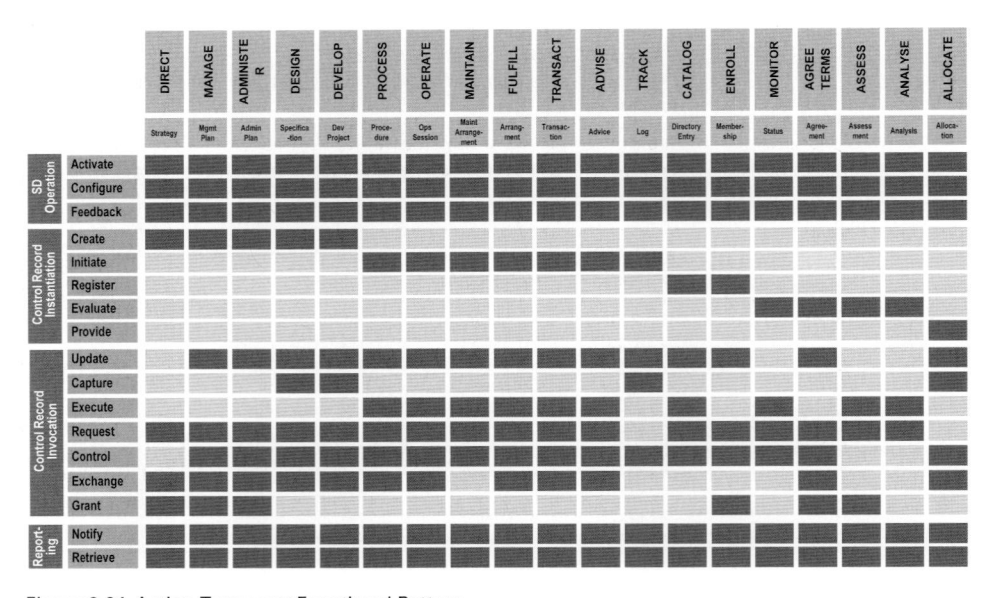

Figure 2-24 Action Terms per Functional Pattern

The BIAN Action Terms can be grouped into four main categories, related to their effect. These categories also apply to the corresponding Service Operations:

- Service Domain (SD) Operations: Action Terms/Service Operations that act on/ influence the overall operation of the Service Domain as a service center (Action Terms: activate, configure and feedback).

- Instantiation: Action Terms/Service Operations that result in the creation of a new Control Record instance, i.e. start a new lifecycle execution (Action Terms: create, initiate, register, evaluate and provide).
- Invocation: Action Terms/Service Operations that act on an existing Control Record instance – typically invoking some function and/or changing/updating its state in some way (Action Terms: update, control, exchange, capture, execute, request and grant).
- Reporting: Action Terms/Service Operations that obtain or subscribe to information for one or more Control Record instances. These actions do not change the state of the instance in any way (Action Terms: retrieve and notify).

The list of Action Terms (AT) and their description can be found in Table 2-5.

Table 2-5 BIAN Action Term descriptions

AT Group	AT Name	AT Description
SD Operations	Activate	Commence/open an operational or administrative service. Example: Activate the ATM network operation.
	Configure	Change the operating parameters of a unit, operational or production function for an ongoing service/capability. Example: Change online ATMs in the network to take machines out of service.
	Feedback	Capture transaction or event details associated with a lifecycle step. Example: An employee logs time spent working on a project against the plan.
Instantiation	Create	Manufacture and distribute an item (terms considered: create/manufacture/make). Example: Create a new analytical model design.
	Initiate	Begin an action including any required initialization. Example: Initiate a payment transaction.
	Register	Classify and capture details of an entity in a catalog/directory Example: Capture a new customer's details.
	Evaluate	Perform a check, trial or evaluation. Example: The eligibility to sell a product is checked against an existing agreement.
	Provide	Assign or allocate resources or facilities. Example: A branch requests an allocation of cash for its tellers.
Invocation	Update	Change the value of some Control Record instance's properties. Example: Update a customer's reference details with a change of address.
	Control	Conclude, complete activity. Example: Terminate the use of a product version.
	Exchange	Provide input/response to handling of a Control Record instance. Example: Accept, decline, confirm, verify.
	Capture	Capture transactional activity details against an instance. Example: Log an event/action, record usage.

AT Group	AT Name	AT Description
	Execute	Execute a task or action on an established facility (note typically creates a result). Example: Apply a payment to a charge card.
	Request	Request for the provision of some service. Example: A customer requests that a standing order is set up on the current account.
	Grant	Allow the execution of a transaction. Example: Regulatory compliance authorizes a product design feature.
Reporting	Notify	Provide details against a predefined notification agreement. Example: A unit subscribes to update notifications from the customer agreement service domain.
	Retrieve	Return information/report as requested. Examples: Obtain an account balance. Request a report covering activity analysis.

2.7.2 Subject of the Service Operation

A Service Operation is a business service that is exposed by a Service Domain.

A Service Operation supports external access to the information and/or functionality offered by a Service Domain. The nature or main purpose of a Service Operation can be inferred from its Action Term. What the Service Operation actually achieves is clarified by the part of the Information Profile it refers to.

The Service Operation can apply to different levels of the Service Domain's functionality and/or information. It can act at the Service Domain level, influencing its overall operation. It can act upon one or more selected Control Record instances (both creating new instances and acting on existing instances). It can, through addressing Behavior Qualifiers, act upon some subset of the functionality and information provided by the Service Domain.

As an example, Figure 2-25 shows a selection of Service Operations offered by the Current Account Service Domain. This Service Domain, with the "fulfillment" Functional Pattern, has Control Record instances called "Current Account Arrangements". The Behavior Qualifier type for an Arrangement is "Features". Hence, the Current Account Arrangement record is broken into parts, representing the different product features that make up the current account product. In this example, we show two Behavior Qualifiers/product features: Service Fees (handles the array of fees and penalties applicable to the current account facility) and Payments (handles the set-up and execution of different types of payment made from the account).

The "initiate" Action Term results in the creation and initialization of a new Control Record instance or a Behavior Qualifier instance for an existing Control Record. For Current Account, the initiate Action Term results in the following response at the Control Record and Behavior Qualifier levels:

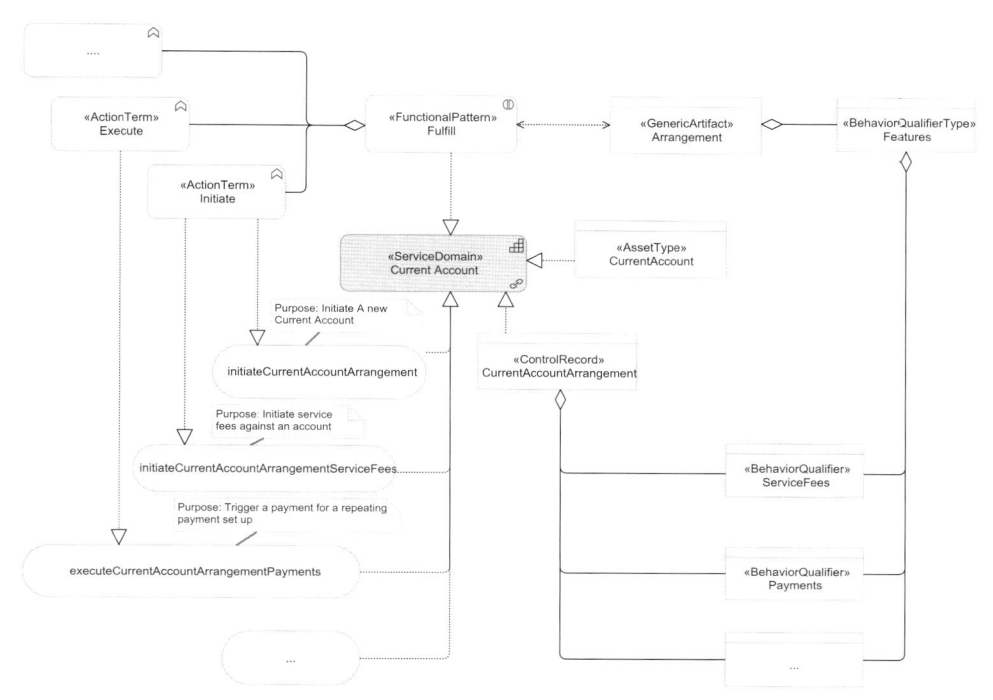

Figure 2-25 Current Account Service Operations work on different levels of the information profile

- "initiateCurrentAccountArrangement" will result in a new current account facility being established and initialized as appropriate.
- "initiateCurrentAccountArrangementServiceFees" will result in fee/penalty handling features being established for an existing current account.

The "execute" Action Term acts on an active Control Record instance or one of its subordinate Behavior Qualifier instances. For Current Account, the "execute" action can result in, for example:
- "executeCurrentAccountArrangementPayment", that will trigger a payment transaction against an existing payment feature.

2.7.3 Semantic API

A **Semantic API Endpoint** is an access point where one Service Operation offered by one Service Domain is made available to the environment. The **Semantic API** is the collection of the Semantic API Endpoints of one Service Domain.

The Semantic API and its Endpoints provide more detail about the Service Operation(s). They can be considered a high-level specification of the Service Operations offered by a Service Domain. The BIAN Semantic API outlines the business purpose and high-level information content of service exchanges.

The BIAN standard is, by choice, implementation agnostic. But in order to support the use of the BIAN Service Domain partitions and Service Operations as a starting point for container-based architectures and the more general use of application program interfaces (APIs), the BIAN definition has been mapped to the REST[22] architecture style.

The assumption is made that the BIAN Service Domain matches the application boundary (the "A") of the API. The Service Domain's Service Operations then make up the collection of program interfaces (the "PI"s) that complete the API's description. A BIAN Semantic API consists of the collection of specifications for Service Operations offered by a Service Domain, with the Service Operation specifications formatted in a manner that is suited for developer enhancement/extension (for example adding bank implementation-specific reference attributes) in view of implementation in the REST architecture style.

Figure 2-26 shows the "Current Account Semantic API" and a sample of its Service Operations related to their Semantic API Endpoints. This specification can be used to design application services and APIs such as "Account Opening Service and associated API" and "Payment Service and associated API".

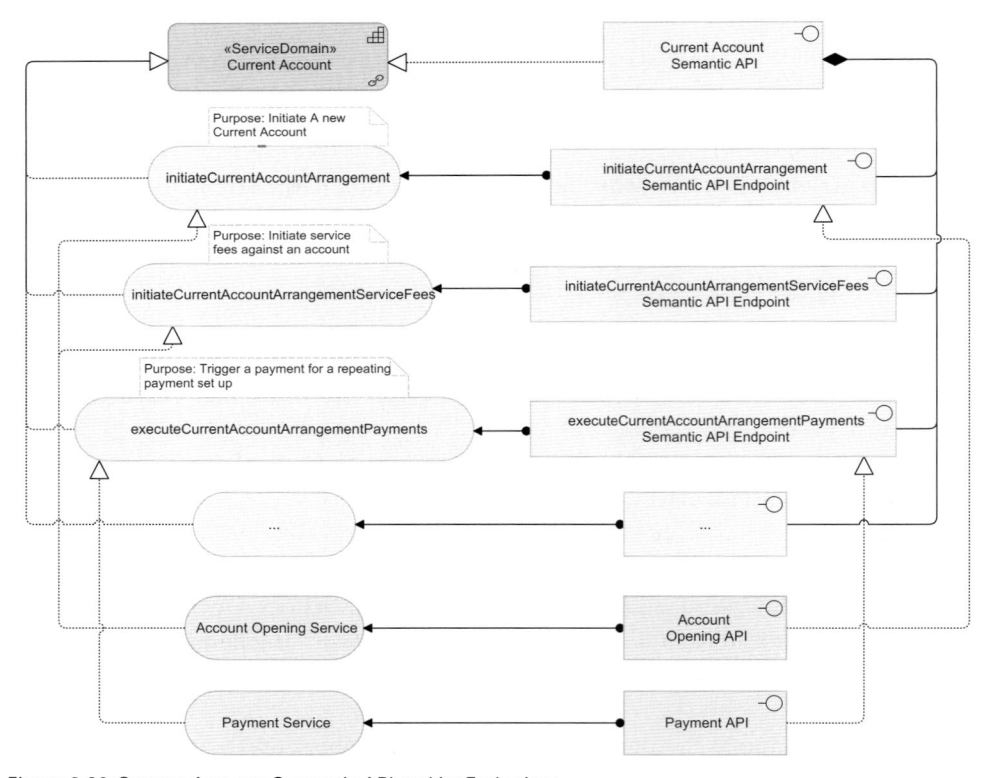

Figure 2-26 Current Account Semantic API and its Endpoints

---

22 Representational State Transfer (REST) is the most popular approach being used for API development in the banking industry at this time.

The Semantic API Endpoints are specified in the REST style as follows.

The Action Term is "converted" into a http method (or "verb") and a "noun".

The BIAN specification includes extensive references to actions and behaviors whereas the REST architectural style, by definition, exchanges only the accessed resource's feature and state information. Therefore, the Action Terms have been converted to their noun form. In this way the action is redefined as the result or outcome of the action being performed, that can then be treated more readily as properties of a resource. The Action Terms, their equivalent http verb and their amended "noun"-forms are listed in Table 2-6.

Table 2-6 Translating Action Term into resources and http verbs

Action Term	Noun	Verb	Action Term	Noun	Verb
Activate	Activation	POST	**Update**	Update	PUT
Configure	Configuration	PUT	**Control**	Control	PUT
Feedback	Feedback	PUT	**Exchange**	Exchange	PUT
Create	Creation	POST	**Capture**	Capture	PUT
Initiate	Initiation	POST	**Execute**	Execution	PUT
Register	Registration	POST	**Request**	Requisition	PUT
Evaluate	Evaluation	POST	**Grant**	Grant	PUT
Provide	Provision	POST			
Retrieve	Maps directly to the HTTP GET method				
Notify	Is not currently used in the BIAN mapping				

Figure 2-27 shows the Semantic API Endpoint specification for the Service Operation "executeCurrentAccountArrangementPayment". This is an example of a Service Operation that acts on the most detailed level specified by BIAN: an individual Behavior Qualifier. This can be derived from the presence of the identification of the individual Behavior Qualifier, Control Record and Service Doman instance. If no such identification is present, all instances need to be addressed by the Service operation.

The input and output information, exchanged in the Service Operation, is expressed in its **Message**. The attributes listed in this Message refer to the attributes of the Control Record Model.

BIAN Endpoint descriptions are far from implementation specifications. The BIAN Service Domain Service Operation descriptions that can be found on the BIAN Semantic API Portal are only formatted to look like a REST endpoint specification in order to ease their adoption by developers familiar with the REST architecture style. It is important

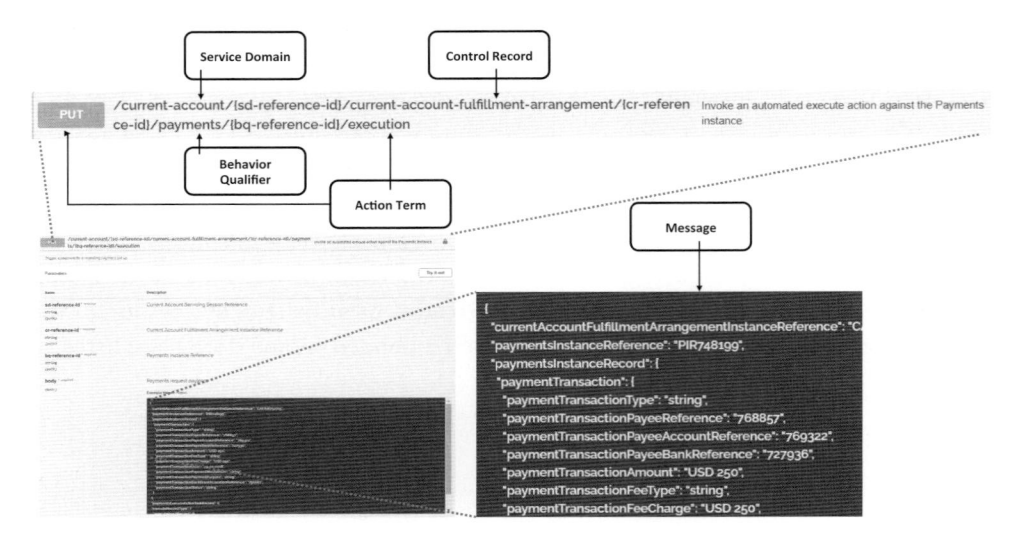

Figure 2-27 BIAN Semantic API Endpoint format

for developers to recognize early on that these semantic descriptions are some way from implementation-level specifications.

2.7.4 Swagger File

A **Swagger** File is a machine-readable format (according to Swagger[TM23]) of a Semantic API description. It can be used as starting point for actual implementations.

BIAN provides a Swagger file, generated from the Semantic API, for each Service Domain.

■ 2.8   THE SERVICE DOMAIN OVERVIEW DIAGRAM

The Service Domain Overview Diagram provides a complete overview of the BIAN model elements, from the point of view of a Service Domain.

Figure 2-28 shows the Service Domain Overview Diagram for "Current Account".

The Service Domain is the result of the Functional Pattern "Fulfill", applied to the Asset Type "Current Account". As the Generic Artifact for "Fulfill" is "Arrangement", with Behavior Qualifier Type "Feature", the Control Record is "CurrentAccountArrangment", with a set of Behavior Qualifiers describing the features of a current account arrangement.

---

23 Swagger[TM] allows you to describe the structure of your APIs so that machines can read them.

On Service Domain level, a set of referenced information is mentioned (for example "Bankrates").

The "Analytics Object" represents the fact that a Service Domain not only manages operational information but also provides "analytical information" (in this example, this could, for example, be the number of current accounts, the amount of time spent on administering these accounts…).

The Control Record Diagram and the Service Domain BOM Diagram are accessible through a hyperlink.

The Service Operation Groups, depicted on the diagram are more of a reminder to click on the hyperlink to the Current Account Semantic API on the API Portal, where the API Endpoints and their Messages provide an overview of the Service Operations as BIAN specifies them.

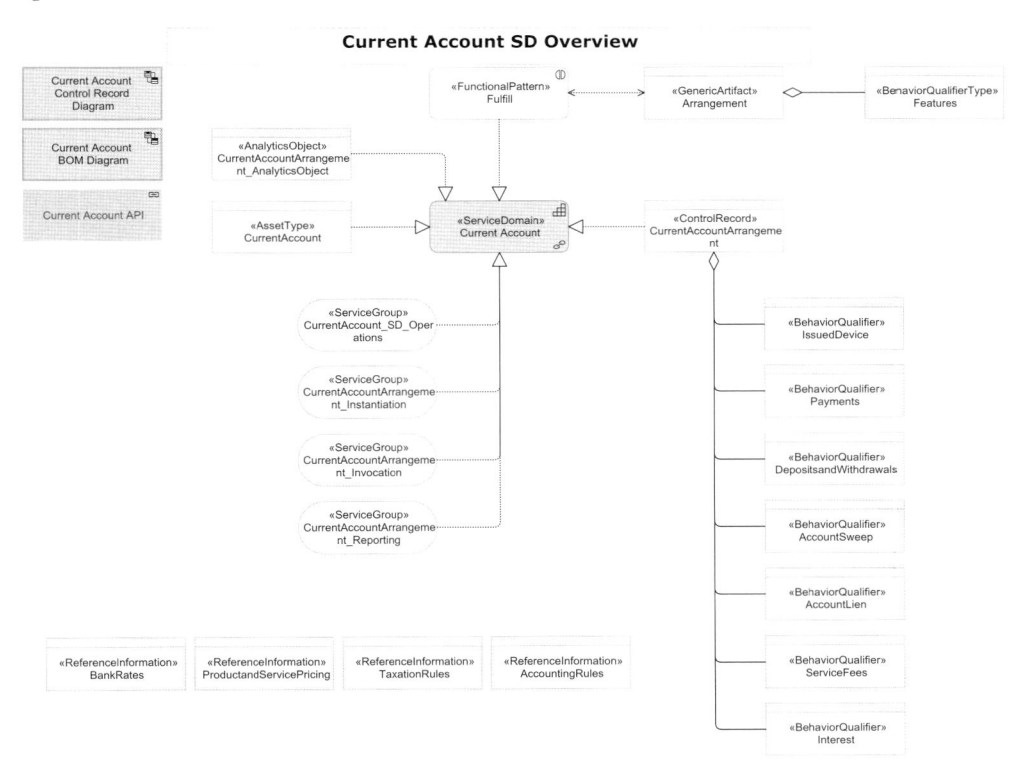

Figure 2-28 Service Domain Overview Diagram for Current Account

2.9 BIAN BUSINESS SCENARIOS AND WIREFRAMES

BIAN **Business Scenarios and Wireframes** provide practical examples of how Service Domains can interact. They are not part of the BIAN standard but are included in the BIAN Framework because they provide a powerful mechanism to illustrate, by example, the roles and interactions supported by the Service Domains.

Figure 2-29 shows the part of the BIAN Metamodel focused on Business Scenarios and Wireframes.

A **Business Scenario** is a depiction of how BIAN Service Domains might work together through Service Operations in response to an event. These **Service Operations** realize the **Service Connections** between the **Service Domains**, required to produce the desired outcome of the scenario.

A **Wireframe** is a depiction that shows the **Service Connections** between a selection of Service Domains.

The service dependency between two Service Domains, one offering the service and one consuming the service, is called "**First Order Connection**".

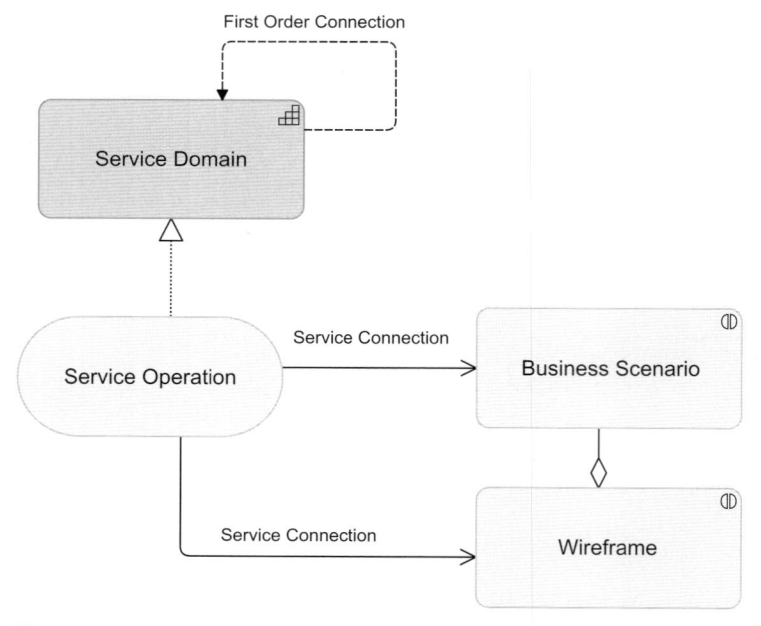

Figure 2-29 BIAN Metamodel, Business Scenario and Wireframe view

2.9.1 Business Scenario
A **Business Scenario** is a linked series of interactions between Service Domains in response to a business event.

2 Explaining the BIAN Architecture

BIAN introduces the Business Scenario as a mechanism to model interactions between Service Domains in order to produce a certain outcome. This simple technique identifies the involved Service Domains and the Service Operation exchanges associated with handling a business event or transaction. Business Scenarios resemble process designs, but their setup is different: the flow is not tightly coupled, just set out to be read in a sensible sequence – each exchange is loosely coupled/asynchronous and any start/end dependencies are not captured formally.

A Business Scenario is not intended to define a standard process but is simply one viable example of possible behavior. Neither is it intended to be exhaustive or complete; it merely needs to include sufficient context to clarify the targeted actions of the Service Domains being considered.

All possible financial services business activity can be modelled as a pattern of collaboration involving a suitable selection of Service Domains taken from the Service Landscape. The BIAN Business Scenario is not a formal design but merely an archetypal instance of one possible pattern of collaboration.

BIAN also uses the Business Scenarios to clarify the nature of the service exchanges between Service Domains and the role of the Service Domains by providing practical examples.

An example of a BIAN Business Scenario is shown in Figure 2-30.

Business Scenarios are visualized in a UML Sequence Diagram. The Service Domains involved in the Business Scenario are represented as lifelines.

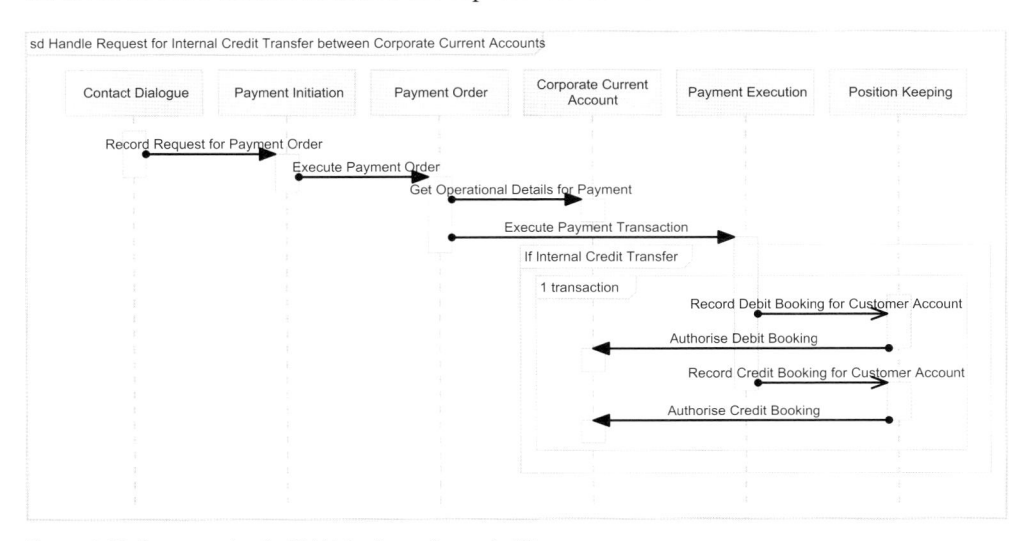

Figure 2-30 An example of a BIAN Business Scenario Diagram

2.9.2 Wireframe

A Wireframe is a set of pathways between a selected set of Service Domains, mediated by Service Operations, as they occur in a selected set of Business Scenarios.

A Wireframe is a static representation of relevant Service Operation connections between a selection of Service Domains. The scope of a Wireframe model is determined to include those Service Domains directly and indirectly involved in a bounded aspect of business operations. It will typically include only those Service Operations that are directly involved in the response to selected business events. A Wireframe provides only viable examples of Service Domain dependencies and interactions for context, it is not a formal/prescriptive design specification.

The Wireframe is a static model, showing the Service Domains and (all pertinent) available connections between them. Conversely a Business Scenario is a dynamic model that shows the pattern of a collection of interactions that are triggered by some business action or event. In other words, a Wireframe is rather like a city map that shows the possible Service Connection "pathways" that connect the Service Domains. A Business Scenario represents one route through the city.

Figure 2-31 shows an example of a BIAN Wireframe. Wireframes are visualized in an ArchiMate Capability Map Diagram.

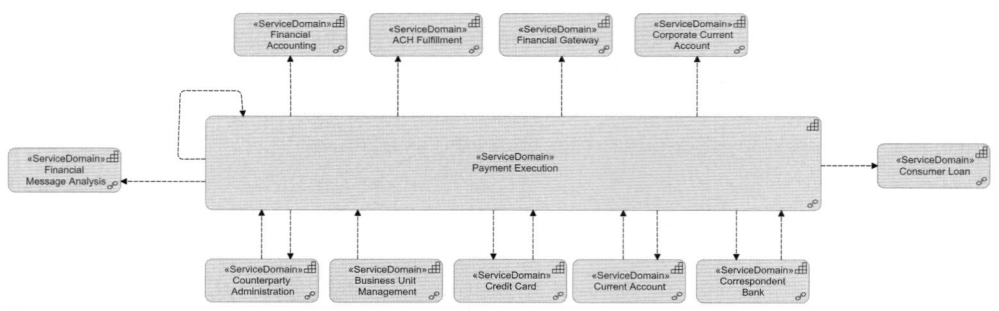

Figure 2-31 An example of a BIAN Wireframe Diagram

2.9.3 Service Connection

A Service Connection is a connection between two BIAN Service Domains realized by a Service Operation.

Figure 2-32 shows an example of a Service Connection. "Execute Payment Transaction" is a Service Connection between the Service Domains "Payment Order" and "Payment Execution". This connection is realized by the Service Operation "initiate a payment execution procedure", which is a Service Operation of the Payment Execution Service Domain.

A Service Connection is represented as a "message" on the UML sequence diagram that represents the Business Scenario. This "message" refers to the Service Operation it is realized by, as illustrated in Figure 2-32. The Service Connection "Execute Payment Transaction" is realized by the Service Operation "Initiate payment execution procedure".

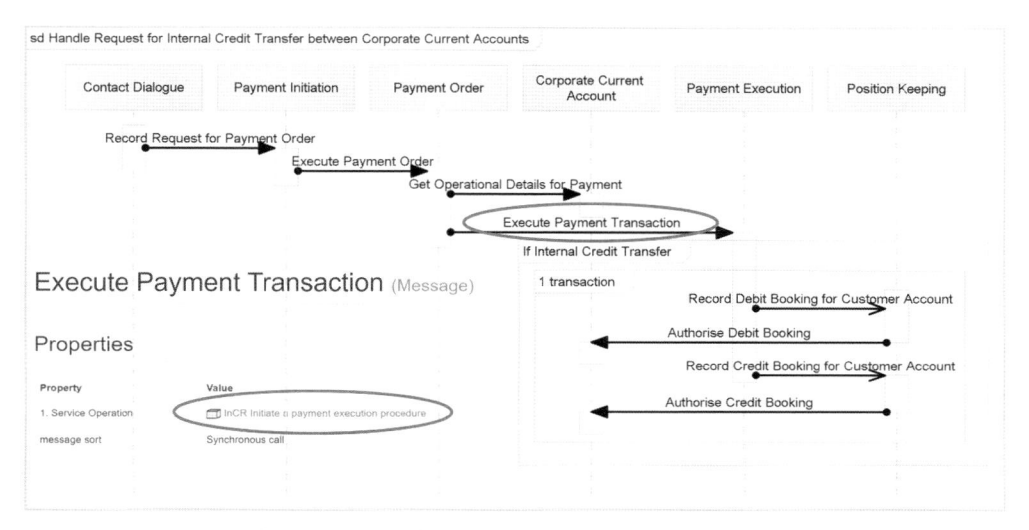

Figure 2-32 An example of a BIAN Service Connection, related to its Service Operation

■ 2.10 BIAN BUSINESS CAPABILITY

A Business Capability represents the bank's abilities and capacities to realize its banking strategies and to create value in its ecosystem. Business Capabilities are an instrument for a bank to define its banking strategy[24].

BIAN defines Business Capabilities that can be used as such or can inspire a bank's own Business Capabilities.

BIAN Business Capabilities decompose into more Business Capabilities. Figure 2-33 illustrates a decomposition view on the "Customer Management Business Capability".

As shown in the view on the BIAN Metamodel represented in Figure 2-34, BIAN offers a set of **Business Capabilities** to realize the **banking strategy** (not part of the BIAN Framework) towards achieving business goals within a financial institution. A Business Capability can be composed of other Business Capabilities. The BIAN **Service Domains** are atomic capability building blocks for these Business Capabilities. A BIAN Business

---

24 A coarse-grained action plan for realizing business goals within a bank or financial institution. (ArchiMate® 3.1 Specification.)

BIAN Business Capability Landscape version 8.0

Enterprise Management and Controlling
- Business Direction Management
- Business Entity Management
- Policy Management
- Risk Management
- Finance Management
- Investor Management
- Fraud Management

Product and Service Enabling
- Financial Plan Management
- «ServiceDomain» Investment Portfolio Management
- Money Movement Management
- «BusinessDomain» Product Management
- Trust Management
- Collateral Management
- Agreement Management
- Financial Instrument Management
- Issued Device Management
- Order Management
- Trade Finance Management
- Payment Management

Enterprise Enabling
- Facility and Equipment Management
- Human Capital Management
- Information Management
- Vendor & Supplier Management
- Legal Support Management
- Task Management
- Intellectual Property Management
- Identity Management

Marketing and Sales
- «ServiceDomain» Brand Management
- Campaign Management
- Event Management
- Market Management
- Message Management
- Loyalty Management
- Lead Management
- Offer Management
- Sales Plan Management

Customer and Distribution
- «BusinessDomain» Customer Management
- Channel Management
- Partner Management

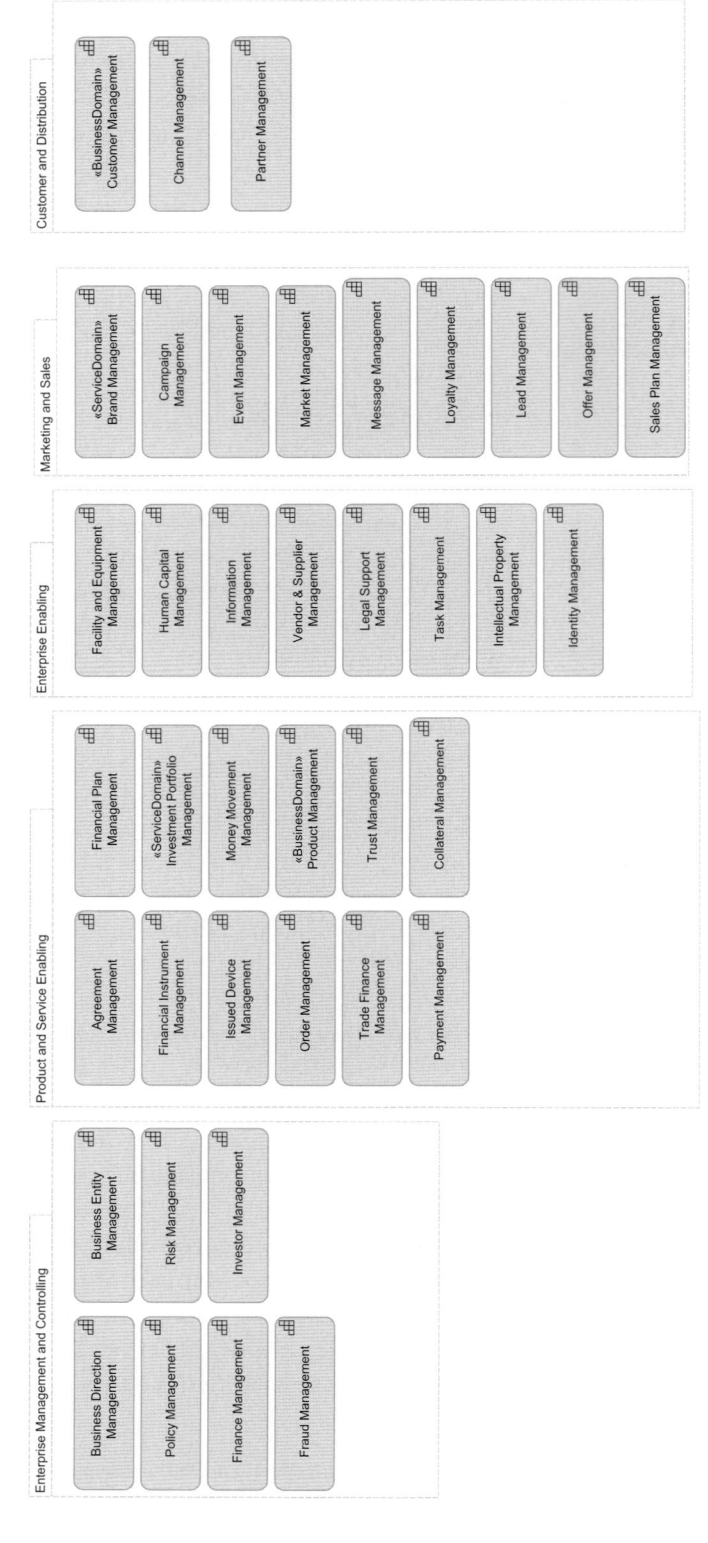

Figure 2-35 Business Capability Model, top level

Capability can be described as a collaboration between Service Domains. A BIAN Business Capability is "served" by a series of Service Domains and each Service Domain can be a building block for more than one Business Capability.

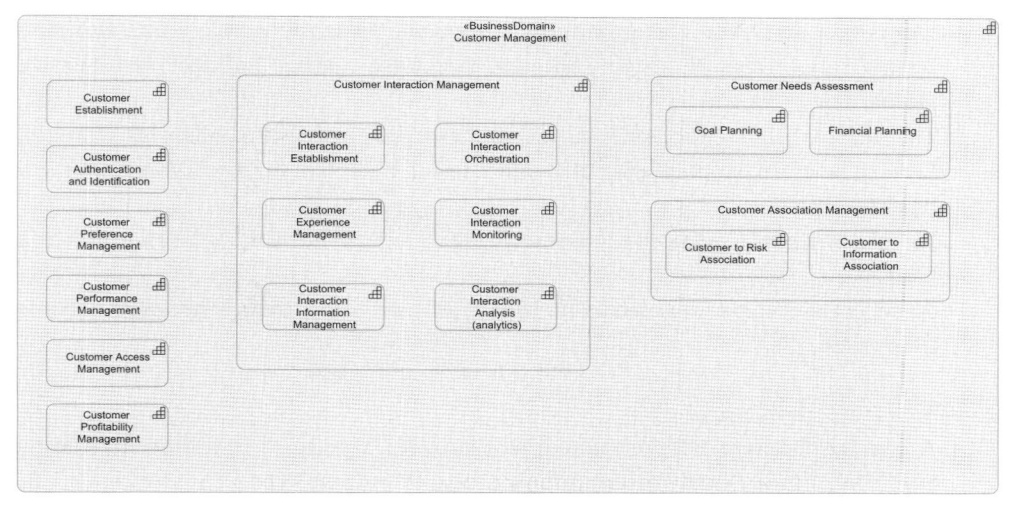

Figure 2-33 Customer Management Business Capability Decomposition view

Where Business Capabilities are established to realize the banking strategy, Service Domains are established to realize the **information systems strategy** (this is explained further in Section 5.1).

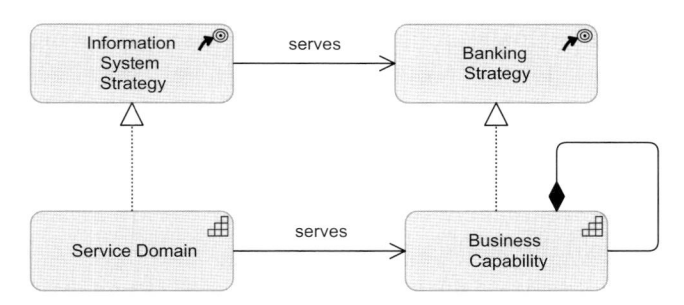

Figure 2-34 BIAN Metamodel, Business Capability view

BIAN represents its Business Capabilities in the Business Capability Model (BCM). Figure 2-35 represents the highest-level overview of Business Capabilities.

A Business Capability is represented as an ArchiMate Capability. The BCM is represented as an ArchiMate Capability Map View.

2.11 TEST YOURSELF QUESTIONS

1. **Which statements are not true?**
   A. The BIAN Service Landscape is a representation that organizes the BIAN Service Domains into Business Domains, which are subsequently grouped into Business Areas. This creates an access path that facilitates finding and accessing Service Domains.
   B. The Service Landscape, with its hierarchy of Business Area, Business Domain, Service Domain, is intended to provide a design blueprint for the organization of a bank.
   C. BIAN's Business Scenarios represent the processes as they should be executed by a bank.
   D. As several Service Domains act on the same Asset Type, their functionality tends to overlap.

2. **Which statements are true?**
   A. A Service Domain is constructed according to a pattern. It fulfills its role by executing a Functional Pattern on instances of an Asset Type.
   B. The Service Domain's Control Record represents the information about the Asset Type combined with the information central to the execution of the Functional Pattern, the Generic Artifact.
   C. The Control Record describes the main business information governed by the Service Domain.
   D. The Service Domain is responsible for executing the Functional Pattern and managing the Control Record accordingly, during the entire lifespan of the Asset instance.

3. **Which statements express how the BIAN BOM can be trusted to provide the financial sector with a reference model for information architecture?**
   A. A Service Domain's Control Record can be decomposed into Behavior Qualifiers, resulting in the Service Domain Business Object Model.
   B. The BOM content and structure patterns ensure the consistency of the Control Record Models.
   C. The Service Domain BOM is the result of modeling the information needs of every BIAN Service Domain, as expressed in its Control Record, according to the Business Object Modeling approach.
   D. The BIAN BOM is the result of the consolidation of the individual Service Domain Business Object Models. Its consistency is ensured by the consistent application of the content and structure pattern in all Service Domain BOMs.

4. **Which statements illustrate how BIAN seeks to provide standards for service interchanges?**
   A. Every Service Domain offers a collection of Service Operations. The purpose of an offered service is characterized by the Functional Pattern of the Service Domain, that acts on part of the Service Domain's Information Profile.
   B. The Service Operation can apply to different levels of the Service Domain's functionality and/or information. It can act at the Service Domain level, influencing its overall operation. It can act upon one or more selected Control Record instances (both creating new instances and acting on existing instances). It can, through addressing Behavior Qualifiers, act upon some subset of the functionality and information provided by the Service Domain.
   C. The Semantic API Endpoint provides more detail about the Service Operation. It outlines the business purpose and high-level information content of the service exchange.
   D. A Swagger File can be generated from the Semantic API specification. This results in executable application services.

PART II

APPLYING BIAN

> **What to expect**
>
> This part of the book is intended to create awareness and understanding of the way the BIAN Architecture can be put to use by an organization.
>
> The objective is not to explain how the activities in which the BIAN Architecture can be utilized should be organized. The various ways the BIAN Architecture can be applied are explained in a way that is as independent of any methodology as possible. The reader is expected to be familiar with the objectives of the supported activities and with approaches[25] for such activities, either in general or as implemented in his or her organization.
>
> We explain the application of the BIAN Architecture for various purposes, illustrated with fictitious but realistic examples as well as real-life examples. Thus, the reader should become aware of the usefulness of the BIAN Architecture and be inspired to apply BIAN in his or her organization. The reader should understand how BIAN can be put to work and be able to apply it in his or her own context, according to his or her own approach.

---
25 Method and techniques.

To fully understand this part of the book, the reader must be familiar with the concept of "architecture layers" (strategy, business, application and technology) together with the "motivation" and "implementation and migration" aspects.

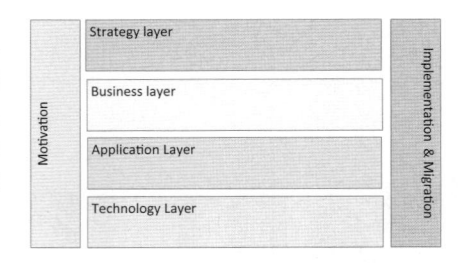

The reader must understand the concept of "zooming levels" on architecture (enterprise, domain, system).

As this is common knowledge for many architects, we will not explain these concepts in this part of the book. Readers who are not familiar with these concepts - or have any doubts about the use of methodology-independent terminology - are advised to read the related sections in Appendix A2.1 and A2.2.

3 Introduction to Part II, Applying BIAN

The (many) ways that BIAN can be of use to a bank have a set of common denominators. These are explained in the first chapter of this part of the book (Chapter 4). The following chapters, that elaborate on the support BIAN can provide for different management viewpoints on the bank and for different architecture viewpoints, relate to these general abilities.

Chapter 5 considers the unique ability of BIAN's Service Landscape and its Service Domains as a Frame of Reference that provides a holistic view on the multi-dimensional reality of a bank.
Service Domains can link strategy to the bank's operations.

They can be used as building blocks for each entity's blueprint, providing a common Frame of Reference for management. This same Frame of Reference can be used by several disciplines, looking at the enterprise from management angles such as value and risk management, requirement management, performance management, architecture management, and investment and change portfolio management. The use of the BIAN-based common Frame of Reference facilitates the cooperation between these disciplines. Used as common reporting canvas, it provides enterprise management with a holistic view.

Chapters 6 and 7 look at the use of "BIAN for the Business Layer" and "BIAN for the application layer". The technology layer is touched upon in the chapter on the application layer.

There are two "transversal" chapters, that look at an aspect of the architecture through the layers. Chapter 8 addresses "BIAN for information and data", whilst Chapter 9 covers "BIAN for interoperability".

Each of the chapters starts with the use of BIAN on the enterprise and domain architecture level and ends with the use of BIAN on system architecture and design level.

The use of BIAN is illustrated with two types of examples. Real-life examples from BIAN members and examples from the fictitious but realistic M5 Banking Group. The M5 Banking Group is included in all chapters of this part of the book. It is based on real cases in real financial institutions, adapted for this purpose.

The illustrations used in this part of the book are all informal representations for illustrative purposes only. They come from different sources; hence different representation styles are used. Even the representations in the ArchiMate language should be understood as informal illustrations, not as architecture documentation.

The representations in ArchiMate and UML are based on version 8.0 of the BIAN Architecture. The other representations are taken from member presentations. They use different versions of the BIAN Architecture that can go as far back as 2015.

The lack of uniformity in the BIAN version and in the architecture and design representation language we have used is a deliberate choice. It illustrates that the BIAN versions are consistent, while each version is richer than the previous one. It illustrates that, though BIAN decided to use the Enterprise Studio tool from BiZZdesign and the ArchiMate and UML languages to document its architecture, members are not obliged to use the same tooling and representation languages.

Presenting the M5 Banking Group

M 5

The M5 Banking Group is a medium sized international group of financial institutions. It is the result of acquisitions and mergers over the past decades.

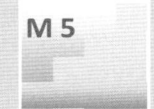

Its origin lies in Homeland, where its head office, the Mfour Bank, is itself the result of a merger between the A Bank and the C Bank. In Awayland, the Mzero Bank is the most important member of the M5 Banking Group. This bank is similar to the Mfour Bank in terms of its enterprise strategy. It wants to be a customer centric, multiproduct, multichannel bank, leading in the Open API economy. It is however the opposite of the Mfour Bank on the level of both application and technology landscapes. The Mfour Bank provides all banks in Homeland with application support. The Homeland application platform is highly componentized, fully service-based and aligned with the BIAN Architecture. Conversely, the Mzero Bank has an application platform that consists of an amalgam of commercial off-the-shelf software, bought by the business.

The Group strategy of "growth by acquisition" is starting to wear thin. The group's profitability suffers, amongst other things, from the high cost of fragmented ICT support. A fragmented ICT support that also impacts upon the quality of the group's management information and its ability to comply with the ever-increasing regulatory demands. It affects the Group's ability to respond adequately to the changing banking environment. The Group Management Board launched a strategic exercise that has resulted in a drastically different banking group strategy. "Group

Synergy" is now one of the key strategic directions. One of its main principles, valid for both the business organization and information system strategies, is "Service is our orientation" (Figure 3-1).

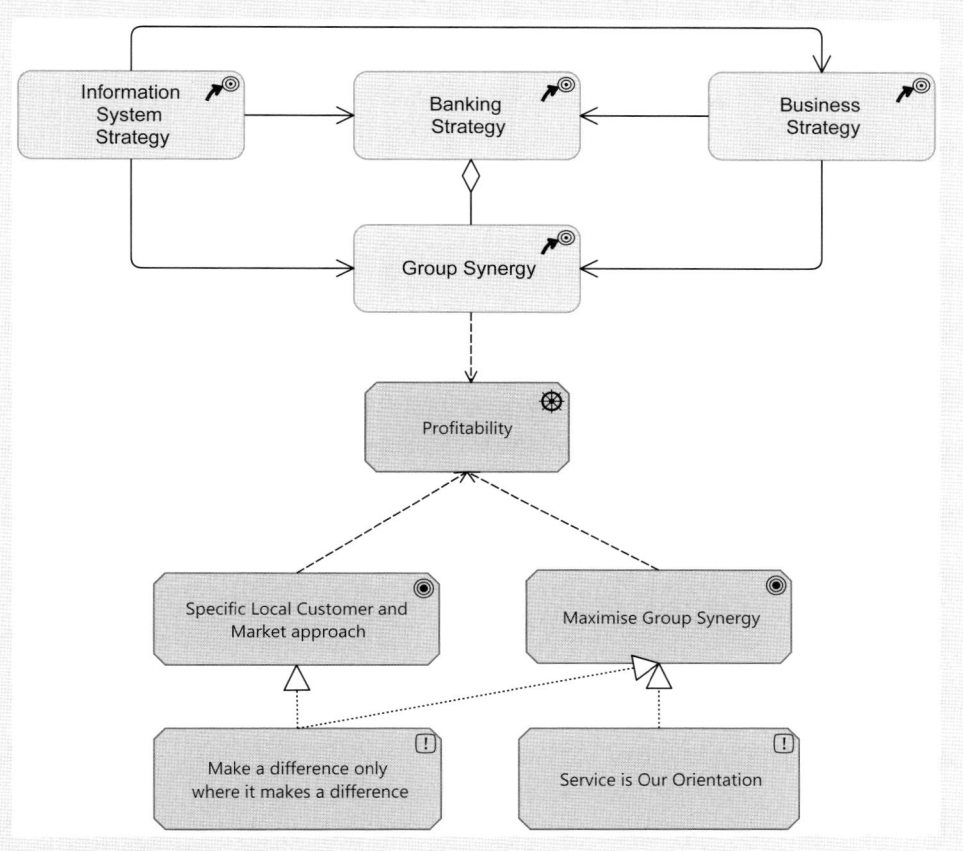

Figure 3-1 M5 Banking Group's "Group Synergy" strategy

4 What BIAN can do: general abilities

This chapter looks at the abilities of BIAN that are the basis for its application in all architecture viewpoints on a bank and for all management disciplines it can support. The next chapters will relate to these general abilities.

The component and service-based nature of the BIAN architecture means that it can serve as a "common Frame of Reference" to unambiguously identify the functionality provided by elements of both the business and application architecture layer. The same Frame of Reference can be used to structure requirements and assessments. It can be used to specify the scope of projects.

This "Frame of Reference" can be used on different ambition levels, from an informal "common vocabulary", to a common Frame of Reference used by several management disciplines and viewpoints, through to steering and structuring the business and application architecture. This is covered in Section 4.1.

The "BIAN-based Frame of Reference" can be tailored to the needs and specific requirements of an individual organization – as long as its principles and patterns are respected. This is described in Section 4.2.

BIAN can be gradually introduced. Growing through ambition levels as well as starting locally and expanding through the organization. This is addressed in Section 4.3.

■ 4.1 BIAN AS FRAME OF REFERENCE

A bank's organization (or "business landscape") and application platform(s) (or "application landscape") are usually the result of years of evolution. More often than not this evolution has taken place on isolated islands, resulting in similar business functionality being realized in several organizations and supported by different applications. Comparison, communication, and cooperation between business islands and application platforms is difficult and prone to misunderstandings.

The "Open Banking" (r)evolution increases the pressure to cooperate with partners outside the bank – a cooperation that suffers from these ailments on an even greater scale.

BIAN offers solutions to this "interoperability" challenge by providing a common language and a common Frame of Reference.

BIAN's Service Landscape contains all of the "elementary capability building blocks" that a bank requires to function. These building blocks, the BIAN Service Domains, are "MECE" (mutually exclusive, collectively exhaustive). They are defined and delimited on a conceptual, purely semantic level – they express *WHAT* a bank needs to be able to do. They are independent of *HOW, WHERE* and *BY WHOM* the bank chose to realize the business (in terms of functions, processes, locations, by organizational units, service providers and partners. . .). They are independent of *HOW* and *WITH WHAT* the application or technology layers support the business layer[26]. As such, a BIAN Service Domain is stable in time.

BIAN's Service Operations, as detailed in the Semantic API Endpoints, are elemental, stable building blocks for services that enable the functionality provided by Service Domains to be orchestrated into services rendered to a bank's customers and other stakeholders.

BIAN's Business Object Model offers the elemental building blocks for the information required by the bank. The collection of Service Operations and Business Objects is mutually exclusive, the "collectively exhaustive" aspect is work in progress.

Thus, BIAN can offer a Frame of Reference that provides a stable, time and organization independent view on a bank, with three points of view: functionality (the Service Landscape and its Service Domains), interoperability through services (the Service Domains and their Service Operations) and information (the BIAN BOM and its Business Objects).

In this section, we elaborate on the usage of the BIAN Service Landscape and its collection of Service Domains as a "common language and Frame of Reference". The subjects that are covered here are also applicable to the other two viewpoints. The specifics with regards to the Frame of Reference viewpoints information and interoperability are treated in Chapters 8 and 9.

---

26 An organization functions through three cooperating layers: the business layer, interacting with and serving the customer, the application layer, providing the information systems that enable and support this, and the technology layer that enables the application layer to function. These layers are explained in more detail in Appendix A2.1 in the section Architecture layers and aspects.

4.1.1 Common vocabulary

BIAN can be gradually introduced in an organization and used on different levels of ambition. A simple use as a common vocabulary is the lowest level of ambition.

Using BIAN as a "common language and Frame of Reference" can be a rather informal one-off. BIAN is used as a **common vocabulary** to resolve language confusion in one project, between several projects, or with potential service providers and software vendors. This does not need to imply a long-term ambition.

> The management team of the XYZ Bank wanted to rationalize the internal organization of the bank. In trying to describe what was done today and how the responsibilities should be divided in the future, they were faced with a language problem. Each department had its own vocabulary, which resulted in many misunderstandings and unclear delimitations of responsibility.
>
> The management team decided to hire a BIAN expert as a language teacher and interpreter, to help them in their discussions and express their requirements and decisions in a common, unambiguous language. They divided the responsibilities among each other using the BIAN Service Domains as elementary responsibility units.
>
> Once the new organizational chart was agreed upon, BIAN played no further role in the implementation of the decisions.

M 5

4.1.2 Common Frame of Reference

The role of Service Domains does not change, even though the way they are implemented and their collaboration patterns can change as new practices and solutions evolve. As a result, they are well positioned for use with a long term, systematic perspective. This level of ambition is required to exploit the full potential of the BIAN Framework.

The BIAN Service Landscape and its Service Domains can be systematically applied as a **common Frame of Reference**[27]. It becomes more than a common language with which to discuss functionality. It is used to systematically and unambiguously **label** the functionality provided by business solutions, such as business processes and business departments. It can be used to label the functionality provided by application solutions. The functionality of each solution can be decomposed according to the BIAN building blocks. The solution is then labelled with the corresponding Service Domain(s). Or one could say that the functionality of the solution is described (on a high conceptual level) by enumerating the BIAN Service Domain(s) it maps on to.

The scope of a project can also be described in terms of the impacted Service Domains (Figure 4-1).

---

27 BIAN (based) Frame of Reference: The set of reference or anchor points offered by BIAN, that enable a unique understanding and positioning of the elements that make up a bank.

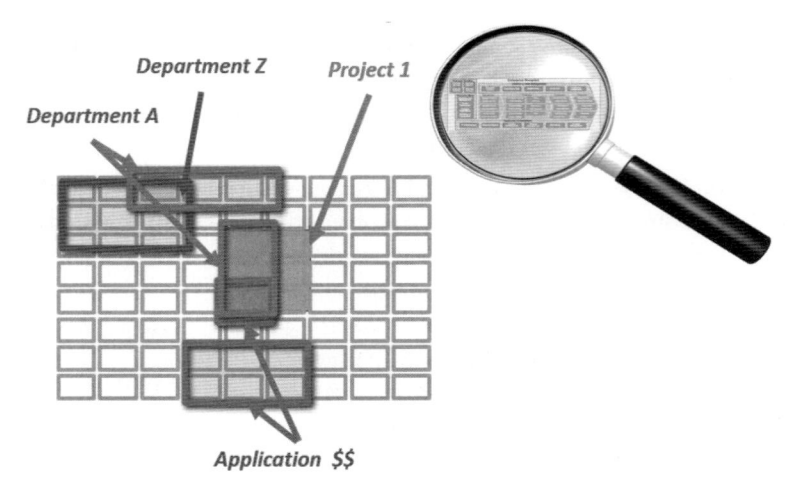

Figure 4-1 BIAN as a common Frame of Reference

This Common Frame of Reference has a whole range of possible applications. A few examples include: comparing the responsibilities of organizations, identifying gaps and duplications in an application portfolio, specifying the functionality of a software package and optimizing the project portfolio. The use of BIAN as a "common Frame of Reference" realizes the main objectives of the BIAN Framework and will be discussed further in the following chapters.

4.1.3 Adding features

The stable, elemental delimitation of the Service Domains also provides excellent **anchor points for documenting "features"**. The BIAN Framework encourages the augmentation of its model elements by adding features.

When discussing "adding features", it is important to keep in mind that the BIAN Service Domains are *conceptual* building blocks. They describe *WHAT* a bank (and/or its partners) needs to be able to do. This is done in a "canonical way", which implies that only the mainstream functionality is described. A bank can add more detailed functionality descriptions, still on the conceptual level, in order to clarify the responsibility of a Service Domain. These features are added to the *actual BIAN model elements*. This is considered part of "tailoring" the BIAN model as described in Sub-section 4.2.1.

Service Domains, as conceptual building blocks, can be realized in different geographies or lines of business. They can also be realized by different applications. In this case, the features are not actually added to the "model element", but to the "implementation of the model element", on a business level or application level. The Service Domain is the *"anchor point" for documentation*[28].

---

28 Delimiting stable, exclusive, and comprehensive documentation "building blocks" is a headache for each architect and designer. BIAN offers strong support – at least for the high-level specifications.

These "anchor points" can be attributed with **requirement specifications** (note, as mentioned above, each implementation of a Service Domain can have different requirements). Consider an example of the benefits of using the common Frame of Reference to document requirements and actual system specifications: the requirements of a new system, structured according to this Frame of Reference, can be easily compared with the specifications of possible solutions, assuming their specifications are also structured according to that same Frame of Reference.

The BIAN-based Frame of Reference can also be used as "anchor points" for (the documentation of) all types of **assessments** (estimations, measurements. . .). As the requirements are specified according to the same structure, the performance against these requirements can be assessed unambiguously. This allows, for example, a one-to-one comparison of the performance of different business units and application solutions that implement the same Service Domains.

4.1.4 Organizing and exploiting documentation

Systematically using BIAN as Frame of Reference implies that all documentation is at least labelled with, and best organized according to, the relevant Service Domains. This can be leveraged by using the BIAN artefacts as an **index on the architecture and solution documentation.** This facilitates the retrieval of documentation relevant to an area of interest –identified in terms of BIAN model elements.

> The international M5 Banking Group has decided to create a Payment Group Service. The scope is expressed as BIAN Service Domains.
>
> **M 5**
>
> Luckily, the Group has already introduced the BIAN model as a common Frame of Reference. During an overall enterprise architecture exercise, a "quick and dirty" mapping of the business functionality of business processes and application systems on the BIAN Service Landscape, has already been done (an example of the mapping of applications is shown in Figure 4-2).
>
> The result of this effort is documented in the Group's architecture repository. An index on Service Domains is implemented.
>
> As such, it is not difficult to find the stakeholders of the project. The business processes with an interest in payment processing can also be easily found. The organizations that need to contribute to the requirements of a Payment Group Service – and those that will be impacted by the migration to that Group Service- can be derived with a high degree of reliability.
>
> As stakeholders from different countries, banks and lines of business are involved, the requirements for the new Payment Group Service are documented in BIAN language and per BIAN building blocks relevant to the solution.

To select the application platform for this Group Service, the business functionality of the payment systems available in the group is compared with that offered by a selection of application service providers and packages. To enable the comparison of the performance of the contenders on the functional and non-functional requirements, some effort must be spent on the internal contenders. They need to map the available performance reports on the BIAN Frame of Reference.

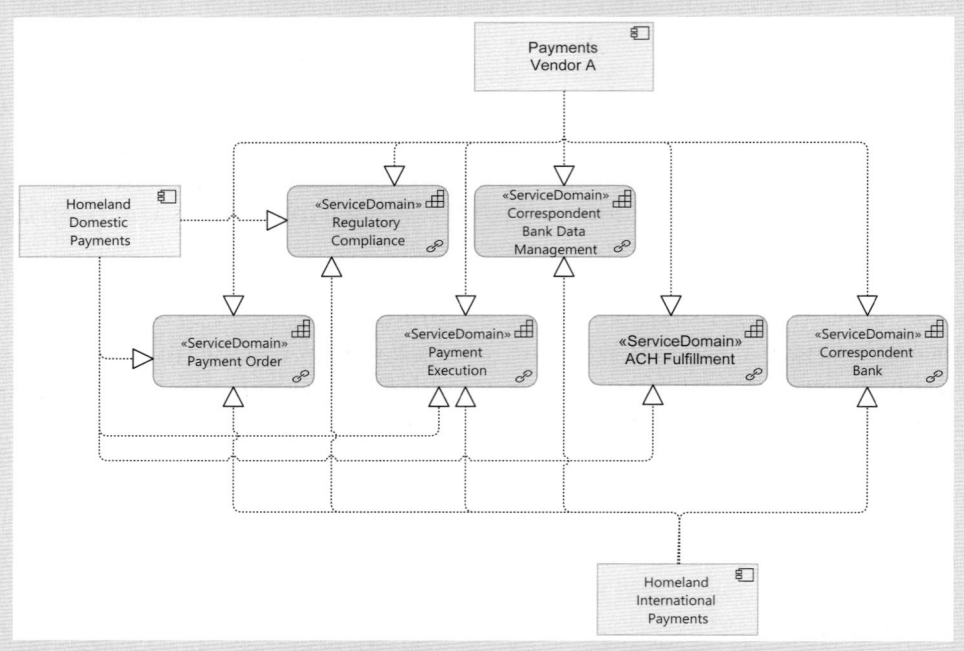

Figure 4-2 Using BIAN as Frame of Reference to find and compare candidate solutions

4.1.5 Building blocks for a reference architecture

BIAN as a Frame of Reference helps to unambiguously identify *what* is done where and by whom on a business level and with what on an application level. This can be seen as a "passive" use.

A bank may want to go further and prescribe patterns and standards for how, by whom and with what things need to be done. It wants to impose an "enterprise reference architecture". The final level of ambition in applying BIAN's common Frame of Reference is to use the building blocks and BIAN's principles as the basis for an **enterprise reference architecture.** BIAN assumes an active role in steering and structuring a bank's business and logical application architecture.

The patterns of a reference architecture prescribe "a repeatable way of putting building blocks into context; a re-usable solution to a problem". The standards prescribe, amongst other things, what actual building blocks to use in these patterns. An example of a standard building block is Mfour Bank's Party Management Application. An example of a pattern is the sequence of applications used to provide a customer with secure access to his or her products. Patterns also exist on a business level, for example all departments to be involved when a new product is introduced.

The problem with these patterns and standards is that they differ "over time" (as business organogram and application platforms change) and can be different "in space" (e.g. depending on the line of business and the application platform).

BIAN provides a solution for this problem: a *conceptual pattern* can be elaborated, consisting of Service Domains. These Service Domains are, at a moment in time, realized by actual business functions/departments/applications. This implementation level needs to be kept up-to-date, but the conceptual level only changes when the environment changes.

A principle in the reference architecture can also be that every solution needs to be conceived as the realization of (a cluster of) BIAN model elements. For example, an application component realizes a (cluster of) Service Domains, encapsulated by application services that are a realization of Service Operations.

The use of BIAN as a basis for an enterprise reference architecture is explained further in the following chapters.

■ 4.2   TAILORING BIAN

BIAN is a generic framework for the financial industry. Recognizing that every (type of) financial institution has its own particularities however, every financial institution can tailor the BIAN Framework for an optimal fit. The only condition is to remain faithful to the principles of the BIAN Architecture and the patterns according to which the model elements are created.

Tailoring BIAN will facilitate its acceptance and enhance its usability for the specific organization. But it can diminish the ease of communication with vendors, partners and other stakeholders such as regulators. Keeping up with the new BIAN versions is also more difficult. It is therefore strongly advised to manage the relation of your own BIAN-based Frame of Reference and the "base level" provided by BIAN.

4.2.1   Detailing specifications and models
The documentation of the BIAN model elements is intended to define mainstream features.

The BIAN definition of a Service Domain considers the internal functionality to be "black box". BIAN does not attempt to specify any internal working patterns. BIAN merely clarifies on a high-level what business functionality a Service Domain should provide to fulfil its business purpose.

Note that the Service Domain description is not the only source of information illustrating its role. The Control Record and the corresponding Service Domain BOM, as well as the Semantic API Endpoints and Messages shed more light on the functionality of Service Domains. The role that a Service Domain plays in the Business Scenarios BIAN provides also contributes to greater clarity.

A bank may want to elaborate the **Service Domain specifications** in more detail. They can be made more concrete and/or aligned with, for example, legal constraints or distinguishing practices of the company. When detailing the specifications, one should be careful to remain on the level of *what* needs to be achieved and not *how* and *with what*. *How* and *with what* things are done will change in the light of evolving insights and practices, laws and regulations, as well as increasing sophistication of information and communication technology (ICT) support. *What* needs to be achieved to serve customers and other stakeholders - or other Service Domains - remains stable.

How and with *what* things are done may differ not only in time but also in place. Each entity may have its own business procedures, applications and technology. Detailing Service Domain specifications should not be confused with describing (requirements for) implementations.

The Service Domain **Control Record** and the **BIAN BOM** are described in varying detail, as a balance between clarity and remaining generic for the sector.

The Control Record can be detailed by adding more attributes and a more detailed structure: Behavior Qualifiers, Sub-qualifiers and so on (as explained in Section 2.5). The BIAN BOM can be detailed by adding attributes and by detailing the structure.

4.2.2 An organization-specific Frame of Reference

The BIAN Service Landscape is meant to support all types of financial institutions. Its Service Domains are intended to be canonical definitions of the elemental capability blocks of a financial institution. This one-size-fits-all may suit a bank perfectly, but equally it may well prefer some adjustments for a perfect fit.

Customizing the Service Landscape and its Service Domains is most likely to happen for – but not limited to – "product fulfilment" related Service Domains, as a bank will want to align these with its product portfolio. The release notes for a new version of BIAN will demonstrate that BIAN itself keeps fine tuning its Service Landscape in all areas, based on the input of its members.

A bank may want to customize the **BIAN Service Landscape** and the **Service Domains** for a better fit to the bank's specificities, to legal requirements...

Moulding the Service Landscape into a bank-specific Frame of Reference involves two steps: "Select", possibly followed by "Customize".

Select
A first (and obvious) step in creating an organization-specific Frame of Reference (or "customizing the BIAN model") is to eliminate those Service Domains that are not relevant for the bank.

Customize
The bank can create its own Service Landscape structure by creating a bank-specific Business Area - Business Domain structure. As this structure defines the "search and access paths" to the Service Domains, customizing this to the bank's viewpoint is a contribution to the adoption of the BIAN Framework.

The bank can also customize Service Domains. This is more pervasive. It requires attention to retaining the principles of the BIAN Framework and the ability to profit from upgrades of the framework.

Customizing Service Domains can imply renaming Service Domains but also splitting and/or merging Service Domains and creating new ones.

Renaming is the simplest customization of Service Domains. Service Domain naming is adjusted to the bank's own terminology. This has no structural impact.

Splitting Service Domains might be done when the bank deems the base Service Domain is too coarsely grained. Alternatively, when the base version is deemed too finely grained, it may involve merging Service Domains.

With respect for the architecture principles
Detailing and customizing activities need to be executed with respect for the principles of the BIAN Architecture.

The Service Landscape and its constituent Service Domains need to stay consistent with the BIAN BOM.

A Service Domain should remain a plausible business service center; it should provide functionality that is recognisable for business and be sufficiently coarse in granularity that one can imagine a dedicated team performing it.

The Service Domain should also be tightly scoped. All functionality that is expected to be independently useful for other Service Domains is "externalized".

A Service Domain should be compliant with the BIAN Service Domain pattern: a Functional Pattern should act on an Asset Type. The Control Record (and its representation as a Service Domain BOM) should be consistent with the Functional Pattern's Generic Artifact combined with the Asset Type and be elaborated in more detail according to the Control Record pattern: its Behavior Qualifiers should be conformant to the Behavior Qualifier Type.

The **BIAN BOM** can also be tailored, but needs to stay consistent with the BOM content and structure pattern. Obviously, it needs to be compliant with information modeling rules. Each Business Object instance needs to be managed by a Service Domain, hence, it needs to appear in its Service Domain BOM.

In view of its new "Group Synergy" strategy, the M5 Banking Group decides to install a groupwide enterprise architecture capability. BIAN has served as a common language and common Frame of Reference during the project, helping to make the strategy actionable. The enterprise architecture team decides to continue with BIAN. They feel the need to customize it to the M5 Banking Group.

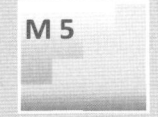

M 5

The team deems it better to work with more general product Service Domains. Each member bank's Product Catalog is different, but the "product factory" (back-offices that ensure the fulfilment of the product agreements) support products based on the type of product features, not on their commercial presentation. Figure 4-3 shows the "merging" of several Service Domains that fulfil loan agreements. The Functional Pattern remains "Fulfil"; the Asset Type is generalized.

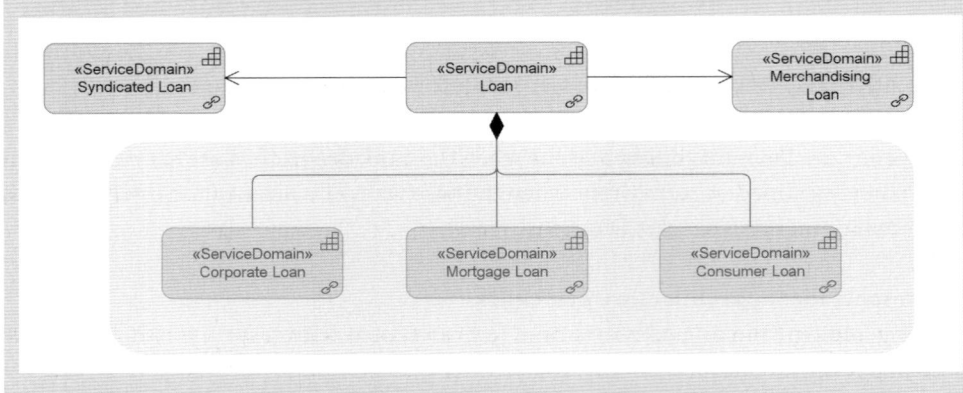

Figure 4-3 M5 Banking Group's generalization of the loan product fulfilment Service Domains

They also decide to create a separate Service Domain "Standing Order", as the Asset Type "Standing Order" is considered independent of "Current Account"[29]. (Figure 4-4)

---

29 This actually happened in version 9 of BIAN. BIAN appreciates input from its member banks and will update its model with their insights.

This new Service Domain fulfils (Functional Pattern) the Standing Order (new Asset Type) Arrangement (Generic Artifact). The Behavior Qualifier "Standing Order" becomes an Asset Type, and disappears from the (Corporate) Current Account Service Domain's Control Record. The "Payment Service Arrangement" in the Service Domain BOM of the (Corporate) Current Account Service Domain becomes "Standing Order Agreement" in the new Service Domain's BOM. This Business Object remains related to the Current Account Agreement through "Payment Instruction Involved Account".

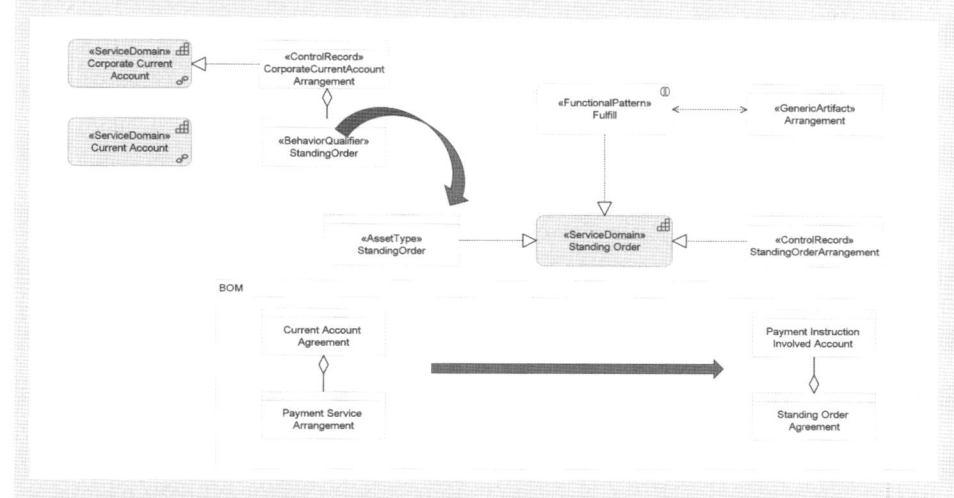

Figure 4-4 M5 Banking Group's very own Standing Order Service Domain is split off from the Current Account Service Domains

4.3   BIAN CAN BE INTRODUCED GRADUALLY

The levels of ambition upon which "BIAN as common Frame of Reference" can be used might be viewed as one dimension in the gradual introduction of BIAN. Other dimensions of a gradual introduction are the impacted business and application landscape areas.

A bank evolving from a "line of business" driven business architecture and a "process-based" application architecture to a "service-based" landscape, is rarely able to migrate in one "big bang" operation. The risk of a gradual migration however is rework, if for example the new components turn out not to be delimited correctly.

A "zooming" approach (described in Appendix A2.2) facilitates the delimitation and prioritization of change areas and the elaboration of a realistic migration scenario.

The BIAN Service Landscape supports such a zooming approach. It provides not only candidate components, it also provides a canvas to delimit the areas in the bank that do not have to be involved in a first phase, and those for whom the "to-be" architecture needs to be elaborated first.

The risk of rework, inherent to elaborating an architecture area by area (in sequence or in parallel), is reduced significantly by the stable and reliable building block delimitation offered by the BIAN Reference Architecture.

The ambition to use BIAN does not need to be company-wide. Obviously, the wider the scope, the greater the leverage of the BIAN model. But even on a project scale, the generic, stable building block delimitation BIAN offers is a recipe for future-proofing the individually designed puzzle-pieces.

The "puzzle piece" itself will require little adaptation when new service users start using it. The service users are enabled with clean and sound requirements in terms of what functionality to exchange with service calls in order to join the enterprise service puzzle.

Gradual introduction and ambition levels go hand-in-hand. While one part of the bank may already be compliant with a BIAN-based reference architecture, another may be using the common Frame of Reference to assess its landscape and yet another may only be a "passive speaker of the common language".

> The Mfour Bank, founder of the M5 Banking Group, was a BIAN user avant la lettre. It elaborated the core of its service-based architecture at the time when its current accounts and savings accounts were migrated from file-based systems to database-based systems.
>
> At the same time, the first access channel outside the head office was created: access for branch employees. Figure 4-5 shows (in grey with dotted line) the first components of the new, service- oriented, component-based application architecture.
>
> A service-based component architecture was elaborated, based on the requirements of only three products: Current Accounts, Payment Orders and Saving Accounts (in dark grey with full line).
>
> The first series of common services (such as Party Authentication, Party Reference Data, Customer Correspondence, Position Keeping, Payment Execution, Regulatory Compliance…. in orange) match well with the BIAN Service Landscape. These applications turned out to be future-proofed. A whole series of other products (examples of the first adopters with bold dotted line) "clicked in" to these service with ease[30]. The addition of new access channels did not require major rework of the product applications, as the "channel logic" was already neatly separated from the "product fulfilment" logic.

---

30 *The Mfour Bank participated in an application development productivity benchmark and came in first, way better than the other participants. This benchmark did not count the "lines of code" achieved over a given period of time by the ICT organization, but instead the "delivered business functionality". Given the number of reusable services when introducing a new product, channel or other new "business choreography", it is not surprising that the productivity of Mfour Bank's ICT department was significantly better than that of the other benchmark participants.*

4   What BIAN can do: general abilities

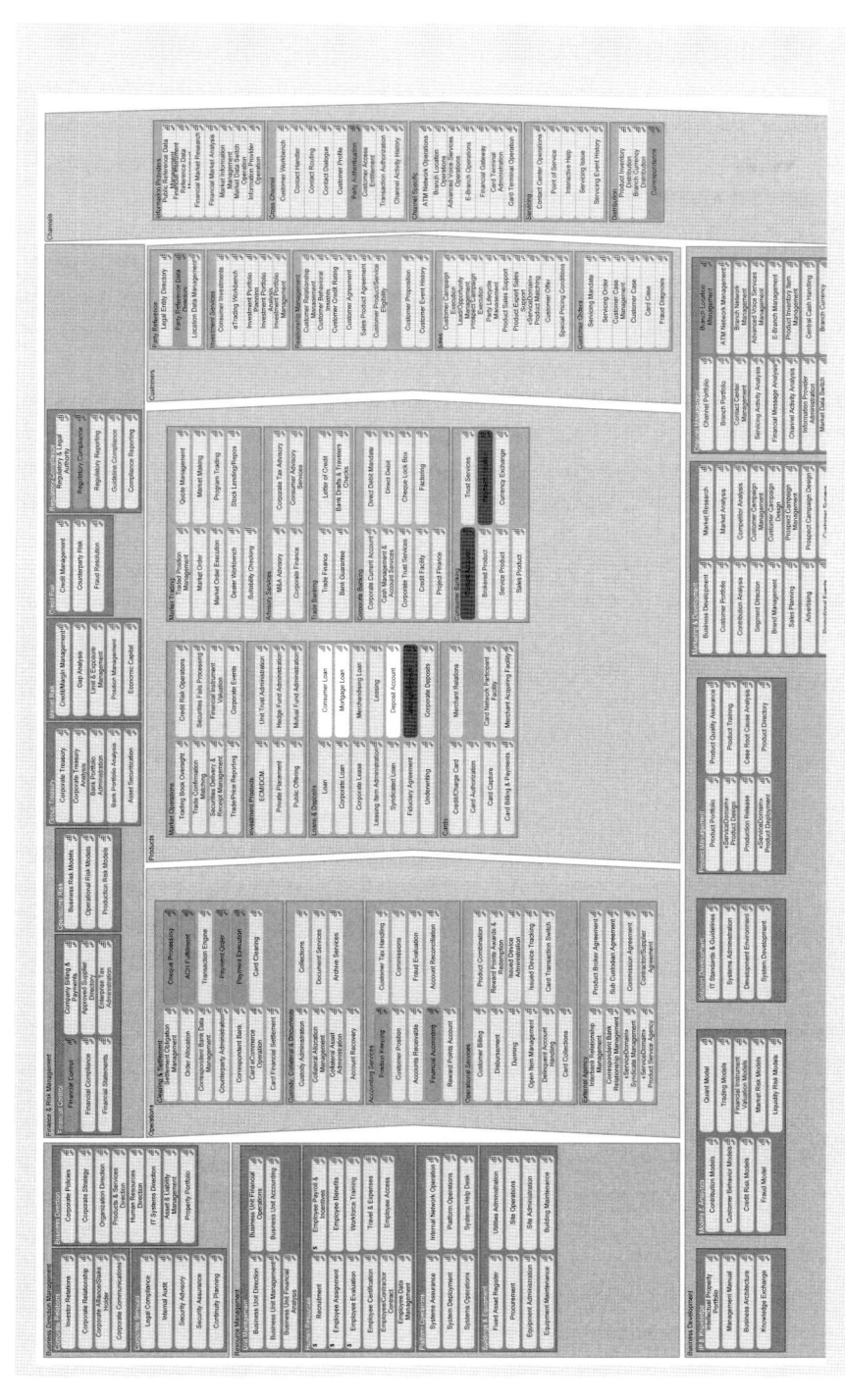

Figure 4-5   The first components of Mfour Bank's "new" application platform (late 1970's) mapped on the BIAN Service Landscape[31]

[31] We apologize for the fact that the names of the Service Domains are not readable. The purpose of the figure is to give you an impression of how well Mfour Bank's systems align with the BIAN Architecture. For online version of this figure see free download at https://www.vanharen.store/bian-2nd-edition-a-framework-for-the-financial-services-industry

4.4 TEST YOURSELF QUESTIONS

1. **Which of these statements express valid reasons for customizing the BIAN Architecture?**
   A. Legal obligations may require a specific delimitation of functionality.
   B. The product portfolio of a financial institution needs to be reflected in the Product Service Domains.
   C. Service Domains will be understood more easily if their names are aligned with the vocabulary used in the bank.

2. **How can the BIAN standards be used, which statements are correct?**
   A. As a common vocabulary to improve communication.
   B. As a common Frame of Reference to chart and compare business functionality of business and application solutions.
   C. As an index to an architecture repository.

3. **Right or wrong: The use of BIAN only makes sense if it is done systematically, for the entire enterprise and in all change initiatives.**
   A. Right
   B. Wrong

5 BIAN for a holistic enterprise view

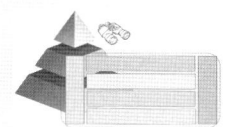

A financial institution is a complex ecosystem, an ecosystem that becomes wider and more complex with the ever-increasing digitalisation, Open Banking and the participation of banks in an Open API economy.

As in any major organization, the "Steer-Operate-Assess-Change[32]" cycle is organized in levels. The enterprise level oversees business lines, that oversee departments… that oversee the operation of actual "systems[33]". Systems that are possibly being changed with a resultant impact on other systems.

A holistic view on this complex ecosystem is a major challenge for management on each level and for professionals active in disciplines serving management with information from different points of view.

The enterprise strategy needs to be passed down effectively, in order to steer operations. Managers (at any level) need information from multiple viewpoints, on multiple systems, to assess their adequacy and possibly decide on changes. Management is provided this information from multiple sources. Sources and viewpoint that do not usually share the same language (Figure 5-1).

BIAN can provide a common language and a common Frame of Reference for this multidimensional information. This facilitates management in acquiring the holistic view they need, and the "practitioners" providing this information in communicating amongst themselves more effectively.

This chapter explores the benefits of the use of the BIAN Architecture as a Frame of Reference for enterprise management and for management disciplines that look at the

---

32 Freely after the 'Plan-Do-Check-Act' cycle for processes and products.
33 An organized collection of parts (possibly organized in subsystems) that are highly integrated to accomplish an overall goal. A system can be on a business, application and/or technology level. It delivers results to other systems or humans.

organization from different points of view, sharing the "big picture perspective" that is the enterprise level.

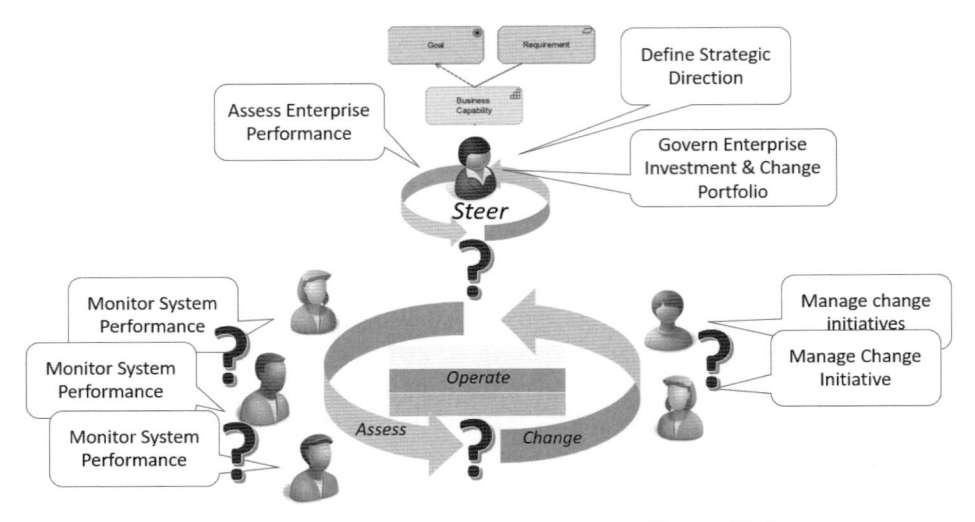

Figure 5-1 Different disciplines in search of a common language and Frame of Reference

This chapter focuses on the role of Service Domains. Similar roles for the BIAN BOM and Service Operations are highlighted in Chapters 8 and 9.

The BIAN Framework supports Strategy Management by offering archetypical Business Capabilities in a Business Capability Landscape. Service Domains are elemental, stable capability building blocks that realize these Business Capabilities. The strategic positioning and requirements of the Business Capabilities can be projected on the Service Domains (Sub-section 5.1.1).

Service Domains are realized by actual "systems" such as business processes or functions, applications… Systems that represent the actual operations of the bank. Systems whose functioning can be assessed in comparison to their requirements and that can be changed in light of an improved alignment with strategy.

As such Service Domains are the linking pin between Strategy and Operations and facilitate the Steer, Operate, Assess and Change cycle (Sub-section 5.1.2.).

Service Domains, as conceptual building blocks, can be realized in different organizational and legal units. Expressing the "enterprise blueprint" in "BIAN language" supports the blueprint decision, creates a common Frame of Reference for the management of different entities and facilitates the comparison of their activities (Section 5.2).

Service Domains are well suited as stable, common documentation anchor points for features such as requirements, assessments and measurements. The collection of Service Domains provides a common Frame of Reference for requirements management and performance management. A Frame of Reference that is stable over time and is able to "funnel" requirements and assessments between architecture layers and from strategic to operational level (Sub-sections 5.3.1 and 5.3.3).

The same Frame of Reference can be 'overlaid' by the business and logical application architecture landscapes, to chart their functionality and detect gaps and overlaps. The availability of (strategic) requirements and assessments on Service Domain level enables the evaluation of the quality of the business and application architecture landscape (Sub-section 5.3.2).

This information is used to delimit areas in need of improvement: investment and change proposals, whose scope and impact are related to Service Domains. The use of the common BIAN-based Frame of Reference facilitates the optimisation of the investment and change portfolio (Sub-section 5.3.4).

The Frame of Reference, based on the Service Domains, provides a common way of looking at the bank, from all "management" perspectives (Figure 5-2). It enables the projection of Strategy and its requirements on the (architecture of) bank's Operations. It structures the Assessment of its operations and the Changes to these operations.

The "bank on a page" representation of the enterprise blueprint can be used as a "canvas" for the visualisation of information from all these viewpoints in all parts of the enterprise. The consistent use of this same Frame of Reference facilitates management in acquiring a holistic view.

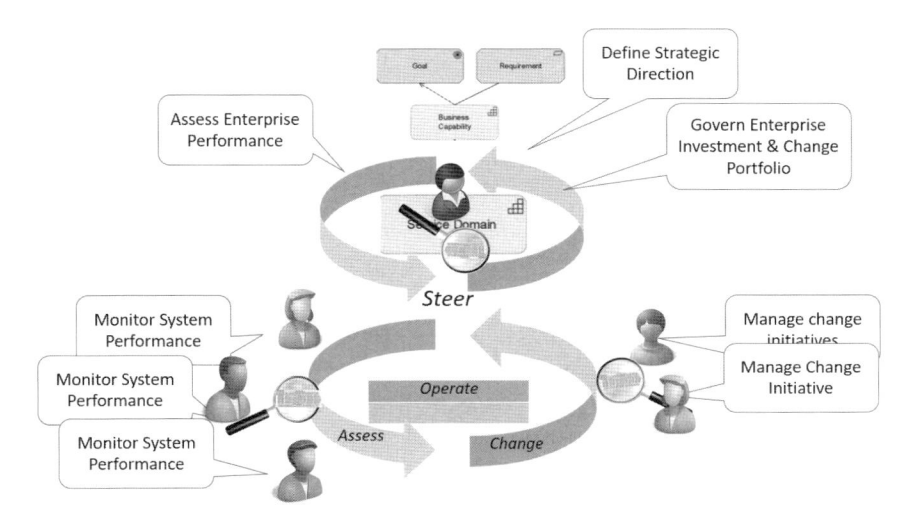

Figure 5-2 The common Frame of Reference provided by BIAN, enables a holistic enterprise view

5.1 DEFINING AND ARCHITECTING BUSINESS CAPABILITIES

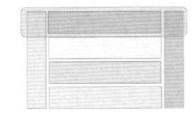

5.1.1 Business Capabilities for strategy

A Business Capability represents the abilities and capacities an organization needs to realize its value proposition.

Strategy is concerned with positioning an organization in its environment and defining the direction to take in order to create value for its stakeholders. Business Capabilities are an instrument for strategy management. The Banking Strategy defines, amongst other things, what Business Capabilities the company needs, specifies the requirements for these Business Capabilities, classifies them according to their contribution (e.g. "commodity" or "key differentiator") and their associated risk.

Resources, such as people, information, applications… are assigned to Business Capabilities, to enable them to realise their objectives. The priority of investments is defined by the strategic importance of the Business Capabilities they support.

BIAN provides archetypical **Business Capabilities,** hierarchically organized in a **Business Capability Model** (Section 2.10). BIAN's Business Capability Model and Business Capabilities can be used by strategists as a basis for defining their organization's Business Capabilities.

The BIAN Service Domains also represent capabilities – the ability to create value. Service Domains are the elemental building blocks for the Business Capabilities as defined by BIAN. A BIAN Business Capability can be described as a collaboration between Service Domains (Figure 5-3). A BIAN Business Capability is "served" by a series of Service Domains and each Service Domain can be a building block for more than one Business Capability.

Given their elemental, stable nature, Service Domains are the linking pin between Strategy and Architecture – as we will explain in Sub-section 5.1.2.

BIAN offers[34] a mapping between its Service Domains and its Business Capabilities.

A bank's strategists can obviously decide not to use BIAN's Business Capabilities. They can still profit from the "universal language" and "linking pin" capacity of the BIAN Service Domains, by mapping[35] their custom-made Business Capabilities on the BIAN Service Domains.

---
34 Work in progress.
35 Or ask the enterprise architects to do the mapping.

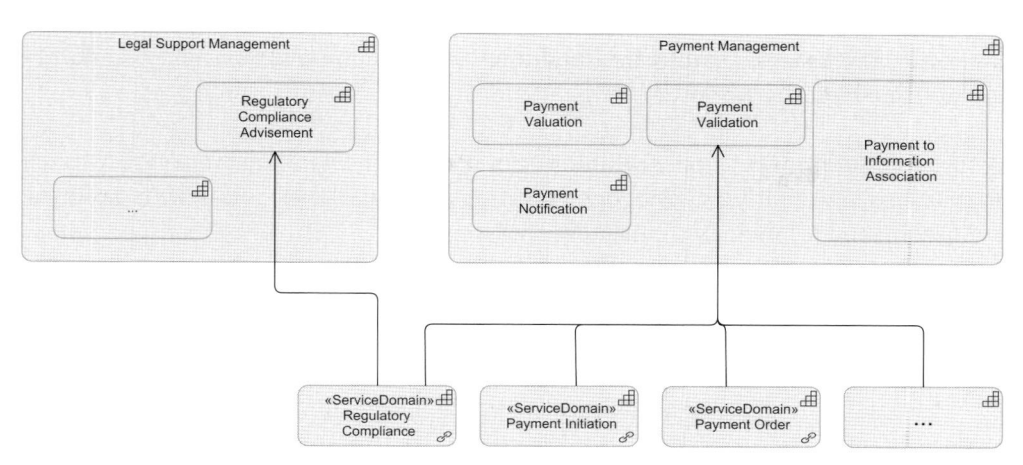

Figure 5-3 Business Capabilities are served by several Service Domains that can serve several Business Capabilities

5.1.2 Service Domains for architecture

Enterprise architecture is about enabling the strategic direction[36] of an organization by optimizing "the structure of business and ICT[37] components, their inter-relationships, and the principles and guidelines governing their design and evolution over time[38]".

For enterprise architecture management, Business Capabilities are a strategic input. The enterprise architecture needs to optimize support, by defining architectural building blocks that can flexibly cooperate in order to realize the Business Capabilities. Business Capabilities must evolve with the environment, their building blocks should be stable and reusable in different orchestrations. Service Domains are stable capability building blocks, that provide anchor points for well delimited architecture building blocks.

Figure 5-4 illustrates the "linking pin" role of the Service Domains between strategy and architecture. The Banking Strategy defines how the bank positions itself in its ecosystem. It is realized by the bank's Business Capabilities, that need to be furnished according to this strategy: their building blocks, the Service Domains, need to comply with their strategic requirements.

The Strategies for the Business Organization and for Information Systems (application and technology) serve the Banking Strategy. They do not aim directly at Business Capabilities – an ever-moving target that evolves with the bank's ecosystem. They aim at the stable Business Capability building blocks, that can be reused for several Business Capabilities. They aim at the Service Domains. These are furnished according to these

---
36 While guaranteeing sufficient manoeuvrability to permit strategy changes.
37 Information and Communication Technology.
38 Inspired by The Open Group (2018).

strategies, by business architecture building blocks and application and technology architecture building blocks.

A such, the Service Domain is the linking pin between the Banking Strategy, expressed by Business Capabilities, and its operations, realized by the elements of its business, application and technology architecture landscape[39].

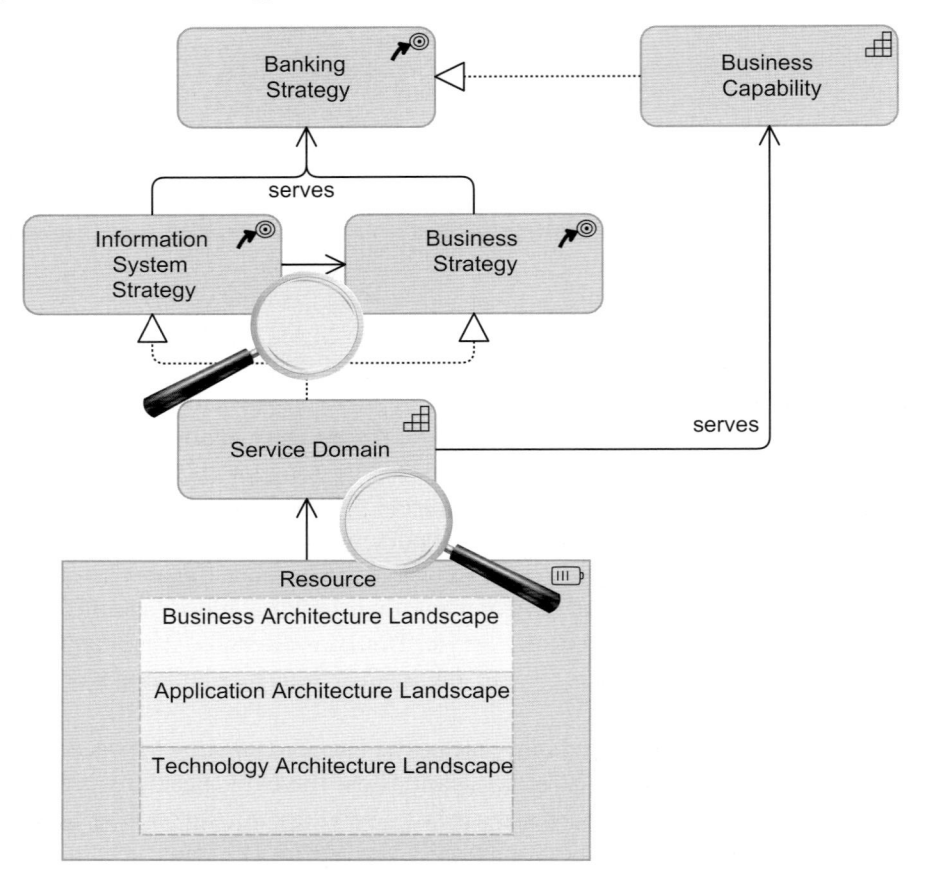

Figure 5-4 Service Domains are the linking pin between strategic business capabilities and the architecture that realizes them

In the following sections, we will see how the common Frame of Reference, provided by the (tailored) BIAN Service Landscape, can become the instrument that enables a holistic view on the multidimensional reality of the enterprise.
The same Frame of Reference view enables enterprise management to link this holistic view to the Banking Strategy.

---

39 In the ArchiMate language, "resources", such as information assets, people (human assets), business processes and functions, application and technology assets, are assigned to capabilities – according to strategic requirements and priorities. This explains the presence of "resource" in this figure.

5.2 ASSEMBLING AN ENTERPRISE BLUEPRINT

An enterprise blueprint is often referred to as "bank on a page". It provides an overview of the capacities, as they are (or should be) available to an entity, that can indeed be visualized on a single page.

An enterprise blueprint can be drawn up for an entire banking group, and/or an individual bank and/or per line of business or other organizational or legal unit. The enterprise blueprint of the bank(ing group) should contain all the capability building blocks required to realize its aspired Business Capabilities. Partial blueprints, such as for lines of business, will only contain a subset of these.

A major advantage of expressing such a blueprint in "BIAN language" is the **common language** it provides. A common language between those involved in developing the blueprint and a common language among the entities whose activities are expressed in the blueprint. The stable, universal nature of the BIAN building blocks creates a blueprint that can be used as a **common Frame of Reference** not only between entities, but also to keep track of evolutions over time.

BIAN's Service Landscape is in fact a generic "bank on a page". Its Service Domains represent the capability building blocks relevant for any bank. The "Value Chain representation" of the Service Landscape (Section 2.3), is an example of an enterprise blueprint representation that appeals well to business. It can be used as a quick start for a bank's blueprint.

Assembling an enterprise blueprint with the help of the BIAN Service Landscape[40] involves three steps:
1. Filter: Select the BIAN Service Domains that match the enterprise activities;
2. Customize the BIAN Service Domains as required;
3. Organize: Assemble the Service Domains in a structure matching the enterprise.

The first step in assembling an enterprise blueprint is to filter out the Service Domains that are not required to support the Business Capabilities of the bank.

The second step is to customize the Service Domains for a closer fit to the bank's specificities, if and as far as required. The descriptions can be augmented for a better understanding and Service Domains can be merged or split.

---

40 Note: Service Landscape as in a "collection of Service Domains". BIAN's Service Landscape structure is not meant to represent a bank's organization.

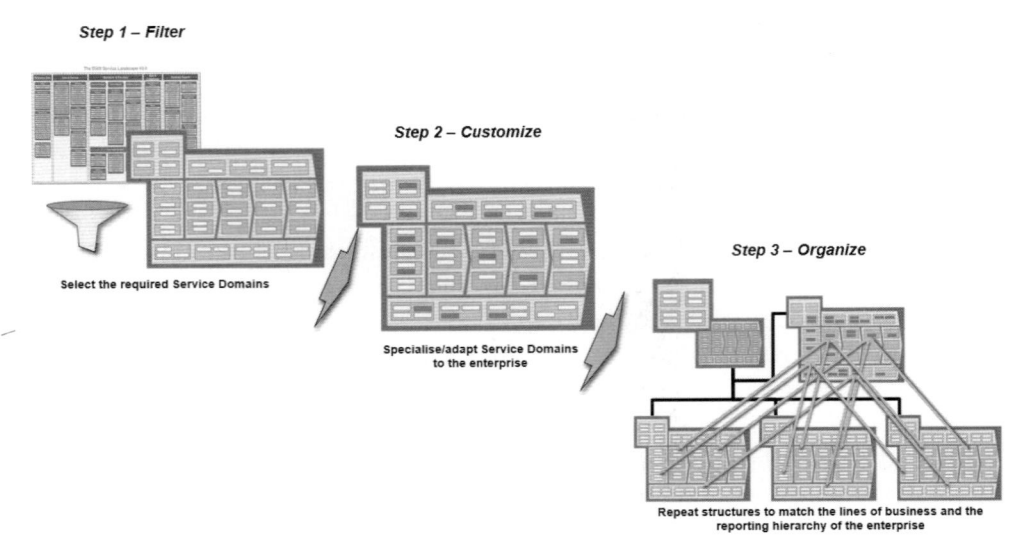

Figure 5-5 Three steps in developing an enterprise blueprint

With these two steps, the bank (or banking group) has created its own BIAN-based **Frame of Reference** (as in Sub-section 4.1.2). These two steps are optional, as a bank can choose to use the base version of BIAN as its Frame of Reference.

In the final step, the building blocks of this BIAN-based Frame of Reference (the Service Domains) are assembled on as many "banks on a page" as the bank deems fit in terms of management views. Angles that can be taken into consideration are for example:
- Lines of business - these can be based on geographical and/or market segments e.g. financial services in a country, retail or corporate banking etc.;
- Centralized operations – these can be regional or global service centers, that support multiple lines of business, e.g. a regional payments center, central training services;
- Legal entity structure – for instance a global holding company with regional and local subsidiaries.

The bank or group as a whole is an obvious blueprint view, that coincides with the entire Frame of Reference.

The blueprint depicts the high-level organizational choices of the company. It is however not an organogram (*"who does what"*). An organogram can be built from the same Service Domain building blocks. We will examine this further in Chapter 6.

The blueprint depicts *"who is responsible for what"*.

What is the difference? The blueprint includes all of the functionalities an entity executes, as well as those it requires but are outsourced. In the organogram, functionalities will only be assigned to the entity that actually executes them.

"Operating model" choices are taken at the level of the blueprint. Issue such as whether data is shared between entities or not and whether functionality is implemented differently or not, are expressed in the operating model of an organization. When assessing the business and application landscape based on the BIAN-based Frame of Reference (as we will see later), it is crucial to take the "operating model" into consideration. Note however that possible differences in how the same Service Domain is implemented for different entities are *not* visible on Service Domain level. The use of the common Frame of Reference to express the blueprint, does imply that it is recognized that *what* needs to be achieved is similar and implies that decisions on differences in implementation (*how and with what*) between entities are taken consciously.

A "bank on a page" diagram can be made for each business line, legal entity, centralized service organization… These representations show the functionality (Service Domains) each unit needs (Figure 5-7 represents two lines of business). Such representations are not just pretty pictures. Because they use "a common language" to represent the functionalities, they are powerful instruments for communication. A diagram can be used as a canvas for heatmaps, highlighting different viewpoints on the bank, resulting in, for example, a clear and consistent management cockpit.

In the following sections, we will show how the common Frame of Reference, consisting of the Service Domains, can be used to provide a "holistic" view on the bank. The view of each entity on the common Frame of Reference is provided by its blueprint.

With appropriate tooling, the common Frame of Reference and the blueprint view of each entity can be exploited fully (see also Sub-section 4.1.4). Each Service Domain from the common Frame of Reference can be linked to the entity it is entrusted to (Figure 5-6 shows this in the ArchiMate® language) as well as to the entities that depend on its execution (those on whose blueprint it appears). The functionality, as implemented[41] in each entity, can also be "indexed" by the Service Domains. Requirements to, assessments of and changes to this functionality, can also be documented *per Service Domain in this entity*. Relationships between implementations of one Service Domain can be documented, such as outsourcing relationships. The layered structure of, for instance, "finance and risk management" activities, that are performed on an entity as well as the enterprise level can also be expressed.

Thus, the "bank on a page" for each entity can be generated, as well as heat maps, using this "canvas" to depict all types of information.

---

41 To be precise, currently implemented (as-is) or planned to-be implemented.

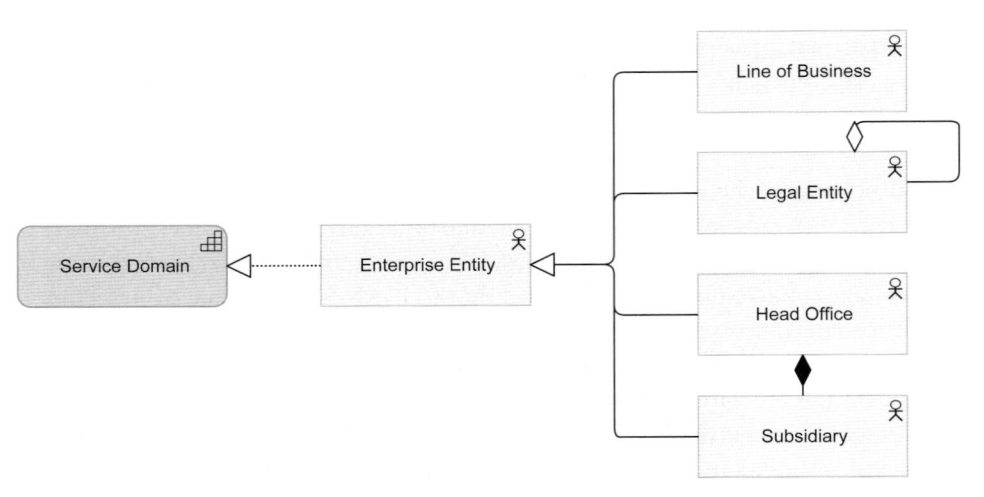

Figure 5-6 Assigning the responsibility for Service Domains in the ArchiMate language

■ 5.3 ENTERPRISE BLUEPRINT AS/OR A FRAME OF REFERENCE

The blueprint, expressed in Service Domains, creates a common view on activities for all management levels and organizational partitions.

Service Domains, as assigned to entities, can be attributed with all kinds of features, such as characteristics of business and application support, performance measurements and estimations, current and future requirements, assessments … This Frame of Reference creates continuity in space and time, as it describes the functionalities in semantic, implementation-agnostic terms.

The blueprint provides a manager with his/her view on the common Frame of Reference according to which all types of analysis are organized and reported to management. The "bank on a page" can be used as a canvas for visualization. Using a consistent Frame of Reference for management reporting facilitates the combination of information from different points of view and different sources. It enables a one-to-one comparison of the same point of view on different entities or over time.

It facilitates communication between disciplines such as requirement management, performance management, architecture and change portfolio management.

The reader may have noticed the difference between the blueprint (and its representation as a "bank on a page") and the Frame of Reference. The (Service Domain) Frame of Reference is the structured collection of Service Domains on which each entity, each business process, each application… can be overlaid. The blueprint provides management with a consistent "lens" on the enterprise. An entity's blueprint sees only that part of the Frame of Reference that is relevant for the management of this entity (Figure 5-7).

Each entities Blueprint is its management's view on

the common Service Domain Frame of Reference that provides a holistic view on

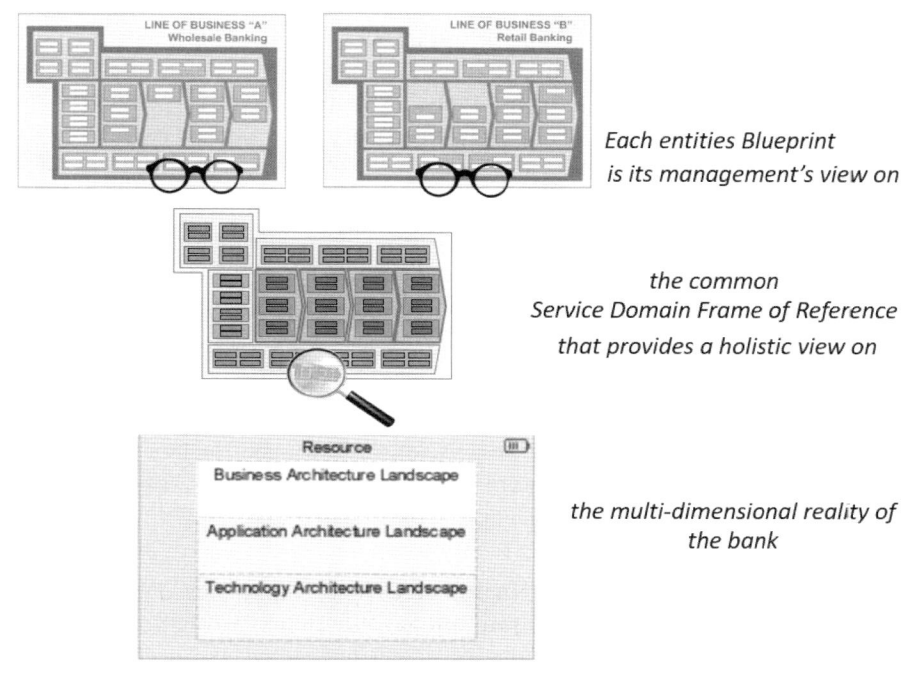

the multi-dimensional reality of the bank

Figure 5-7 The "bank on a page" for a line of business is its view on the common Frame of Reference

From this point on, we will use the term "blueprint" and its representation as "bank on a page" for the view provided to management. The term "Frame of Reference" is used for the instrument that is used to structure the information related to the bank's operations.

5.3.1 Defining and documenting strategy direction and requirements

Service Domains are building blocks for Business Capabilities, which in turn are instruments for defining the Banking Strategy. Service Domains are the instruments used to express the Business and Information System Strategies that realize the Banking Strategy.

The strategic positioning of the Business Capabilities is "projected" on the Service Domains that realize them. The **value and inherent risk** of each Service Domain, as well as the strategic **requirements** that are imposed on it, can be derived from its support for the Banking Strategy, through the Business Capabilities it supports. *These attributes can of course be assigned directly to Service Domains, if a bank so chooses.*

Service Domains in their turn impose those requirements on the business and on the application and technology landscapes.

Requirements (and goals and objectives, value and risk) become more detailed and more concrete as they descend from the "strategic" to the "tactical" to the "operational" level. They are passed through from business requirements to application requirements to technology requirements. Obviously, BIAN does not provide full support for requirements lineage and traceability. What it does provide, however, is stable anchor points for documenting and exploiting requirements from all management levels and from all points of view. This anchor point is the Service Domain.

5.3.2 Charting and evaluating the "operations" landscape down the stack

This use of BIAN for the architecture layers is discussed in more detail in Chapters 3 to 6. This overview highlights the value of the BIAN-based Frame of Reference for architecture management, in view of improved cooperation between architects and with other disciplines, and in support of a "holistic enterprise view" for enterprise management.

A bank can be seen as an ecosystem consisting of three cooperating layers, each organized as an architecture landscape (as described in Appendix A2.1). The business landscape, providing the banking services to customers and other stakeholders, is supported by the application landscape that is supported by the technology landscape.

However, obtaining a clear view on these landscapes and their ability to support the bank's objectives may not be evident, as business functionality might be expressed in different "dialects" and application functionality is not clearly and uniformly defined. The BIAN-based Frame of Reference is an instrument to acquire insight in this heterogenous, complex ecosystem.

The **business architecture landscape** can be "overlaid" on the Frame of Reference. The functionality of business processes, functions and organizational units can be expressed in terms of the Service Domains they realize. This delivers a "map" with a clear and universal "legend" of the available business functionality in each part of the organization.

Expressing business functionality as a choreography of Service Domains is key for BIAN's role in supporting a holistic enterprise view. It clarifies the concept of a "functionality building block" for management and helps them in using this lens on various management aspects.

Expressing business functionality as "implemented Service Domains" facilitates an optimization of the business landscape. For example, it improves the cooperation between business architects, the detection of overlaps, gaps and synergy opportunities within the bank. It facilitates the detection of outsourcing or insourcing opportunities and the evaluation of business service provider offerings. It facilitates the opportunity for alliances with partners in the Open API economy.

The **application architecture landscape** can also be overlaid on the Frame of Reference. This delivers a "map" of the business support each application and the entire application portfolio provides. This is a powerful support for application portfolio management, as duplications and gaps will clearly show.

As application architects and designers share the same language with business architects and designers, the communication between business and ICT will be improved. Application architects will have an easier job at optimising the application portfolio, providing shared application support for different entities and developing or selecting appropriate vendor solutions. Interoperability with partners who share the same Frame of Reference is facilitated.

Communication with enterprise management will also improve, as applications can be described in the BIAN Service Domain language they are familiar with.

The usefulness of BIAN as a Frame of Reference for business and application layers is very similar. The landscapes will almost certainly not be identical, as business architecture decisions and application architecture decisions are based on different criteria. But business and logical application architectures share one important criterion for delimiting their building blocks: the provided business functionality. Neatly componentized business functionality is exactly what the BIAN Architecture offers.

This does not apply to the **technology layer**. This layer does not offer business functionality, but it enables applications to function[42]. As such, technology resources cannot be mapped directly to Service Domains.

Technology landscape elements can, however, be mapped indirectly on the BIAN-based Frame of Reference. The support provided by the technology landscape elements for the application landscape elements should be clear from the bank's configuration management.

As a result, it is possible to show the technology support for each building block of the Frame of Reference and evaluate the adequacy of the support they offer. For example 24/7 availability or big data abilities.

Thus, the Frame of Reference can provide a consistent and cohesive view on the operations of the bank, throughout all "architecture layers".

---

42 Technology functionality, such as printing, exchanging messages, executing programs etc. is not specific for the type of business functionality it supports, and is certainly not bank-specific.

Each building block on this map is attributed a strategic value and associated requirements: the Business and Information System Strategy assigns a strategic value and imposes requirements to the business, application and technology landscapes. These requirements are "funnelled down the stack" and "down the management levels" according to the Service Domain Frame of Reference.

5.3.3 A uniform and stable base for performance management

Service Domains can provide a common, stable Frame of Reference for monitoring the performance of the business landscape elements and of the applications and technology landscapes.

Performance management that addresses different entities, or over time within an entity, often struggles with a comparison base. The architecture elements that are monitored, such as processes and organizational units, are delimited differently in space and time. Applications are replaced, their functionality is extended. This problem can be solved by using the stable, canonical, elemental functionality building blocks which Service Domains represent, as performance reporting anchor points.

As demonstrated in the previous section, Service Domains can link all architecture layers together: business functionality as supported by applications, as supported by technology. They can also "funnel" requirements "down the stack": from the strategic business capability requirements to business, application and technology requirements.

Thus, if the performance of the operations of the bank, on business, application and technology layers, is *measured* per Service Domain delimitation, it can be *assessed* in relation to the requirements.

Performance measurements and assessments can be attributed to each Service Domain implementation. It may not be easy to map existing performance instruments on Service Domains. If, however, the performance of different organizations must be compared, or performance information needs to be consolidated, there is never an easy solution.

The "bank on a page" representation of the blueprint can be used as a heatmap, allowing an easy visual comparison of performance measurements and assessments over time and between entities.

Examples of measurements are shown in Figure 5-8. They are quantitative (such as the number of staff per unit outcome, the processing cost per unit outcome), semi-quantitative (such as the information quality) or qualitative (such as customer satisfaction) and relate to business or ICT performance, or to a combination of both.

5   BIAN for a holistic enterprise view   113

SYSTEMS RELATED COSTS
- Development & deployment
- Training, support & assurance
- technology/platform operations
- Licensing/subscription/purchases

NON-SYSTEMS RELATED COSTS
- Workforce utilization
- Workforce training
- Location/equipment/utility/consumables
- Fixed capital allocation
- Fees/licensing/agenc
- Management overhead &support

Costs can be further analysed in terms including:
- Own Vs allocated
- Fixed/variable
- Book value/depreciating costs
- Repeating/ad hoc
- Volume discounts

SYSTEMS PERFORMANCE MEASURES
- Machine utilization
- Operating profile – schedule
- Security/resilience
- Performance profile
- User headcount, skill level & schedules
- Variability/configurability
- Advanced technology/practices

BUSINESS PERFORMANCE MEASURES
- Staff utilization/productivity
- Operating budgets
- User headcount/skills profile
- Working/commited capital
- Business criticality/contribution
- Reputational/customer exposure/risk profile

Different systems and business cost and performance measures can be associated with the Frame of Reference

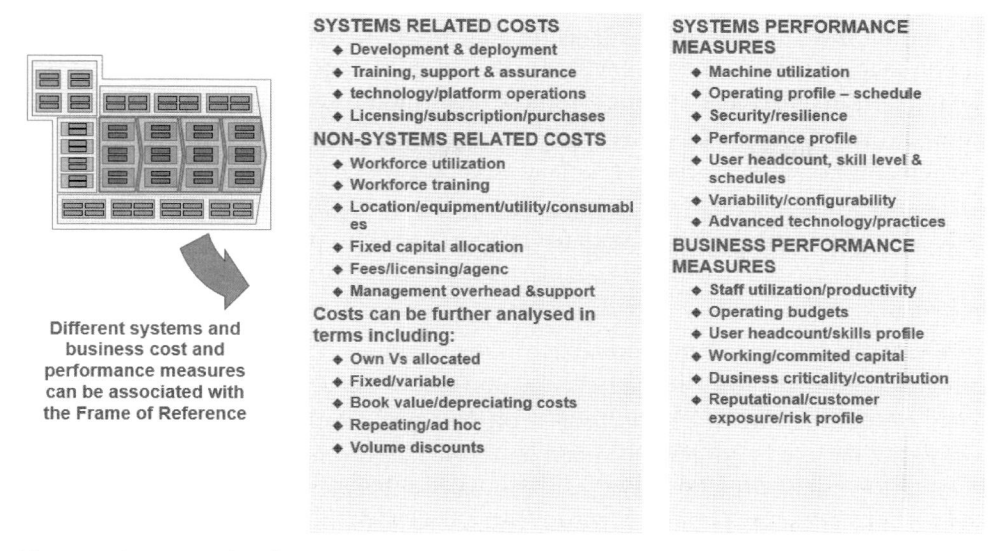

Figure 5-8 Examples of performance measures

Each building block of the bank's operations is now also attributed with performance information.

5.3.4   BIAN for investment and change portfolio management

The enterprise investment and change portfolio contains the desired, planned and ongoing initiatives (projects and programs) intended to fill gaps between the "as is" situation and the "to be" situation of a bank's operations. Defining and managing the investment and change portfolio initiatives can benefit from the Frame of Reference. This closes the "plan-do-check-act" cycle.

As described in the previous sections, each building block of the bank's operations ("do"), on each architecture layer is now labeled with the BIAN building block it realizes. It has a strategic position attributed to it, as well as requirements ("plan"), and its performance is measured and assessed on the same scale ("check").

This information enables the architects to assess the quality of the operations of the bank, on each architecture layer and throughout the stack. The readiness of the stack for the strategy (looking upward from the Service Domains to the strategy they support) can be objectively assessed. Problem areas can be delimited, their importance (such as impact on strategic goals – or on operational risk and continuity) can be defined.

The architects can now define change proposals, to mitigate problems with the as-is situation and to improve the strategic fit of the bank's landscapes.

These change proposals ("act") can also be described along the BIAN-based Frame of Reference. The scope is expressed as impacted Service Domains, whilst the gaps that need to be filled and the requirements for the "to-be" situation are also documented accordingly.

The quality of the change and investment portfolio, as a whole, will also improve.

The impact of changes on the existing business and application landscapes can be identified more easily and with a higher reliability through the same "Service Domain lens".

Expressing the scope of change initiatives in the common "Service Domain language", facilitates the interaction between change portfolio managers and project managers. Touch points (the impact of one project on another), overlaps and conflicts can be more easily detected and portfolios can be revised accordingly. Change management for initiatives impacting the same areas can be coordinated, and common initiatives detected and isolated. Migration strategies can be elaborated for a combination of projects.

All this leads to a more efficient and effective delimitation of the required change initiatives and a more reliable estimation of the costs. The enterprise change portfolio will correspond better to the strategic priorities and will be more coherent.

Expressing the scope of investments and change initiatives in the "Service Domain language" and sharing this with strategy and performance management, facilitates the communication with enterprise management and improves investment and change portfolio governance.

Management will gain a better understanding of the scope, as this is expressed in a common language. Their evaluation of the impact of a change initiative on the existing organization is improved.

Management gains a better understanding of the business case of change initiatives for the application and technology landscapes, as their contribution to the business landscape and the strategy can be "translated up the stack" along the Service Domain "funnel". Hence, they can be a better judge of the importance and priority of investment and change proposals from different sources. It will also be easier for them to evaluate the impact of factors such as a lack of progress or a change in project costs on the business case.

Figure 5-9 Illustrates how a BIAN member used its "bank on a page" to communicate the scope of a project to management. Similar heatmaps with goal contribution and paintpoints in the business landscape, support the business case for this project.

5 BIAN for a holistic enterprise view

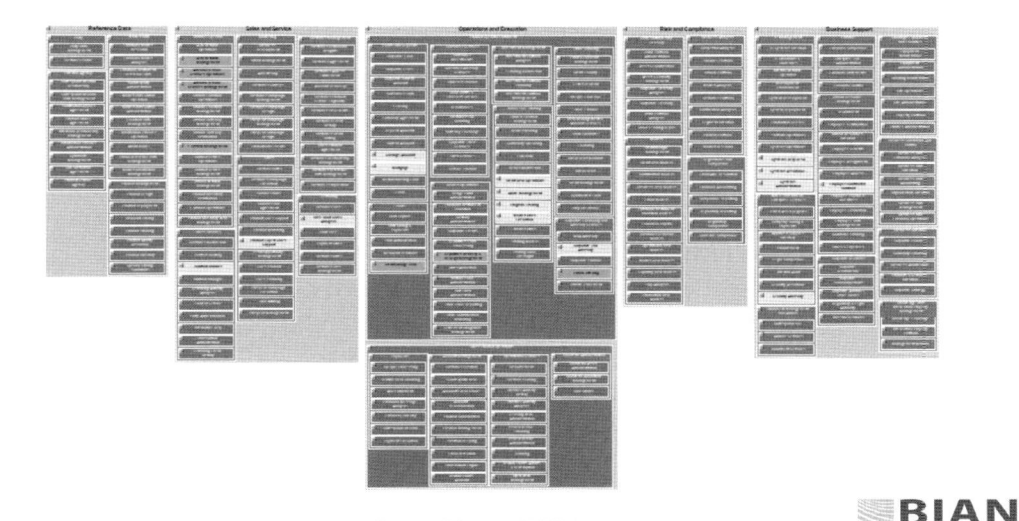

Figure 5-9 Using the enterprise blueprint as a common Frame of Reference for change management[43,44]

The international M5 Banking Group has grown organically over the years through mergers and acquisitions. As a result, many activities are duplicated, ICT platforms are incompatible, information quality suffers and maintenance costs rise. After careful consideration, Group management decides on a new strategy: "Group Synergy". For all activities, except those that a member bank specifically uses for its local customers and market, optimal group synergy needs to be realized.

A strategy working group is established, to develop a long-term plan (LTP) for implementing the new strategy. This group consists of enterprise architects, organization specialists and strategists from different banks within the group. They are in need of a common language and a shared Frame of Reference and decide to adopt the BIAN Framework.

The working group decide to document their work and conclusions in the architecture repository available in Homeland and hire a consultant with BIAN and ArchiMate experience as secretary. The first job of this secretary is to assign all Service Domains to the M5 Banking Group entity, as an enterprise blueprint for the Group and to visualize this as the Group's "bank on page".

The first step in the LTP is to decide which activities are likely to profit from group synergy and which ones should remain specific for each bank's customers and markets.

The working group decides on following approach:

---
43 Freely after BIAN Architecture Working Group (2017a).
44 We apologize for the fact that the names of the Service Domains are not readable. The purpose of this figure is to illustrate the power of the Service Landscape to manage and communicate the scope of change initiatives. For online version of this figure see free download at
https://www.vanharen.store/bian-2nd-edition-a-framework-for-the-financial-services-industry

Every Service Domain is considered a "generic activity". Each one will be assigned a "integration eligibility" requirement, i.e. the level to which it can profit from common ICT support, common business procedures and centralized management.

The strategy working group of the M5 Banking Group draws up a series of criteria to decide on the "integration eligibility" of a Service Domain. They assess each Service Domain on each of these criteria. They document the results of these assessments in the repository (Figure 5-10, left side).

From these assessment results, they derive the strategic "integration eligibility" requirement that expresses whether a Service Domain should be centralized, harmonized or diversified. This result is also documented in the repository.

Each level of "integration eligibility" requirement is made more explicit. Centralized activities must be brought under central management and must have one set of procedures and be supported by one ICT platform. Harmonized activities remain under distributed management but must share procedures and ICT support. Diversified activities decide on their own process design. ICT synergy is still to be pursued. These requirements are also documented for each Service Domain (Figure 5-10, upper right).

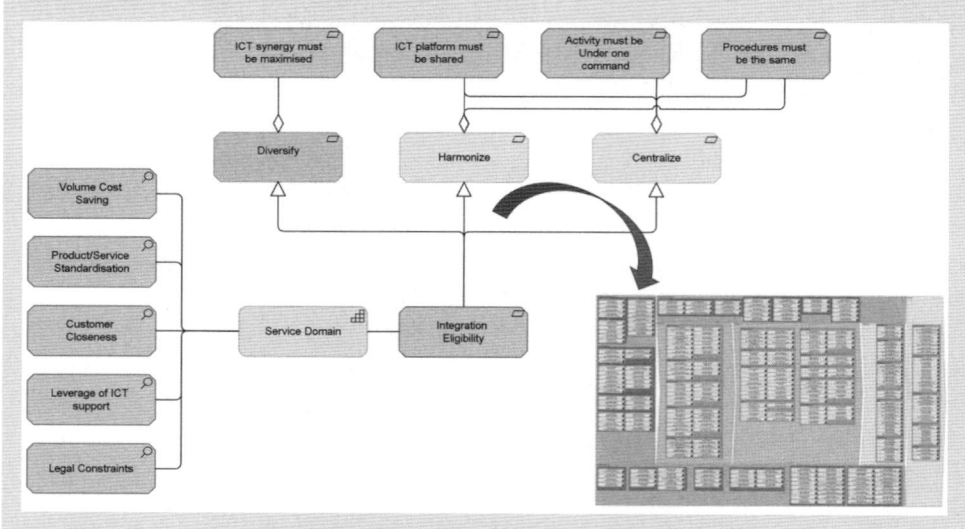

Figure 5-10 M5 Group's strategy: assessments lead to requirements, both attributed to Service Domains

The group "bank on a page" is used to visualize the conclusions of the working group for Group management (Figure 5-10, lower right).

The strategy working group recommends establishing a separate legal entity "Group Services". Its "to-be" blueprint contains all those activities with the integration eligibility "centralize". (Figure 5-11).

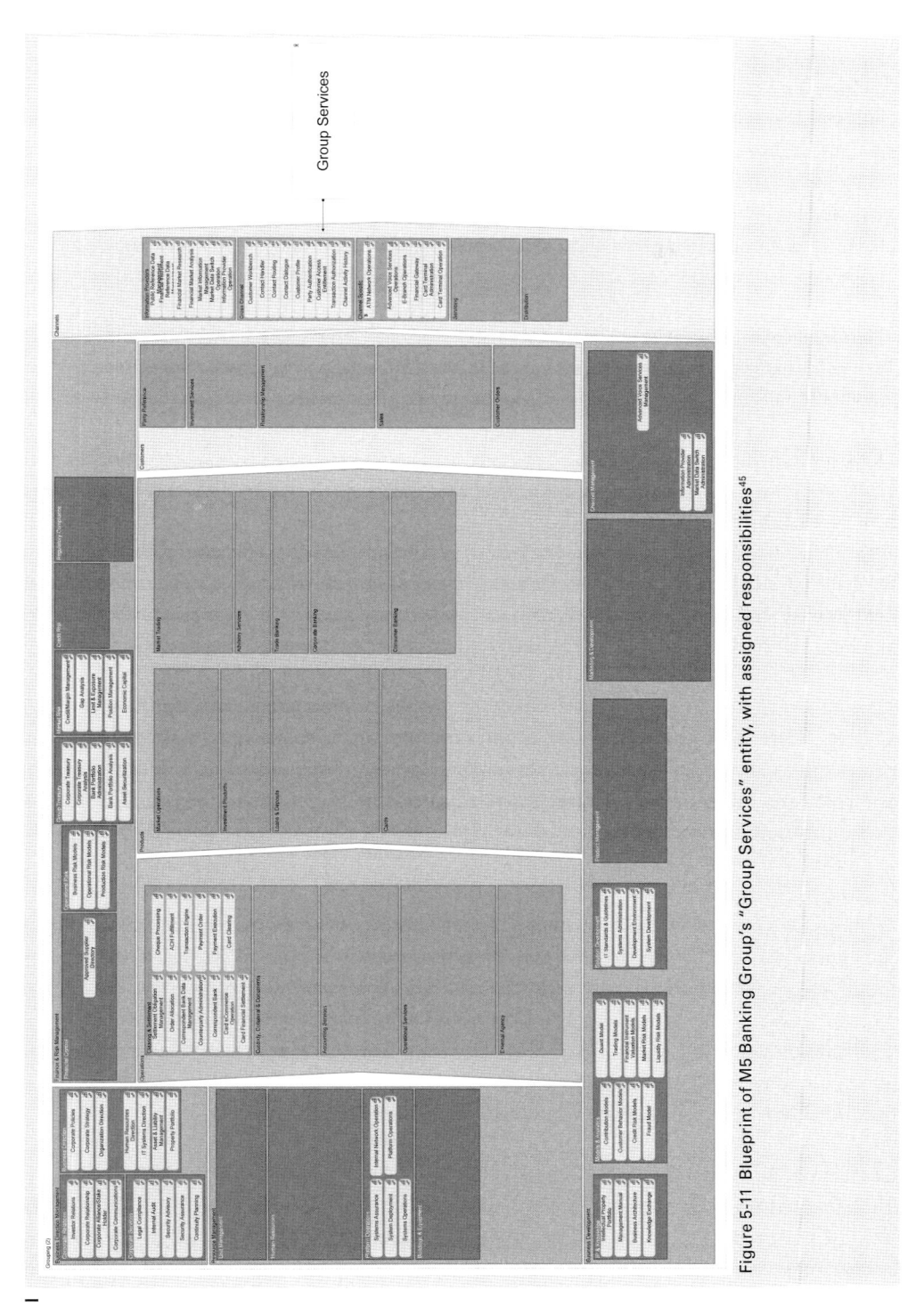

5 BIAN for a holistic enterprise view

Figure 5-11 Blueprint of M5 Banking Group's "Group Services" entity, with assigned responsibilities[45]

---

45 Our apologies for the fact that the the names of the Service Domains are not readable. The purpose of this figure is to illustrate what an entities blueprint could look like, using the common Frame of Reference of the bank or banking group as a canvas. For online version of this figure see free download at https://www.vanharen.store/bian-2nd-edition-a-framework-for-the-financial-services-industry

> The working group defines an initial project portfolio, containing proposals for the "quick synergy wins", such as the centralization of the audit function. It describes the scope of these integration projects as collections of Service Domains. The quick wins are selected in view of their high "integration eligibility" scores and based on limited interactions with other activities.
>
> The working group concludes that an overview of the "as-is" business and information systems landscapes in the different banks is required before launching other centralization or harmonization initiatives, because a solid impact analysis is needed.
>
> The working group strongly recommends the establishment of an enterprise architecture capability (both business and ICT) on a group level, to enable the transition to the service-oriented business organization and ICT platform required for the Group Synergy strategy.

■ 5.4 TESTIMONIAL

In the first edition of this book, Steven Van Wyk, Executive Vice President, Head of Technology and Operations, PNC Financial Services Group, explained the benefits of aligning the bank's enterprise architecture to the BIAN model:

"The BIAN model fits perfectly in line with how we view enterprise architecture (EA) at PNC. One of the first steps we took as an organization was to bring a business perspective to enterprise architecture. To us, technology is not just a collection of servers and software, but rather a set of technical solutions that are aligned to specific Business Capabilities and functions.

Adding the business view
To begin, we looked at every application that existed in our portfolio and mapped it to the aligned BIAN Service Domains (specific business functions) in our EA management tool.

This gave us a clear view of systems that were providing similar or overlapping solutions, which could be optimized, while also creating a consistent and replicable way to evaluate proposed new solutions for our application portfolio.

Creating a "bank on a page"
This allowed us to create a business-driven "bank on a page" heat map, using BIAN's Value Chain representation, to show what areas were suffering from obsolescence and compliance issues. As we move forward, we can align our risk and project portfolio views to the same "bank on a page" overview.

Using the BIAN Framework, we can move our core platforms into a componentized framework, which allows us to manage our transformation in logical steps that are aligned with the overall business strategy.

Positioning for disruptive industry change
Defining our technology into capabilities in this way also sets us up for future innovation. The proliferation of FinTech is setting new expectations with new business models that sometimes compete directly with banks. We are evolving our core banking capabilities into a componentized framework that will allow us to embrace evolving business expectations and customer demands. The search for innovation partnerships becomes easier when you are no longer tied to the past era's monolithic application approaches. We are exploring Open Banking APIs, for example, in a collaborative project with BIAN and Carnegie Mellon University.

By aligning with the BIAN Framework we are assured that our enterprise architecture can continuously adapt to new market and technology demands."

■ 5.5   TEST YOURSELF QUESTIONS

1. **Which statements correctly express the role of the Service Domain Frame of Reference?**
   A. A blueprint expressed in Service Domains whose functionality is required for each entity, provides a common Frame of Reference to management.
   B. Requirements for, and assessments of, business functionality can be documented per Service Domain.
   C. By overlaying the application landscape on the Service Domain Frame of Reference, the functionality of each application can be expressed in a common language.
   D. The coverage and quality of the support by applications can be indicated on the Frame of Reference.

2. **Which statements correctly express why the Service Landscape (especially the Value Chain representation) is well suited as a quick start for an enterprise blueprint?**
   A. The BIAN Service Domains provide well defined, elementary, mutually exclusive, commonly exhaustive building blocks to describe any bank's functionality.
   B. The BIAN Service Landscape's business areas, as presented in the Value Chain representation, define organizational units as present in any bank on a semantic level.
   C. The Value Chain representation of the Service Landscape appeals greatly to business management.
   D. The BIAN Service Landscape enumerates the Service Domains that are always present in all banks.

3. Which of these statements do not represent the possible use of an enterprise blueprint as a Frame of Reference for analysis?
   A. Assign strategic value and risk to Business Capabilities.
   B. Attribute requirements to the Service Domains as implemented in an entity.
   C. Attribute assessment results to the Service Domains as implemented in an entity.
   D. Express the scope of projects in impacted Service Domains.

6 BIAN for the business layer

The banking ecosystem is changing at a rapid pace. A bank can no longer afford a business organization that consists of islands connected by some bridges and hourly ferries. It needs to be a well-oiled, agile service organization, both on the inside and outwards towards the open finance ecosystem.

Even though the (r)evolution that is changing the financial ecosystem is enabled and even triggered by the capabilities of the technology and application layers, it is the business layer that provides the bank's value to customers and other stakeholders. The business organization needs to be manoeuvrable, able to provide services in differing and evolving orchestrations.

The BIAN Framework provides a Frame of Reference for the business landscape that promotes modular "service center thinking" in view of manoeuvrability – or (still crucial) in view of processing efficiency and effectivity (Sub-section 6.1.1). It can be used to create the most effective organizational chart (Sub-section 6.1.2).

This Frame of Reference enables the exploration, charting and evaluation of the business landscape (Sub-section 6.1.3).

It can be used to "parcel out" the business landscape in view of architecture governance. As the Service Domain is the linking pin between enterprise strategy and its operations, the Frame of Reference can be used to link strategic assessments of, and requirements to, the business landscape elements implementing Service Domains (Sub-section 6.1.4).

The BIAN Framework provides the building blocks and principles for a conceptual reference business architecture (Sub-section 6.1.5). Such reference architecture improves the integration of business activities within the enterprise. It improves the quality and completeness of business requirements and impact analysis for new functionalities or changes.

The Frame of Reference supports the evaluation of opportunities for mergers and acquisitions. It facilitates the delimitation of investments and change proposals. The shared Frame of Reference facilitates the cooperation with ICT, improving the quality of business cases and an adequate scoping of projects and programmes (Section 6.2).

The "building block thinking", enforced by the Frame of Reference, can be applied in business process management and in business requirement analysis (Section 6.3). This can improve the agility of the design. It facilitates the cooperation between process managers as well as with business solution providers and partners (Section 6.3).

■ 6.1   BIAN FOR BUSINESS ARCHITECTURE

This section describes the use of the BIAN Architecture on overview level – the enterprise and domain levels (as described in Appendix A2.2).

6.1.1   A Frame of Reference for the business landscape

In Sub-section 4.2.2, we explained how BIAN supports the elaboration of a Frame of Reference, tailored to the bank. This Frame of Reference depicts the elemental "capability building blocks" that the bank requires. It provides a common language and a common Frame of Reference to express functionality, between the different "speech communities" in the business organization, such as business lines, departments, or even processes.

6.1.2   Elaborating the organogram

The organogram depicts the assignment of operational activities and their grouping along reporting lines.

When discussing the best organogram for the enterprise, expressing the responsibilities according to the Frame of Reference creates a common language between those involved in the proposals and management that takes the final decision. It helps to look at the business organization with a fresh view: to think in terms of provided contributions (services), instead of processes.

Reporting lines are a way to create a manageable span of control. Business processes and customer services tend to be transversal. If the responsibility of departments, as well as process steps, is expressed in Service Domains (as in Sub-section 6.3.1), the responsibilities of each "actor" in an end-to-end process can be defined in the same language as the organogram.

6.1.3   Charting and assessing the business landscape

The business landscape can be overlaid on the Frame of Reference. This provides an overview of what functionality is performed where/by whom. This business functionality is expressed in a universal language, not one that is specific for one bank, one line of business or one process. It enables an inventory and comparison of the functionality between, for example, organizational units, banks in a banking groups, within alliances….

BIAN provides the ability to look at business processes as an orchestration of elemental capability building blocks: the Service Domains. This provides an inventory of the responsibilities of an organizational unit, or an overview of what actually happens in processes, on a rather fine-grained scale and in a common language (Figure 6-1).

The overlay allows the detection of activities that are duplicated – or that seem to be missing. The more fine-grained Service Domain "grid" enables the detection of gaps that one would not have expected based on a process inventory. Whether, and to what extent, duplications and gaps are a problem, needs to be evaluated by business architects and management[46].

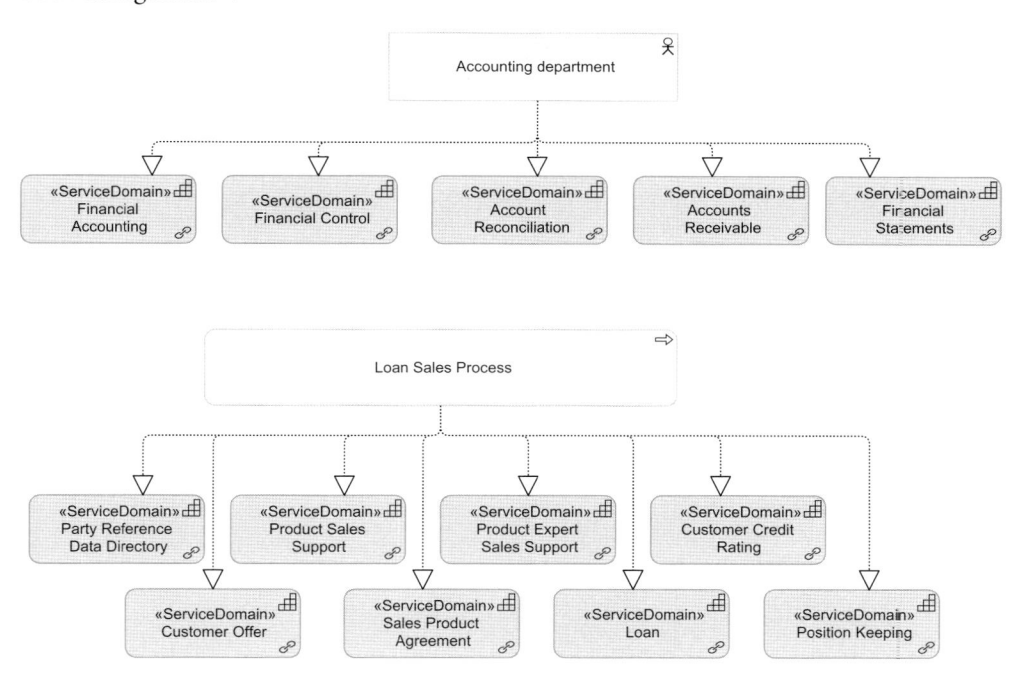

Figure 6-1 The responsibilities of an accounting department and a loan sales process clarified

The performance of business organizations and business processes can be analysed and documented on this more fine-grained scale. This provides an organization-independent view, in space and over time, of business performance. As/if the same "overlay" is used for applications (as in Sub-section 7.1.2), then the root cause analysis of performance issues is more precise and can involve causes on all architecture layers.

---

46 And by the audit department.

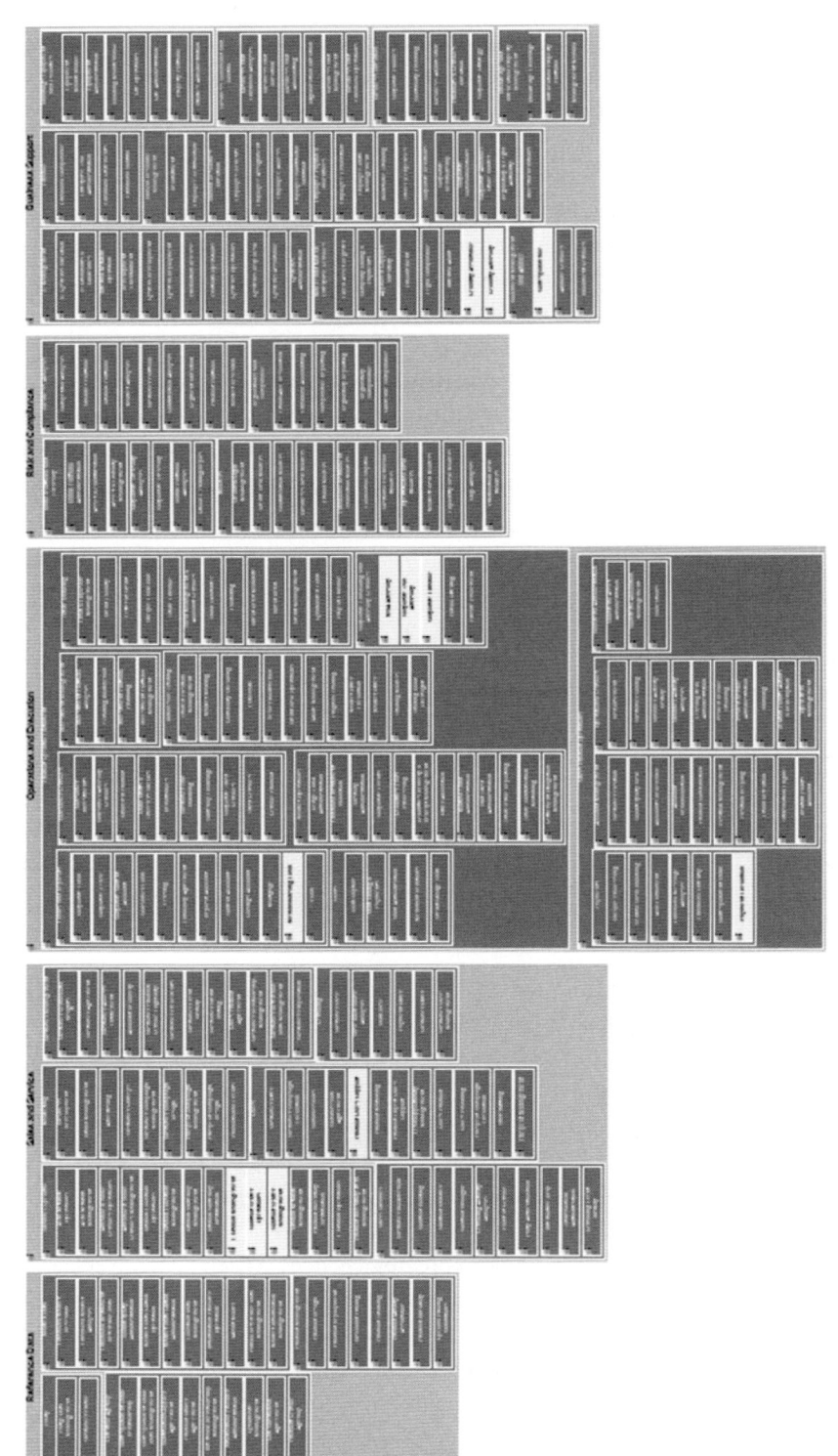

Figure 6-2 Business pain-points visualized on the "bank on a page" of a BIAN member [47,48]

47 BIAN Architecture Working Group 2017 (a)
48 We apologize for the fact that the names of the Service Domains are not readable. The purpose of this figure is to illustrate the power of the Service Landscape to manage and communicate the quality of the business landscape. For online version of this figure see free download at https://www.vanharen.store/bian-2nd-edition-a-framework-for-the-financial-services-industry

6 BIAN for the business layer

In Figure 6-2, problem areas are visualized on the enterprise blueprint canvas (or "bank on page") of a BIAN member. This is intended for management communication.

The enterprise architecture team, inspired by the recommendation of the strategy working group, has decided to continue using the BIAN Framework as a common language and a common Frame of Reference. They have also decided to upgrade the Homeland repository to a Group architecture repository.

Their first project is to develop a high-level overview of the business landscape of each member bank (and its application support – see Chapter 7). Each department's activities are mapped on the Service Domain Frame of Reference. This is documented in the repository.

The blueprint for each bank can be derived from this information. The "bank on a page" representation of this blueprint will be introduced as a canvas for (new) management reporting.

A first evaluation of the business landscapes is undertaken. This reveals several duplications within the banks. It also reveals some gaps, for example the loan sales process in the Mzero Bank does not consider "customer credit rating". The enterprise architecture team entrusts the risk assessment of these gaps to the audit department[49].

6.1.4 Governing the business architecture

For an enterprise of significant size, it is necessary to split architecture responsibilities between different individuals, whilst it is also crucial to ensure cohesion and consistency in the architecture. This is done by distinguishing architecture levels, with increasing detail as the scope diminishes (as in Section 13.2) and assigning responsibilities for these "zooming levels".

Contrary to a process-based architecture, the component characteristics of the BIAN Service Domains makes them suitable for a clear responsibility delimitation. The BIAN Service Landscape and its Business Areas and Business Domains can be used to delimit coherent and "loosely coupled" business architecture domains. Or a bank can assemble Service Domains in governance units as it sees fit.

---

49 It turns out there is already an audit recommendation to "fill the gap", as it creates an inacceptable risk exposure for the bank. The internal audit activity has scored very high on "integration eligibility" during the Group Strategy exercise. It will be the first to be centralized. The audit integration team sees the Service Domains as an excellent starting point for the "audit universe" on a Group level: it provides an implementation-independent, common Frame of Reference to describe the activities in the Group and to assess the risks involved in these activities. The Frame of Reference will now also be shared by the Group Internal Audit department. Another contribution to the holistic enterprise view.

> The Mfour Bank has defined a "business architect" role. Business architects are responsible for an effective and efficient business organization, in line with the business strategy. They are also responsible for defining the investment and change portfolio, required to align the business and information system architectures with the requirements of the Banking Strategy.
>
> To keep things manageable, the bank is divided in business architecture domains. The "distribution domain", for example, overarches the customer service and interaction channels (brick, click and paper), as well as marketing and sales activities. The "product factory" domains are responsible for product design and fulfillment. To clarify the delimitation of responsibilities between the distribution domain and the product factory domains, the BIAN Frame of Reference is used.
>
> A by-product of this exercise is an improvement in the "customer interaction script". This part of the reference business architecture describes the "pattern" for how customers are able to access products and services (as in Sub-section 6.1.5).

Strategic assessments and requirements

As described in Sub-section 5.3.1, strategic assessments (such as value and inherent risk classifications) and strategic requirements can be documented for each Service Domain. Either passed down through their contribution to Business Capabilities, or directly assigned.

Strategic requirements can be documented per Service Domain. For example, Party Reference Data Management and Legal Entity Directory are "commodities", but the completeness and correctness of party information might be a "unique selling proposition"[50].

The strategic position of Service Domains (or better: types of business activities delimited and labelled by Service Domains) is made explicit in a cascade of more detailed requirements. For example, Party Reference Data Management in the example above, "must reach a maturity level of at least 4".

Figure 6-3 shows an example of a BIAN member that assessed the "process maturity" per Service Domain. Combined with the strategic requirements, such assessments lead to an evaluation of the ability of the business landscape to support the enterprise strategy. (Notice again the "heatmap" representation on the enterprise blueprint canvas. This visualization helps enterprise management to evaluate the consequences of this

---

50 If customer proposition and risk evaluation are precise, agreements can be closed in an instant. *Actually, the Mfour Bank is making money with its "legal entity directory". It has excellent data on group structures that can support instant credit decisions for corporate customers. It is now selling this information to other interested parties.*

assessment, as the strategic requirements are presented on the same canvas – according to the same BIAN-based Frame of Reference.)

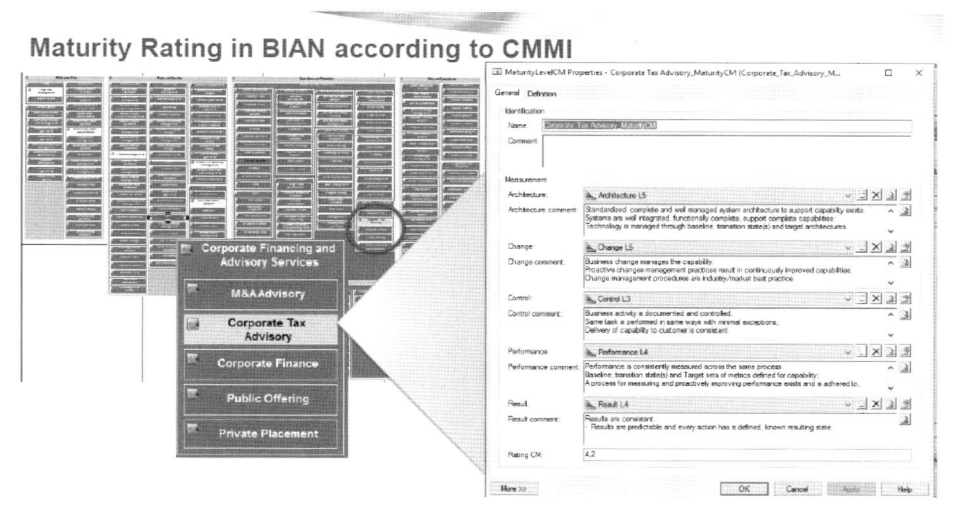

Figure 6-3 Maturity rating per Service Domain, represented on the "bank on a page" of a BIAN member[51]

Figure 6-4 visualizes the "group synergy" aspect of the business organization strategy for the M5 Banking Group. The integration eligibility is shown for each business activity, according to the Frame of Reference. For management communication purposes, it is displayed as a heatmap, on the "bank on a page" canvas. The colors represent the overarching "integration eligibility requirement", which incorporates a range of more detailed requirements (represented in Figure 5-10).

Sourcing strategy

The Frame of Reference and the "blueprint view" of an entity on it, is also an instrument to define the bank's sourcing strategy.

Each Service Domain is a possible business service center, given its internal coherence and service encapsulation. It provides a sensible, stable delimitation of responsibilities and is an excellent anchor point for requirements specification – or for service-offerings specification. As such, the Service Domain is well suited to structure service-offerings and outsourcing agreements between a bank and a business service provider - or by the bank as a business service provider.

---

51 BIAN Architecture Working Group (2017a).

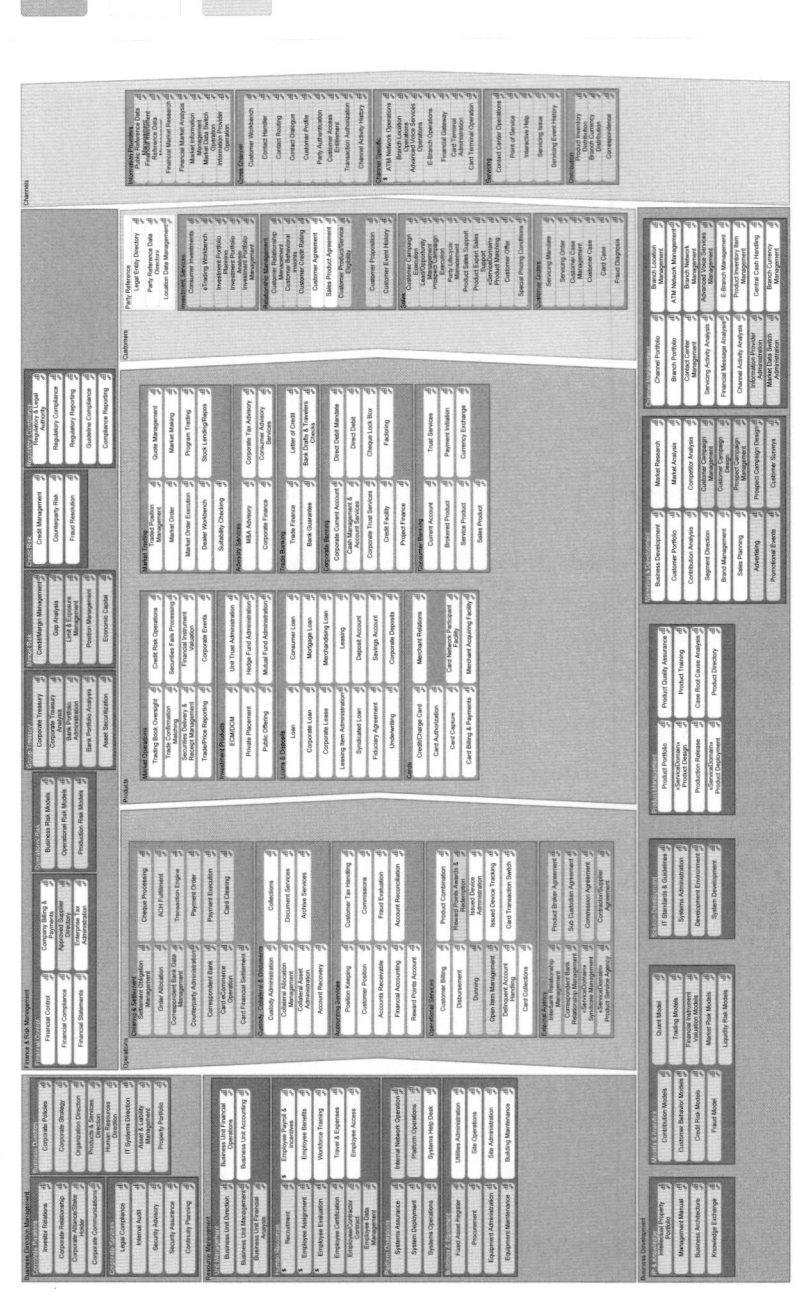

Figure 6-4 Strategic requirements per Service Domain presented as a heat map on the "bank on a page" of M5 Banking Group

6.1.5 Building blocks and principles for a reference business architecture

The BIAN component design maximizes the cross-product re-use of Business Capabilities and defines standard integration boundaries such that new product facilities can be integrated quickly, as only the new product specific logic is required and many requirements will be supported by re-use of established facilities. This ability is leveraged by an enterprise reference architecture.

The BIAN-based Frame of Reference provides the building blocks for a conceptual enterprise reference architecture. This expresses what functionality building blocks need to be present and how they need to cooperate to ensure the secure and controlled end-to-end operation of the bank.

If the Frame of Reference is positioned with a view to streamlining the company's architecture, great care should be given to the tailoring effort, as the customized Service Domains will act as the capability building blocks of the company's conceptual enterprise reference architecture. Still, a clear link with the base BIAN version should be maintained, in view of the potential cooperation with partners and the sourcing of services in the Open API economy – and the new versions of the BIAN Framework.

A bank's primary purpose is to provide financial services to customers. The provision of financial services to customers is enabled by a whole range of supporting and surrounding activities. For example, apart from providing secure access to financial services for customers, managing currency and party information, sending bills and account statements, managing customer risk… is also required.

The bank also needs to ensure its services are provided in a controlled way. For instance, it needs to comply with laws and regulations; it needs an overview of its activities in view of enterprise risk and financial management; it needs to report to regulatory authorities.

These "supporting and surrounding activities" usually support and surround sales and product-agreement fulfilment activities. They provide their services according to **patterns**. How Service Domains cooperate to provide secure access, for example, does not depend on the product type this "service orchestration" provides access to. Neither does the fact that product information needs to be provided to the "Risk and Finance Management" and "Business Direction" Business Areas.

Figure 6-5 shows where types of patterns can be situated on the Value Chain representation of the Service Landscape. Patterns that support secure access to and delivery of financial services and enable the required control activities such as compliance checks and registration in the financial control systems.

Whilst BIAN does not actually provide such patterns, its Business Scenarios can be an inspiration for these patterns.

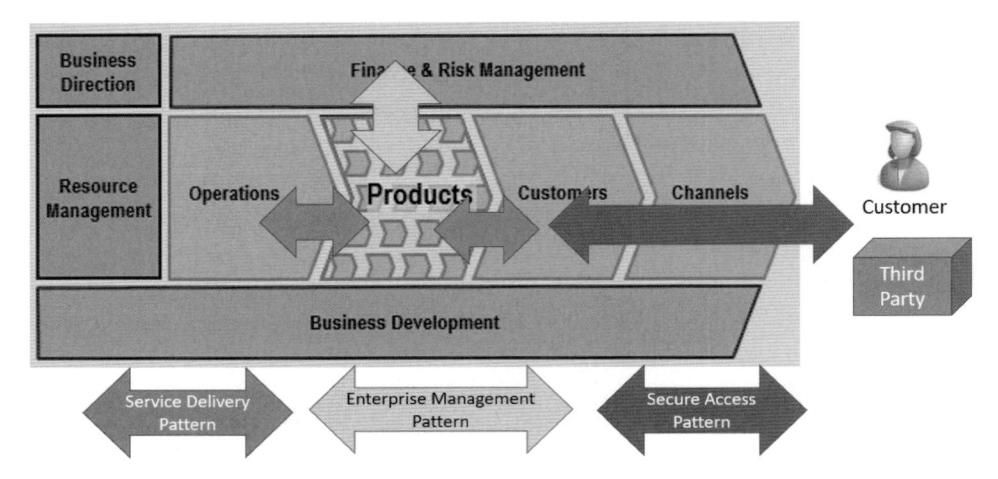

Figure 6-5 Service Domains cooperate in patterns, enabling a secure, controlled delivery of financial services

The patterns can be documented as part of the conceptual enterprise reference architecture, expressed as orchestrations of Service Domains. Such descriptions are organization-independent and stable over time. The patterns can evolve with the evolutions of the banking ecosystem[52].

These patterns ensure that, for example, new products or new access channels are correctly embedded in a bank's end-to-end ecosystem.

The "conceptual level" of these patterns is expressed in Service Domain terms. It applies to both the reference business architecture and the reference application architecture. For the business layer, the stable "conceptual patterns" (which Service Domains need to be involved) will be complemented with, for example, directions about which department needs to be involved and for what purpose. This level evolves with the actual business landscape, as responsibilities can be transferred to different organizational units.

> The business organization department of the Mfour Bank maintains a "reference business architecture manual". The department heard about a "reference application architecture" initiative set up by the chief enterprise application architect. She is seeking to mitigate the recurring problem of project delays due to forgotten service connections. These gaps only surface during end-to-end testing. The business organization department realizes this is in fact a business problem. A new business functionality is never stand alone. It needs to be embedded in the end-to-end enterprise, to ensure a smooth, secure customer journey and a secure and controlled functioning of the bank.
>
> M 5

---

52 For example, in the last decades lots of "control" activities have been imposed on banks. Technology evolutions have enabled new architecture styles that require new secure access patterns.

The business organization department decides to join the initiative and develop a reference business architecture, consistent with the reference application architecture.

The reference business architecture describes how product sales and product agreement fulfilment are embedded in the enterprise, e.g. how it interacts with party reference data, financial accounting, risk management, compliance…

It contains several "scripts", describing which business responsibilities need to be involved for particular situations, such as the introduction of a new product or access channel.

This manual is much appreciated by other departments such as business unit management, who are often overlooked in new product or channel launches and need to work with impossible deadlines and insufficient information when including the new product in their statistics.

The change portfolio management department is also happy, as the reliability of scope definition and business cases for change proposals is improved. Project budgets are more accurate in predicting project costs.

The business organization department and the application architects decide it is better to create a "conceptual" layer for the reference architecture. The responsibilities of business departments change, as do applications. The patterns and scripts on this conceptual level are expressed in Service Domains. These are mapped on an "operational" reference business architecture manual and its application counterpart. The business manual describes, amongst other things, the departments and business roles that need to be involved and guidelines on what needs to be discussed.

■ 6.2 BIAN FOR BUSINESS INVESTMENT AND CHANGE PORTFOLIO

6.2.1 Supporting mergers and acquisitions

Decisions regarding mergers and acquisitions are often based on opportunities for synergy or complementarity between the candidates.

Expressing the "enterprise blueprint" of the involved institutions using the common BIAN language facilitates the assessment of the opportunity for a merger or acquisition.

The mapping of the business and application landscape using the BIAN-based Frame of Reference, enriched with performance assessments expressed according to this Frame of Reference, enables a one-to-one comparison of the available business organization(s) and application platform(s). This supports the selection of the best fit for the new organization – or the merging of best practices. It also supports the development of an appropriate migration strategy.

> The Mfour Bank is the result of a merger between the A Bank and the C Bank. The A and C Banks are active on the same market, have well-developed retail and corporate lines of business and "customer centric, quality above price" strategies. Their "BIAN-based enterprise blueprints" are remarkably similar. The decision to merge has been taken in view of economies of scale.
>
> C Bank has only recently upgraded itself to a multi-line-of-business bank through an acquisition. It was strong in retail banking, but not in corporate banking. It acquired the I-Bank, a corporate bank, with a complementary enterprise blueprint.
>
> Both the merger and the acquisition were preceded by due diligence that (amongst many other things) corroborated the assumption of synergy and complementarity respectively, by comparing the business activities. The BIAN Service Landscape was used as the common Frame of Reference for this purpose.
>
> The C Bank acquired the corporate I-Bank and incorporated it into its legal structure. Back-office and not sales organization synergy was the main objective of the acquisition. Both organizations remain independent as separate lines of business. The "partner and regulator facing" processes, however, needed to be merged. The I-Bank had a more sophisticated business and application support for "Correspondent Bank", and "Correspondent Bank Relationship Management". C Bank's "Correspondent Bank Data Management" on the other hand, was better. The newly merged Correspondent Bank team will use a combination of those best practices.

6.2.2 Business change portfolio

The business architect provides his/her contribution to the bank's change portfolio by evaluating the quality and strategic fit of the business landscape. Change proposals are delimited based on the quality of the business landscape and its strategic fit.

In the current age, business change is seldom possible without application and technology change. The common Frame of Reference facilitates a comprehensive impact analysis, hence scope definition, all through the layers.

The existence of a BIAN-based reference architecture improves the impact analysis and scope definition even further, as the end-to-end embedding of the change will be included in the scope.

Project stakeholders can be more easily found, as all areas of the business that "map" on the change scope, as defined in Service Domains, can be identified.

When considering the benefits of the common BIAN-based Frame of Reference for an optimized portfolio management and for communication with management, we refer to Sub-section 5.3.4.

6.3 BIAN FOR BUSINESS DESIGN

This section describes the use of the BIAN Framework on the "system" level.

6.3.1 BIAN for business process management

Processes are important assets of an organization, that must be well designed and managed (measured, improved) in order to deliver value to customers and other stakeholders.

Although BIAN's Business Scenarios do not imply a sequence in the Service Domain interactions, they are comparable to processes. They can certainly inspire a bank when it comes to designing its processes. The Wireframe technique can be used to make a "city plan" that can support the different routes a complex process can follow. Such a Wireframe is a consolidation of the different Business Scenarios that describe one of the possible "branches" of the process[53].

The most important added value of BIAN in business process management lies in the use of the Frame of Reference[54].

Processes are conditional sequences of process steps. Elementary steps are often process-independent building blocks. Expressing a process design as (a) sequence(s) of Service Domains, has several advantages. Some examples follow.

A Service Domain delimits a "cohesive, loosely coupled" unit of functionality. Those who have iterated between attempts to delimits process steps, will acknowledge the usefulness of BIAN's stable, pre-defined process steps. Expressing the process according to the Frame of Reference, creates a common language between Business Process managers.

The detection of "business service centers" that can serve several processes is made easier.

Measurements and assessments need to be executed on a process step level, not just on a process level. If these process steps are expressed on an even basis, i.e. according to the Frame of Reference, comparing the performance of processes in different entities becomes more objective. Comparing alternative process flows and explaining the

---

53 For this purpose, *related* business scenarios are consolidated. To delimit application components and encapsulate them with application services (Sections 7.4 and 9.3, it is important to use business scenarios from *different* contexts, as they are more likely to provide a representative sample of the demands imposed on the Service Operations that are in scope.
54 BIAN is not useful for detailed process design – i.e. for "the inside" of a Service Domain. It is useful for high level end-to-end process design, where each process step is a process in itself.

differences in performance becomes more "quantitative"[55]. Best practices can be more easily exchanged, as "the best performer" can be detected on a process step level.

The "best performer" is not necessarily found within the boundaries of the bank. The clean BIAN-based delimitation of (high level) process steps, facilitates outsourcing such a step (or insourcing it). Figure 6-6 shows an example of possible partners that could provide services in a mortgage loan underwriting process (Plais 2020).

Process step	Review & Add Conditions	Get Overall Customer Position	Get/Review Customer Credit Score	Get Collateral Risk	Get Mortgage Lending Risk Model	Conduct Regulatory Compliance Checks
Service Domain	Underwriting	Customer Position	Customer Credit Rating	Collateral Asset Administration	Credit Risk Models	Regulatory Compliance
Possible Partners		CDR Aggregator	FICO / BIG DATA SCORING	Finicity / PLAID	Finicity	genpact

Figure 6-6 Process steps expressed as Service Domains facilitate the selection of business partners

Expressing processes as a sequence of Service Domains is especially important in view of the relationship with the application layer. In an agile application architecture, processes are supported by an (application component that conducts the) orchestration of application components. These components are re-used in a whole range of process orchestrations. Such application components benefit from a delimitation according to BIAN Service Domains. Expressing the process according to the Frame of Reference, creates a common language between business process managers and application architects who are in search of optimal synergy.

Process improvement often requires investments and/or change initiatives. If business process management and investment and change portfolio management use the same Frame of Reference, the integration of process improvement proposals in the enterprise investment and change portfolio is facilitated.

Last but not least, using BIAN Service Domains as process steps reinforces the attention on information. Information that should be available for the process, as specified in the information profile of each Service Domain. Information that should not only be available within the process, but should, according to the BIAN principles, also be sharable on an enterprise level.

---

55 E.g. is "the sales process" in bank A the same as "the sales process" in bank B? What explains differences in cost and success rates? The absence of process steps, the orchestration of the process steps, the performance of each process step. . .?

6.3.2 BIAN for business requirements
Structuring business requirements
The BIAN Frame of Refence can be used to organize the business requirements analysis (see also Sub-section 5.3.1). The use of the BIAN standards as the Frame of Reference for business analysis and requirement specification, facilitates "building block thinking". It helps to break free of existing thinking patterns.

> Testimonial (Ginsburgh 2015)
> "It is important to map the requirements on the Service Domains. By injecting this thinking as early as possible, it helps to get the stakeholders thinking in terms of business capability building blocks rather than in monolithic systems".

To gather these requirements, the different Business Scenarios that play a role in the new functionality are described. The functional and non-functional requirements for each involved Service Domain and service interaction are gathered. The Service Operations that are exchanged are specified (Figure 6-7 - see also Section 9.3). BIAN's Business Scenarios can be used as inspiration, as a quick start for the bank's actual business scenarios.

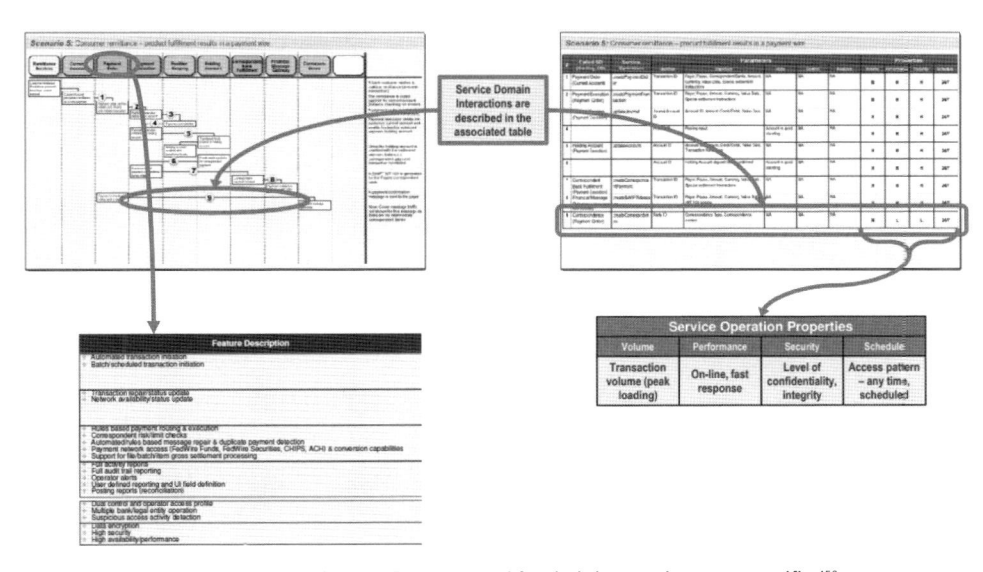

Figure 6-7 The requirements for Service Domains and for their interactions are specified[56]

The Business Scenarios are consolidated into a Wireframe, describing all "roads" that can be "walked". The associated requirements are also consolidated to cover the needs of each Business Scenario that "walks that road" (Figure 6-8).

---
56 Freely after Ginsburgh 2015.

Figure 6-8 Business Scenarios are consolidated into a Wireframe, a holistic view on the requirements[57,58]

| 57 Freely after Ginsburgh 2015.
| 58 Our apologies for the fact that the text in this figure is not readable. Elements are better readable in figures 7.6 and 7.8. For online version of this figure see free download at
https://www.vanharen.store/bian-2nd-edition-a-framework-for-the-financial-services-industry

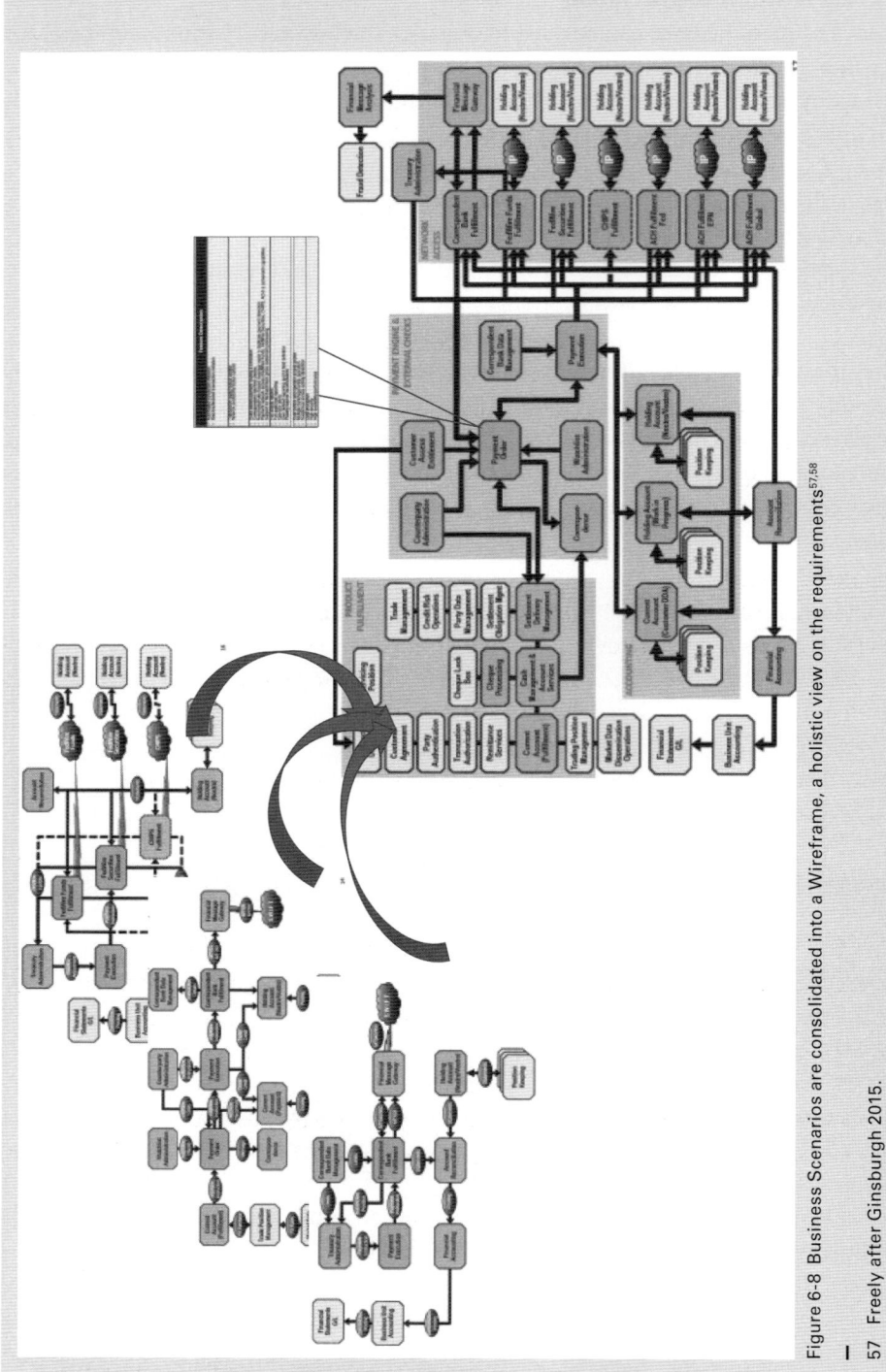

This Wireframe should represent the holistic overview of the business requirements for the new functionality and its end-to-end embedding in the bank.

Integration requirements: embedding in the enterprise
When introducing a new functionality, it is important to ensure its end-to-end embedding in the organization. For example, a new product obviously needs to be sold (through which channels?) and its arrangements need to be fulfilled, but is also needs to be included in accounting, in risk management, in customer relationship management…[59]

If the bank has a "reference business architecture" (as in Sub-section 6.1.5), the task for a business designer becomes much easier and the quality and completeness of the specifications will be more reliable. The reference business architecture will provide patterns, e.g. from customer to product agreement, from sales to product arrangement fulfilment, from product arrangement fulfilment to accounting… The requirement analyst can select the patterns that are relevant for the new functionality and ensure that the necessary business scenarios are elaborated to cover each of these "embedding patterns".

To implement the new functionality, each entity providing a service relating to the new end-to-end functioning and embedding of the new functionality, needs to be contacted. It needs to be prepared to provide its contribution to the new functionality. The mapping of the business landscape on the Service Domains supports the impact analysis and ensures that project scope covers all stakeholders.

> The Group Synergy strategy of the M5 Banking Group labelled the payment execution-related Service Domains as "centralize". After some time, the Payment Management meeting (a coordinated structure addressing the payment domains of all banks within the group) decides it is time to act.
>
> **M 5**
>
> Business Scenarios of the different payment processing process variations are described, taking care to cover a representative selection of banks (at least one per country). The use of Service Domains as high-level process steps enables a uniform representation and facilitates a correct understanding of all variations. These scenarios are consolidated into a Wireframe (Figure 6-8). This Wireframe shows the Service Domains involved in the core functionality of payment processing. Functional and non-functional requirements are consolidated and documented per Service Domain and service interaction.

---

59 In Chapter 7, we refer to the new functionality as "the system". Combined with the functionality required for its embedding in the enterprise, it becomes "the solution".

> The Wireframe also shows the Service Domains immediately involved in the functioning of the core functionality, as well as those required for the end-to-end embedding in the bank. The conceptual chapter of the reference business architecture manual of Mfour Bank's organization department is used for this purpose[60].

Communication of business requirements to solution providers

Business requirements can lead to the inhouse development of a new system, or can be used to select a software package or application service provider. They also need to be formulated with care when outsourcing is considered.

In the case of inhouse development by the ICT department, the common Frame of Reference facilitates communication.

Should the requirements need to be realized by a software vendor or business service provider, the use of the BIAN standards as the Frame of Reference provides an even greater advantage. Vendors and service providers are more likely to correctly understand such an open Frame of Reference rather than a bank's proprietary view on functionality. Vendors might also use the common BIAN-based Frame of Reference to document their offering.

The embedding of an activity in the enterprise is as important for its success as the quality of the activity itself. The availability of a common, standardized language (read "business reference architecture" in BIAN language) with software vendors and business service providers increases the success of the communication for these integration requirements.

---

60 *The enterprise architecture team thinks the introduction of the Payment Group Service is a perfect opportunity to take the ambition level of the BIAN support for business architecture a step further. The impact of this new group service on the business processes of each bank will be major. This is the time to introduce the BIAN-based conceptual reference architecture in all banks. The reference patterns will "sell themselves", they will prove their value by supporting the impact analysis of the switch to the Payment Group Service in each bank.*

■ 6.4　TEST YOURSELF QUESTIONS

1. **Which statements do not correctly describe why BIAN can provide support for business architecture?**
   A. BIAN's Service Domains can be used as process steps and its Business Scenarios can be inspirational for process design.
   B. BIAN's Business Scenarios are standards for a bank's process designs and are benchmarks for their quality.
   C. Service Domains can be used as building blocks for a conceptual reference business architecture.
   D. Using Service Domains for the specification of business requirements helps stakeholders to think in terms of business services instead of monolithic systems.

2. **Which statements correctly describe what overlaying the business landscape on the Service Domain-based Frame of Reference facilitates?**
   A. The detection of duplication of activities between organizational units.
   B. A like-for-like comparison of the performance of business services as provided by different service providers.
   C. The exchange of best practices.
   D. The evaluation of the opportunity for mergers and acquisitions.

3. **Which statements express why BIAN can provide support for business architecture?**
   A. Wireframes can be used as anchor points for documenting business requirements from the strategic level up to the operational level.
   B. Service Domains can be used as anchor points for documenting measurements such as the cost and assessment of business performance.
   C. Using Service Domains as the common Frame of Reference for the business landscape and the application landscape supports the root cause analysis of performance and quality issues.
   D. It is most effective to assign changes to Service Domains belonging to the same Business Area to one project.

7   BIAN for the application layer

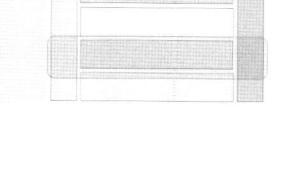

Application components and their functions, the data they need and manage and the services they exchange, are a trinity that defines the success of an application architecture. One cannot be successful without the other. Still, they are separate viewpoints on the application landscape and often separate architecture specializations. In this chapter, we focus on the application components and functions, and touch on their relationship with the other elements. We zoom in on data architecture in Chapter 8 and on application services in Chapter 9.

Technology enabled the (r)evolution that the financial sector has been going through during the last decades. It is, however, an agile logical application architecture[61], consisting of carefully crafted, service-based components, that enabled and still enables this business (r)evolution without a major disruption of the information systems architecture. The importance of this "service-based, components-based structure" grows with the level of digitalization and exposure to the Open Finance and Open API environments.

The BIAN Framework supports an agile application architecture, composed of carefully crafted, elemental components, interacting through elemental services. The value of the Service Domain partitions from a logical application architecture perspective, is that they define discrete elemental application building blocks that can be developed and deployed incrementally. When properly implemented, they define discrete operational capabilities that can be reused in multiple business contexts, thereby eliminating operational redundancy and supporting optimization for each individual functional component.

---

61 The logical application architecture describes how the application layer provides its business functionality. This is the work area of BIAN and the main subject of this chapter. The physical or technical application architecture describes with what technology this functionality is implemented. This is not BIAN's work area.

The BIAN-based Frame of Reference can be used to chart and evaluate the logical application landscape (Sub-section 6.1.3), detecting duplications, gaps and opportunities for synergy. It can also be used for application architecture governance (Sub-section 7.1.4).

The BIAN Framework provides building blocks and principles for a reference application architecture (Sub-section 7.1.5). Such a reference architecture steers system development and maintenance of the application landscape. It is an instrument with which to evaluate and compare the adequacy of solutions. It can steer the renovation of legacy platforms (Sub-section 7.1.6).

The technology landscape is linked to the application landscape by "configuration information". As such, elements of the technology architecture are indirectly linked to the BIAN-based Frame of Reference (Section 7.2).

The Frame of Reference can also be used to delimit investments and change initiatives. Impact analysis of the application landscape is facilitated, improving the quality of business cases and the scoping of projects and programs. A common Frame of Reference for business and application landscape optimizations enables a project portfolio and the associated business case(s) where considerations of the application, data and technology landscape quality are evaluated on an equal basis with business considerations (Section 7.3).

System development – or the selection of application solutions available in the marketplace - can profit from the BIAN-based Frame of Reference that is shared with business. A BIAN-based reference application architecture leverages BIAN for system development even further. This approach is useful in all types of "architecture styles" (Sections 7.4 and 7.5).

*This chapter addresses the **logical** application architecture. The logical application architecture defines how the application layer provides business functionality. The "physical" or "technical" application architecture defines with what technology the elements of the logical application architecture are implemented. While the latter can evolve with technology, the delimitation and functionality of the first can remain stable.*

■ 7.1   BIAN FOR APPLICATION ARCHITECTURE

This section describes the use of the BIAN Framework on an overview level – the "enterprise" and "domain" "zooming levels" (as described in Appendix A2.2).

7.1.1 A Frame of Reference for the application landscape

In Sub-section 4.2.2, we explained how BIAN-supports the elaboration of a Frame of Reference, tailored to the bank. This Frame of Reference depicts the elemental "capability building blocks" the bank requires.

The Frame of Reference is suitable for both business and logical application architectures. Sharing this Frame of Reference facilitates the cooperation between business and application architects and designers. It also improves the alignment between the business and application landscape.

7.1.2 Charting and assessing the application landscape's coverage

When the application landscape is overlaid on the Frame of Reference this creates an overview, in a "common language", of the business functionality that is supported by the application landscape. It can be done for the landscape as a whole and for each application component in particular. This enables an overview of the application portfolio on an enterprise level, on the level of a financial group, within alliances etc.

The Frame of Reference provides the ability to look at application components not as monolithic blocks (such as an ERP[62] or CRM[63] packages), but as an orchestration of elemental functionality building blocks: the Service Domains. For example, the CRM application turns out to support much more than Customer Relationship Management (Figure 7-1). The inventory of the support provided by the application portfolio becomes far more fine-grained.

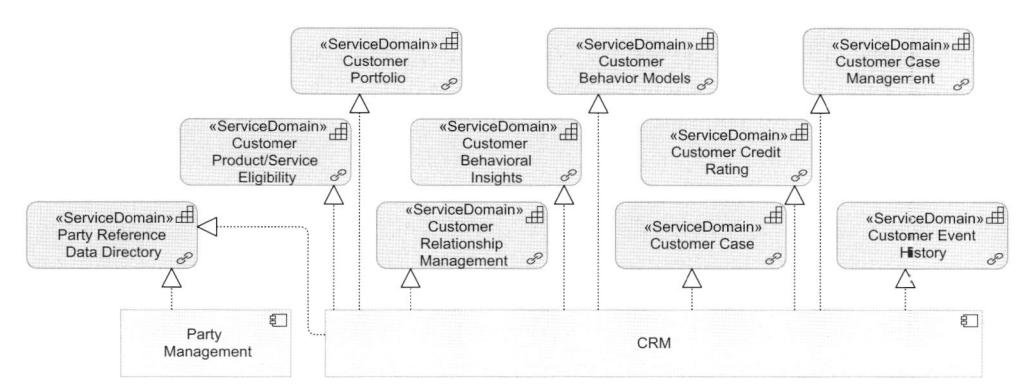

Figure 7-1 Mapping Service Domains on application components reveals the variety of business functionality they support – and identifies duplications

This overview can be used for application portfolio rationalization and optimization.

---

62 Enterprise Resource Planning.
63 Customer Relationship Management.

The overlay of the application landscape(s) on the Frame of Reference provides an insight into the functional coverage of the application portfolio. It enables a comparison of different application portfolios and an evaluation of their coverage.

Duplicates, gaps and misalignments in the support of business functionality within an application portfolio can be detected. Figure 7-1 for example, reveals that two applications support party reference information.

The BIAN-supported mapping reveals *possible issues*. The question of whether they are indeed issues should be evaluated by an application architect within the context of the bank. The advantage of the BIAN overlay is that these things can be pinpointed and hence managed.

Duplicates
A Service Domain may map on several application components. The absence of, and ability to avoid, duplication provides an application architecture with competitive advantage in an age of digitalization. Professionally managed duplication, however, is not necessarily a problem, it can even be an architectural decision (e.g. for performance reasons). The type of precautions that need to be taken depends on the role of the duplicated Service Domain.

The duplicated Service Domain's responsibility can be to provide information (e.g. party reference data, term deposit information as collateral in a loan application). In this case, information consistency must be ensured. For this, data architecture competences are mobilized. There can only be one "'System of Record"[64] when it comes to data, i.e. one source responsible for the management and quality of data instances[65]. If Service Domains with a data responsibility are implemented in more than one application component, a reliable "data integration" architecture needs to be elaborated (see Subsection 8.2.1).

Figure 7-2 illustrates that the duplication of the "Party Reference Data Directory" functionality in the CRM package is mitigated by the data integration architecture. The party data is managed in the "master" (or "System of Record" - the Party Management application) and propagated to the "slave" (the CRM application).

The "duplicated" Service Domain can provide functionality (e.g. position keeping). In this case, it must be ensured that the business rules for this functionality are implemented correctly and consistently over all duplicated occurrences.

---

64 Data store and the application that manages it, that is the authoritative source for the designated set of data.
65 In other BIAN publications the following terminology is used: in the "SoR" application, the Service Domain is "core". In other applications, it is a "proxy".

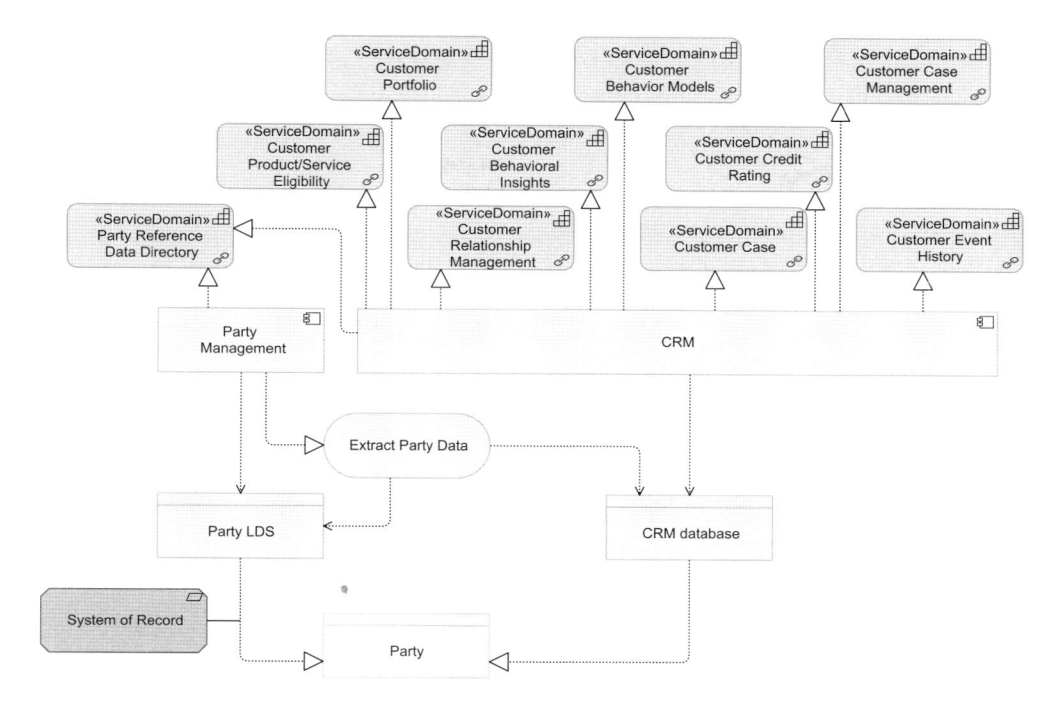

Figure 7-2 A potential Service Domain duplication issue is mitigated by the data integration architecture

Cleaning up duplication can involve eliminating the doubles, or elaborating an integration approach. In both cases, a "System of Record" application should be selected (the remaining one, or the one to take the lead in the integration). Criteria should (obviously) address functionality, but also non-functional criteria and architecture fit.

The application portfolio overview should clearly state which application is the "System of Record" for the support of which Service Domain. This will steer the development and maintenance teams in their usage of the existing landscape.

> The Mzero Bank, a member of the M5 Banking Group, has two applications supporting investment portfolios. New functionality was either added to one or the other. Data is duplicated between the applications and users need to know which application to address for which type of support.
>
> M 5
>
> This is revealed by the Service Domain mapping that creates a high-level overview of the application landscape of the M5 Banking Group, a mapping that is executed at the introduction of the enterprise architecture capability. The application architect, assigned to the Mzero Bank, decides to cut this situation short. An evaluation is made of both applications. Functional criteria are assessed, but also non-functional criteria such as performance and exploitation costs, and factors that are an indication of the embedding in the application service landscape (such as the availability and usage of services, modularity, stability, maintainability, technical fit). One of the

> applications is selected as the best fit for an agile application landscape. A deprecation strategy for the other one is developed and executed step-by-step. The reduction of both maintenance and correction costs contribute to the business case for these actions.

Gaps
The criticality of gaps in application support – i.e. business functionality that is not supported- depends on the criticality of that particular business functionality and the level to which ICT support is critical for that functionality.

Misalignments
Applications may support a strange amalgam of Service Domains. For example, an application might support both "Counterparty Risk" and "Marketing". On the other hand, an application supporting both "deposits" and "loans" is probably an example of abstraction in its design. The mapping alerts the application architect to *possible issues*, but the application architect ultimately makes the decision on whether or not there is actually an issue.

Mapping on the Frame of Reference and undertaking a rough assessment based on the coverage, is a first step in the evaluation and a like-for-like comparison of the application landscapes. The BIAN Reference Architecture and its principles offer other assessment criteria for a more thorough evaluation of the landscape level[66]. This is covered further in Sub-section 7.1.5.

7.1.3 Utilities vs Service Domains

Applications can be developed on a lower level of granularity than a Service Domain.

Service Domains define discrete assignable and reusable business responsibilities. Application components represent a (reusable) unit of application logic.

The systems that support such discrete assignable responsibilities may include application logic that is an assembly of widely reused utility software. For example, an interest calculation component can provide its services to both loans and deposits[67].

7.1.4 Governing the application architecture

In an enterprise of significant size, it is necessary to divide architecture responsibilities over different individuals, but it is also crucial to ensure cohesion and consistency. This is achieved by distinguishing architecture levels, with increasing detail as the scope diminishes (as described in Appendix A2.2). The BIAN Service Landscape and its Business Areas and Business Domains can inspire a bank in **delimiting application architecture domains**.

---
66 Evaluation on a "system" level is covered in Sub-section 7.4.2
67 *Actually, the Mfour Bank has such "utility". This greatly diminishes the cost and speeds up the roll-out of new products.*

The Information System Strategy is developed taking into account the support of the Banking Strategy by the application and technology layers[68]. The overlay of the application landscape on the BIAN-based Frame of Reference enables the assignment of "i**nformation system strategy requirements**" on a finer grain than the often-monolithic legacy application components. Such requirements can be assigned on a Service Domain level, i.e. on the level of supported business functionality. **Strategic assessments** of (for example) value and risk[69] can also be assigned on that fine-grained level.

The CRM package depicted in Figure 7-1, for example, supports functionalities that can be classified as "System of Record", as well as "system of differentiation" and "system of innovation"[70].

The Frame of Reference that is shared with business, facilitates linking the Information System Strategy with its contribution to business goals.

The Frame of Reference is also an instrument to define the bank's **application sourcing** strategy. Each Service Domain is a possible application component, that can be either developed in-house or sourced from a software vendor or application service provider. The vendor is preferably "BIAN-compliant[71]", as this will facilitate the participation of his product in the bank's application orchestration.

The Frame of Reference, represented as a "bank on a page", is a strong communication instrument towards enterprise management.

For example, Figure 7-3 illustrates the strategic position of application support per Service Domain, on the "bank on a page" of a BIAN member. With such an instrument, combined with the Service Domain map of an application, the motivation for investments in such applications becomes more transparent for management.

---

68 As explained in Chapter 5, Service Domains are elemental capabilities, they are the building blocks for Business Capabilities. They can be used as the "linking pin" between the Business Capabilities and the business and application landscapes, depicting the bank's operations.
As such, the success of the Information System Strategy can be measured in the way that Service Domains are implemented.
69 Such as availability risk in line with the Disaster Recovery Plan.
70 As in Gartner's Pace-Layered Application Strategy, a methodology for categorizing, selecting, managing and governing applications to support business change, differentiation and innovation (www.Gartner.com).
71 BIAN is developing a certification program for software vendors.

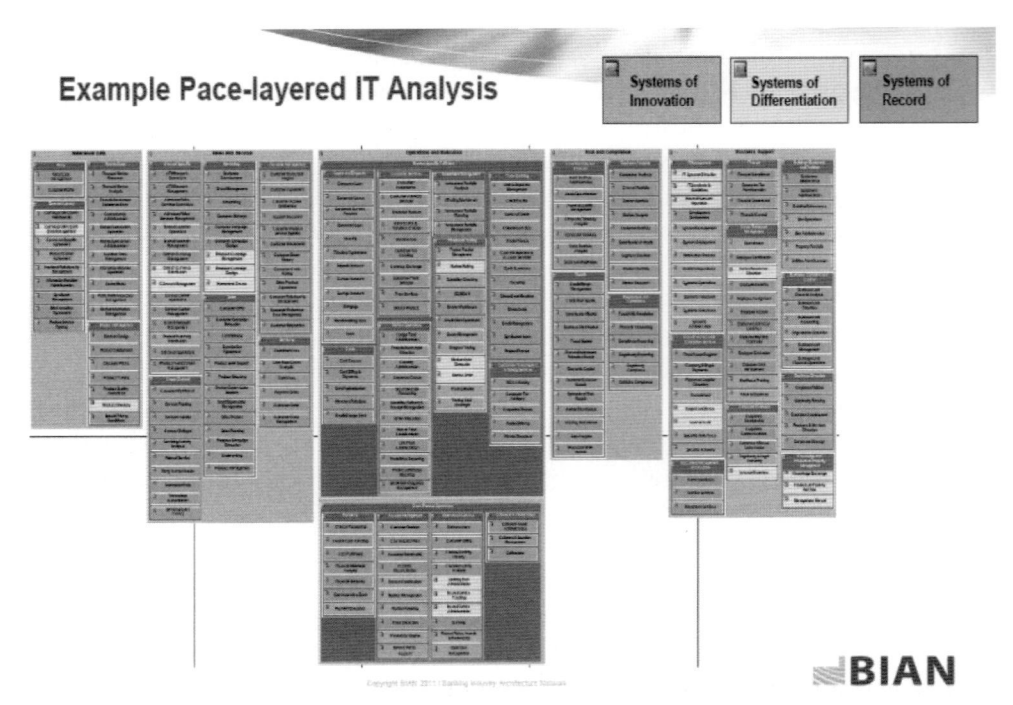

Figure 7-3 The "bank on a page" of a BIAN member being used to communicate an aspect of the application architecture strategy to management[72,73]

7.1.5 Building blocks and principles for a reference application architecture

The BIAN component design maximizes the cross-product re-use of business functionality. It defines standard integration boundaries such that new product facilities can be integrated quickly, as only the new product specific logic is required and many requirements will be supported by re-use of established facilities. This is greatly leveraged by a "reference application architecture".

A reference architecture provides guidance for the actual landscape architecture with principles, guidelines, pattern and standards. The BIAN Framework can support the elaboration of a bank's reference application architecture in several aspects:
- Provides descriptions and delimitations for application components;
- Provides principles and guidelines for application component responsibilities;
- Provides the elemental building blocks for the definition of reference patterns.

---

72   BIAN Architecture Working Group (2017a).
73   We apologize for the fact that the names of the Service Domains are not readable. The purpose of this figure is to illustrate the power of the Service Landscape to manage and communicate the strategic positioning of building blocks of the application landscape. For online version of this figure see free download at
    https://www.vanharen.store/bian-2nd-edition-a-framework-for-the-financial-services-industry

Candidate elemental application components
A logical application architecture benefits from a structure based on business logic building blocks. Which is exactly what the BIAN Reference Architecture offers.[74]

The Service Domains of this Frame of Reference provide a semantic description for elemental logical application components.

As elaborated in Chapter 9, BIAN also offers "reference application services", that encapsulate each reference application component.

Delimiting actual application components and application services according to (a cluster of) Service Domains and Service Operations, provides manoeuvrability for the application architecture. These elemental building blocks can be flexibly mobilized for varying orchestrations (think digital transformation and participation in the Open Finance ecosystem).

Principles and guidelines
In Sub-section 1.2.3, we elaborated on the **agile principles** that lead to the **componentisation and service orientation** of the BIAN Architecture.

The unique responsibility of a Service Domain implies that each "information instance" is managed and provided by one and only one Service Domain. A Service Domain needs to provide information about the operational information it manages in its Control Record. This ensures **information consistency and information openness**.

Apart from the Control Record information, the Service Domain Information Profile also contains "Service Domain Information". A Service Domain is also responsible for gathering and providing **Service Domain Governance information**[75]: this is information about its own functioning (e.g. availability, volumes, performance). The availability of "application component governance information" contributes to the overall quality management of the application landscape. This should not be forgotten when designing a system. It should be part of reference architecture guidelines.

Building blocks for reference patterns
In Sub-section 6.1.5, we explained how business architects and application architects share the **conceptual patterns** of Service Domain orchestration that ensure secure access to, and an effective, efficient and controlled provision of financial services. The **standards** and **guidelines** that make these conceptual patterns concrete on the application level, will (obviously) be different from those for the business level. Application architects will

---
74 These building blocks can be tailored, in a "bank-specific Frame of Reference" (Section 4.2.2).
75 In the "Service Domain Information" part of the Service Domain Information Profile.

define standards for each platform/environment. In other words, they will add the actual application components and services that need to be used to implement the patterns.

The "standards", that is the actual applications and application services, may differ due to the different application and technology platforms, as well as varying architecture styles[76]. They might (will) evolve in light of technological evolutions. But the "conceptual pattern" expressed in Service Domains, will remain stable.

The "conceptual layer" for such patterns does not need to be provided by business architects. Application architects can elaborate the conceptual layer themselves. They will probably have to extend certain patterns (e.g. secure multichannel customer access) anyhow, as such patterns require technology competences rather than business competences. Figure 7-4 shows a fictitious example of a pattern for secure, multichannel customer access. This is an aggregate pattern, consisting of elemental patterns.

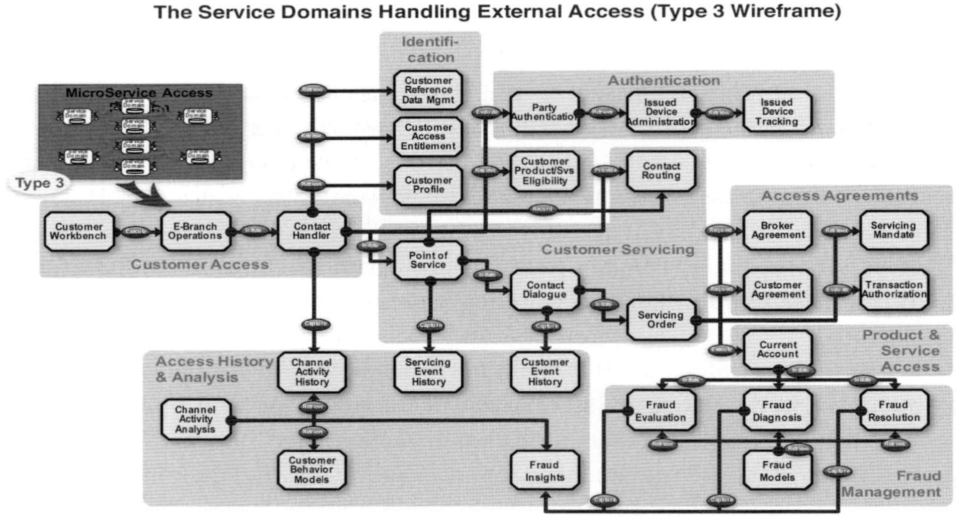

Figure 7-4 Conceptual reference architecture pattern for secure customer access

The availability of reference application patterns and standards will enhance the quality of the application platform. It will improve system development and maintenance efficiency and effectiveness. In fact, patterns are a checklist for the introduction of new products, channels, enterprise management approaches etc. as they describe the coherence of all "partitions" of the bank. They provide guidance for designers and developers – which saves valuable architecture time. They ensure completeness of project and testing scope.

---

76   As in Section 7.5 "BIAN and application architecture styles".

The enterprise application architecture team of the Mfour Bank maintains an "enterprise application blueprint". It started out as a checklist for projects, to mitigate the recurring problem of project delays due to forgotten service connections that only surface during end-to-end testing. It soon evolved into a full-scale reference architecture exercise, in cooperation with the business organization department.

M 5

The "business layer" of the reference architecture describes how business functionalities such as product agreement sales and fulfilment should cooperate with party reference data, customer and financial accounting, risk management, customer correspondence etc.

The application level describes how the cooperation between product agreement systems and the supporting applications (such as party and currency management, product catalog, correspondence, position keeping etc.) needs to be implemented. It contains several "scripts", describing which applications need to be involved, in what pattern, for which particular business requests, such as the introduction of a new product, or a new access channel.

The application architects and the business organization department decide to create a common conceptual layer for the reference architecture. The responsibilities of business departments change, as do applications. The conceptual layer expresses the patterns and scripts in Service Domains. This conceptual layer is common to business and logical application architecture.

The chapter on "secure channel access" is written by the application architects, supported by security and technology architects. This chapter is part of the "conceptual blueprint", but it is not expected to be common knowledge for business or even application designers. These patterns are implemented in applications that are developed by a specialized team. They provide standard interfaces for product applications. The Business Scenarios relating to customer access that BIAN provides inspire this team.

The enterprise application blueprint is much appreciated by the development teams. They are used to working in an environment that provides a lot of reusable components, but often forget one or other vital element in the "end-to-end" orchestration that delivers the "end-to-end" solution.

The application maintenance teams are equally satisfied, especially those responsible for systems that are often overlooked. They are now more often involved on projects in a timely manner.

7.1.6 Assessing and improving the application landscape

The mapping on the BIAN-based Frame of Reference provides an overview of the business functionality that an application landscape supports. The *coverage* provided by the application landscape can be assessed.

To fully assess the *quality* of the functional support, each application's performance regarding the business requirements for that functionality would need to be evaluated. The mapping of both business activities and applications on the common Frame of Reference enables a more accurate evaluation than the monolith level presented by business organizations, processes and applications.

The Service Domain mapping and a comparison with the BIAN-inspired reference application architecture can provide an overall evaluation of the *quality* of the *application landscape*.

The **mapping** reveals gaps in coverage, but also the presence of duplicated functionality and monolithic applications. Duplications either lead to inconsistencies in information and/or the "behavior support" provided, or require continuous integration efforts and result in higher maintenance costs and operational overheads. Monoliths often imply duplication and risk to provide low manoeuvrability.

An application landscape whose components correspond well to the Frame of Reference has a good starting position for the next level of evaluation. This level involves assessing compliance with the BIAN principles and **reference architecture** – or the bank's BIAN-based reference architecture.

Examples of such criteria are:
- Service Domains are supported by only one application component;
- Application components map to (clusters of closely cooperating) Service Domains;
- Application components interact through services, corresponding to (cleanly combined) BIAN Service Operations;
- Data is opened up by data services.

Charting and assessing the application landscape is relevant in different contexts.

Firstly, a bank will always want to keep track of its application portfolio and rationalize it where required. Other contexts are, for example, **mergers and acquisitions** and acquiring enterprise-wide vendor solutions.

In the case of mergers, duplication of logic is a certainty. Mapping the application platform (and the business organization) on the Frame of Reference provides insights into the overlaps and is a first step towards selecting the best candidates for the combined application platform. Apart from coverage, the quality of the application landscape is an important selection criterion, as it defines the ability to support the bank in its strategy.

The quality of the application platform of the merger partner or acquisition target is also evaluated during the due diligence stage preceding the decision. The "BIAN overlay" provides a common language with which to evaluate the application platform.

The Mfour Bank is the result of a merger between the A Bank and the C Bank. As economies of scale is one of the objectives of the merger, the back-offices as well as the branches of both banks are merged. A common application platform is required. The application platforms of both banks are compared, in order to select the best fit for the new Mfour Bank. The platforms are compared on two main criteria. The first is the ability to support the business functionality of the new Mfour Bank, as it will provide the combined services of the A and C Banks. The second group of criteria is the quality of the platform in terms of, amongst other things, agility (componentization, service orientation etc.) and data quality.

M 5

The first thing to do is make an inventory of the business activities of the new Mfour Bank, as the sum of the activities of A and C. The BIAN Framework is selected to create the common language, required to compare the business activities of both banks.

The second step is to map the activity inventory (expressed in BIAN terms) on the application portfolio of the A and C Banks. The A platform covers almost all of the required functionality, while support for certain product features and enterprise level processes is missing on the C platform.

On the other hand, the A platform shows significant duplication of functionality, in rigid monolithic applications. Data is duplicated in several applications without a proper data integration architecture. This results in data quality issues and costly, untrustworthy consolidation in the enterprise data warehouse.

The C platform consists of service enabled application components, each with a responsibility that maps on (a cluster of closely related) Service Domains. Data is opened up by information services and its quality is ensured by assigning responsibility to one and only one application. Adding the missing functionality would not require rework, only implanting the extras in the existing application service landscape.

The Merger Working Group advises the Merger Steering Committee to choose the C platform and add the missing functionality. They argue that the C platform is better equipped for a future that requires an agile application platform and qualitative, open data. The Steering Committee agrees with this proposal: The C platform is upgraded and becomes the application platform for the Mfour Bank. All activity is to be migrated from the A platform to the Mfour platform, not as a big bang, but step-by-step, on the pace of the upgrade of the platform.

Elaborating a step-by-step upgrade strategy for the Mfour platform and a consistent migration strategy of customers and products from the A platform to the gradually adapted Mfour platform, requires serious architecting and problem solving skills. The maps of business and application functionality provided by the "BIAN Service Domain overlay" are used intensively during the planning phase and adapted continuously during the implementation phase. The impact analysis of the subsequent changes turns out to be reliable, as the upgrade and migration program is executed according to the initial planning and (give or take) within the initial budget.

Evaluating the fit of a (combination of) **vendor solutions** in support of a bank's business functionality profits from using the common Frame of Reference, expressing both the business functionality and the vendor's coverage. The coverage of a vendor's solutions, represented on the "bank on a page" canvas, can convey the message to management in the blink of an eye.

BIAN is working on a certification program for vendor solutions. This involves the development of criteria to evaluate whether the solution complies with the BIAN Architecture, in terms of both model and principles.

Externalisation: a technique for legacy rationalization
Legacy environments - both business and application - often date from the age of "process island thinking". Such a rigid, closed environment is not equipped to support a bank in this age of digitalization.

The BIAN Architecture offers support for diagnosis of the issues and presents the concept of "Externalization" as a solution. Externalization is a core concept to avoid (or eliminate) duplication and to enable reuse. It is applied in the validation of the BIAN Architecture.

What it involves depends on the context.

Externalization aims at sharing resources (business and technical). The term "externalization" is used for optimization of the delimitation of Service Domains. A Service Domain performs only its core responsibilities and provides the related services. It delegates other functionality to other Service Domains through the use of their services.

Here, we use the term 'Externalization' to indicate the optimization of the delimitation of applications in the same fashion.

'Externalization' is facilitated by the BIAN Framework. Service Domains are the result of structured "externalization thinking": deciding which logic is core and which logic needs to be delegated to other Service Domains. The pattern-based approach for Service Domains (as explained in Section 2.4) ensures a clean delimitation of responsibilities.

In a context of designing new systems, externalization involves the "embedding" in the application service landscape: only the core functionality is implemented in the system. All supporting functionality is delegated to application services. Sub-section 6.1.5 elaborates on the embedding concept and how BIAN supports this.

In a context of optimizing a legacy environment, externalization involves the reduction of functional duplication and fragmentation through two considerations:

- Reducing redundancy by eliminating functionality from legacy applications and replacing it with application service calls.
- Creating the ability to reduce redundancy by service-enabling legacy systems functionality and creating application services that are in line with a Service Domain and corresponding Service Operations.

Both types of effort are facilitated by the BIAN-based Frame of Reference.

The mapping of the Frame of Reference on the application landscape shows which Service Domain functionality is implemented in specific applications. This demonstrates where functionality is duplicated within monolithic applications. The Service Domain partitions clarify which functionality should (could) be delegated to other, specialized application components/services.

The application service catalog, organized according to BIAN Service Domains and Service Operations (see Chapter 9), can demonstrate gaps in the application service portfolio. Services provided by certain Service Domains might be missing. This Service Domain may well be implemented in some applications, but it is not service enabled.

The isolation of functionality and the encapsulation by application services, does not necessarily involve the creation of a separate application component. What is important is that the application services can be reused by other applications. The aspired result can also be reached by "wrapping" the legacy application.

It is possible that more than one application contains logic that is a candidate for externalization in view of the same services. The application architect will decide which application will become "the System of Record", i.e. be recognized as the authentic source for these services. The other implementations will either have to be eliminated and replaced by (a) service call(s), or become a "slave"[77].

The elimination of functionality and the switch to service calls or a "master-slave" relationship is not always that simple. Neither is the "service enabling" of existing application logic. It might be cheaper/easier to replace the solutions with new ones, or to do nothing (with higher maintenance costs and higher risks on inconsistencies). BIAN supports the diagnosis of the problem. Whether or not to propose a cure, is left to the discretion of the application architect. Technical considerations, risk assessments and the strategic position of the application can be considered as part of the decision-making process.

---

77 The "master-slave" relationship is usually used in the context of data, where the SoR is the authenticated source and the slaves are synchronized. Here, we also use these terms to express the fact that the implemented functionality needs to stay tuned.

Externalization proposals are part of the application architecture change proposal portfolio.

The Mzero Bank in Awayland is a member of the M5 Banking Group. The mapping of the Group's application platforms on the Frame of Reference (as one of the first initiatives of the Group Architecture capability), reveals major Service Domain clustering and serious duplications in big monolithic applications. One of them is the Loan application. It supports a whole range of loan product types (which is a good thing) but also duplicates a lot of supporting functionality. The most critical issue, the duplication of current account positions (see M5 example in Chapter 8) is tackled immediately, as it presents an unacceptable risk. This is not a completely negative experience, as it reveals a quite acceptable internal "component" structure. Future step- by-step externalization efforts are deemed feasible. There is no business case for replacing the application with new, component-based systems.

Figure 7-5 depicts the gradual externalization and service enablement of the application. In view of the Customer Relationship Management program, the loan application externalizes its Party Reference Data Management functionality and switches to the services of the Party Management application. It isolates its Party Credit Risk functionality in a separate "Party Risk Management" application. This will provide credit risk assessment services to other processes.

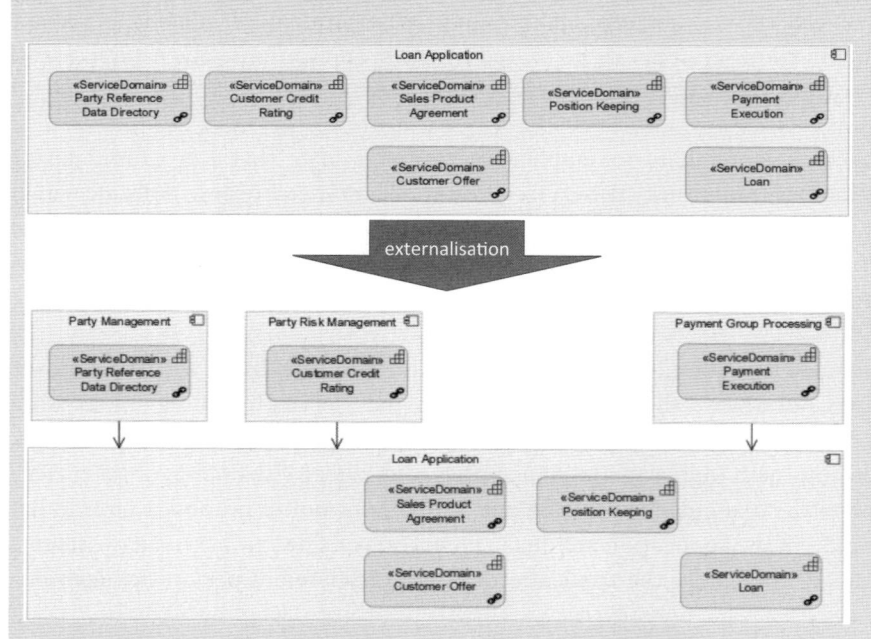

Figure 7-5 Mzero Bank's monolithic Loan application is decomposed step-by-step

The next step in the componentization of the (former) monolith will be the elimination of the payment functionality. As part of the program that is introducing the Payment Group Service into the M5 Banking Group, the loan department of the Mzero Bank will no longer perform its disbursements and collections itself, but instead will delegate the execution of these payment instructions to the Payments Group Service organization and its Payment Group Processing application. The Loan application will eliminate the corresponding logic and replace it with interactions with the services of the Payment Group Processing application.[78]

■ 7.2 LINKING THE TECHNOLOGY LANDSCAPE TO SERVICE DOMAINS

The technical application architecture defines how technology is used by the application layer. Technology does not offer business functionality, but it enables applications to function. As such, technology resources cannot be mapped directly to Service Domains. The BIAN Framework does not provide support for defining and delimiting technology services. It is technology agnostic and does not express a preference for one or other technology.

The support of the technology landscape for the business layer can, however, be expressed according to the Service Domain Frame of Reference and evaluated accordingly.

Configuration information should enable the tracking of how technology resources support each other along with elements of the application landscape. This can be refined to show the support for each Service Domain. As the application support for the business layer is also expressed per Service Domain, an overview of the support for each (implemented) Service Domain can be described through the three architecture layers: business, application and technology. As the requirements are also "funnelled down" the Service Domain, the adequacy of the technology support for each building block of the Frame of Reference can be evaluated, e.g. 24/7 availability, big data abilities etc.

Shortfalls can be identified on a finer grain, so that the opportunities for technology available on one platform can be linked to needs on other platforms more easily.

The positive impact of technology investments and changes can be linked on a rather fine grain (a Service Domain) to application and business functionality that will benefit from them. These investments can be linked to the strategic position of the application and business building blocks. This improves the integration of technology investments in the enterprise investment and change portfolio. Technology investments, application-level investments and business investments can be compared on a more equal base. The result is that the added value of technology can be more clearly communicated to management.

---
78   The Loan department remains responsible for the follow up of the disbursement and collections. A such, the loan application keeps track of the execution status of the payment instructions. Externalization does not mean loss of responsibility. . .

> **M 5**
>
> One of the first actions undertaken by the newly installed enterprise architecture team of the M5 Banking Group is a quick and dirty high-level architecture inventory, using the BIAN Service Domains as the Frame of Reference.
>
> An inventory of the technology that is available in the Group is undertaken, linked to the applications supported. A lot of similarities lead to the decision to start renegotiating contracts on a Group level. A pleasant surprise is the discovery of "rule-based technology" that successfully supports one bank's Regulatory Compliance application. Application maintenance at the point of (regularly occurring) regulation changes is minimal and the business rarely needs to perform manual checks anymore. This technology could be extremely useful on a Group level. Such technology could support other Service Domains that rely on complex, but predictable business rules.

■ 7.3 BIAN FOR APPLICATION INVESTMENT AND CHANGE PORTFOLIO

The "overlay" of the reference application architecture on the application landscape facilitates the detection of problem areas that (could) cause operational problems (e.g. uncontrolled duplications, the usage of services marked as "deprecated" etc.). A Business Strategy, expressed along the lines of the BIAN Frame of Reference, combined with the Information System Strategy, facilitates the evaluation of the readiness of the application platform.

Based on these insights, the application architect can compose a change proposal portfolio, aimed at optimizing and future-proofing the application landscape.

The impact of application landscape changes can be projected upwards to the business layer according to the Service Domain Frame of Reference. Thus, it is not only the areas in the business that currently use the application support which can be identified (those that will be impacted). In addition, the potential synergy for other areas of the business, implementing the same Service Domains, can be investigated.

The BIAN-based reference application architecture supports the completeness of the scope definition of the change.

For further investigation of the benefits of the common BIAN-based Frame of Reference for both optimized portfolio management and communication with management, we refer to Sub-section 5.3.4.

The Service Domain Frame of Reference as a management communication instrument is even more important for change initiatives that originate on the application (and technology) layer. It explains the impact and benefits of these initiatives in clear and undisputable business terms.

■ 7.4 BIAN FOR APPLICATION SYSTEMS

As explained in Chapter 6, the analysis of the business requirements for a new functionality involves two levels:
1. The requirements for the new functionality, e.g. a new product, a new customer access channel or a new type of risk management. For the sake of this section, we will call this "the system".
2. The requirements for the end-to-end embedding of the new functionality in the enterprise. Examples include the connection of the new product to customer access channels, the way it needs to be treated in terms of financial accounting or risk management, and possible the impact of the new type of risk management on sales and operations. For the sake of this section, we will call the system plus its embedding in the enterprise "the end-to-end solution".

7.4.1 End-to-end solution architecture
The Frame of Reference for expressing requirements
If the system development methodology consistently exploits the Frame of Reference, the business requirements for the new solution are documented for each Service Domain and Service Connection that participates in the end-to-end solution. Using a common language and Frame of Reference improves the communication and alignment between business and ICT.

If the business requirements are not expressed using the Service Domain and Service Connection structure, the application architect or system designer can reorganize the business requirements in accordance with the BIAN-based Frame of Reference. The requirements for the end-to-end solution are now structured as a choreography of Service Domains (whether or not customized). Figure 7-6 represents the Wireframe from Figure 6-8 in a readable format[79].

---

[79] The M5 Banking Group worked with the 2015 version of BIAN. For the purpose of the Payment Group Service project, the M5 Group indicated that the ACH fulfillment Service Domain is implemented differently for each Automated Clearing House that the group works with.

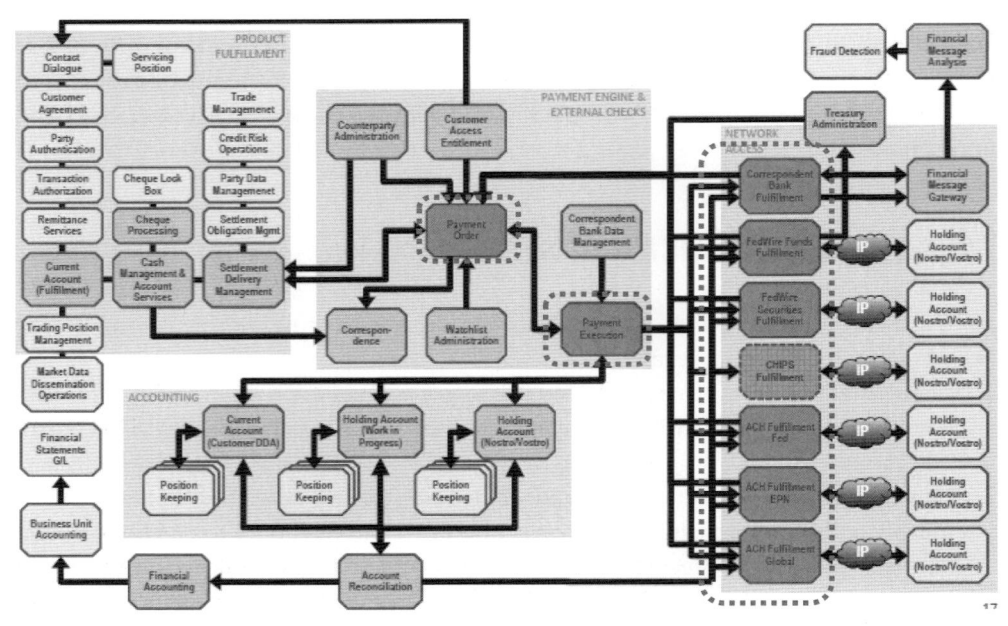

Figure 7-6 Wireframe for the end-to-end embedding of a payment solution[80]

The BIAN-based reference architecture to ensure embedding in the enterprise

If there is a reference business architecture, expressed in BIAN building blocks and patterns (as in Sub-section 7.1.5), the business requirement will very likely cover the entire end-to-end solution. The impact of the new functionality on the enterprise will be accounted for. The application reference architecture patterns might need to add the more technical stuff such as multichannel access, until the Wireframe for the solution covers the end-to-end embedding of the new functionality in the enterprise. Or at least, the checklist provided by the reference architecture can minimize the risk that the connections required for the end-to-end embedding in the enterprise might be forgotten.

BIAN's Service Domains are well suited for the delimitation and high-level specification of an application component[81]. The Wireframe is used to discern the Service Domains – as potential application components - that are "core" to the new functionality (dotted line in Figure 7-6) from those that interact directly with the core functionality (medium grey) and those that are required for its end-to-end embedding in the organization (lighter grey).

The Wireframe is now ready to be "projected" onto the application landscape.

---

80 Ginsburgh 2015, freely applied.
81 "An encapsulation of application functionality aligned to implementation structure" (The Open Group (2019)).
    "It is independently deployable, re-usable, and replaceable. An application component performs one or more application functions. It encapsulates its behavior and data, exposes services, and makes them available through interfaces".

In a process-based architecture, a lot of Service Domains of the Wireframe would probably be implemented in a "process-island" solution. In a component and service-based architecture, only the core functionality needs to be built. It can plug in to the required services already available on the application platform. Missing services will be implemented in separate, reusable components.

The "Service Domain labels" attached to the application components that are already active in the application landscape facilitate the selection of the services the new solution will plug into.

The application service catalog, searchable according to the same Frame of Reference, facilitates an even more fine-grained selection of the most suitable application component and application services (see Section 9.1).

The reference application architecture makes the job really easy: it provides the patterns of application component interactions that have to be used when introducing a certain type of functionality. It also provides the standard application services that a new system needs to plug into.

Ensuring a complete project scope
The end-to-end Wireframe is also useful in defining the project *management* scope. Obviously, the new functionality is part of the project scope. If changes are required to application components that are reused, this should also be part of the project management scope.

All application components that are used in the end-to-end solution should be part of the project *test* scope.

7.4.2 Creating "the system"
The new functionality can be introduced in the application landscape in different ways:
– Reuse: add the new functionality to an existing (set of) application(s);
– Buy: select a software package or an application service provider;
– Build: develop a custom made new (set of) application(s).

The BIAN Architecture can play a role in all these scenarios.

REUSE or BUY: find and evaluate the candidates
If the system is to be purchased (buy) and/or one or more existing systems within the bank are candidates (reuse) for the new functionality, then an evaluation of the possible fit of the candidates in relation to the requirements should be organized.

Candidate systems available in the bank's application stack, will be traced based on their "Service Domain labels" (Figure 7-7).

Software vendors that are BIAN compliant will be able to document their coverage of the requirements according to the Frame of Reference.

This common Frame of Reference facilitates the comparison of solutions. It enables the areas that need to be added or adapted to fit the requirements to be pinpointed. Figure 7-8 shows an example of how the conformance of different vendors with requirements is evaluated per Service Domain.

The ability to plug in to the services that are available on the bank's application platform, in line with the "end-to-end solution", is an important requirement for the new system. The reference application architecture will provide these and other criteria for the evaluation of the candidate systems. If services that the system needs to plug into (the "medium and lighter grey" Service Domains in Figure 7-6) are duplicated in the candidate system, it needs to be demonstrated how the integrity of the landscape can be ensured. If data is duplicated, the vendor solution needs to be able to plug in to the data integration architecture (i.e. source the data from the System of Record, with a quality sufficient for the core functionality)[82]. If logic is duplicated, the consistency with the logic available in the bank needs to be ensured.

> The Payment Management meeting of the M5 Banking Group agrees with the specifications for the new Payment Group Service and its implantation in the ecosystem of the banks.
>
> **M 5**
>
> The project team now needs to decide whether to build or buy a system, or to adapt one of the application systems already available in the group.
>
> The Service Domain mapping on the application landscapes of the banks (obviously) reveals the presence of payment functionality in many applications. More often than not, as part of a big "cluster" with product-agreement functionality.
>
> This is considered useful information for the impact analysis of the introduction of the Group Service (this functionality will need to be "externalized" and switched to the Group Service).
>
> Such applications are deemed not to be suitable for adaptation/upgrade to a Group Service application. However, the project team detects two candidates, both on the Homeland platform.

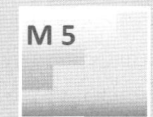

---

82 Section 8.4 "BIAN for information and data on the system level" describes BIAN-inspired requirements relating to data architecture.

7   BIAN for the application layer

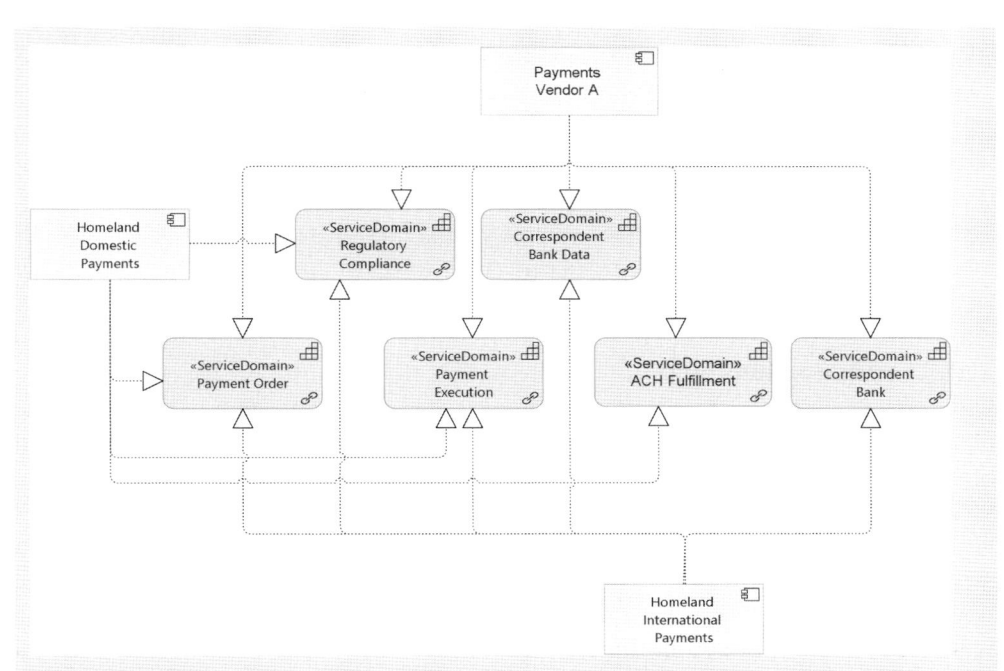

Figure 7-7 Mapping of the "Reuse" candidates and a vendor offer ("Buy") on the Service Domains required for the new Group Payment application

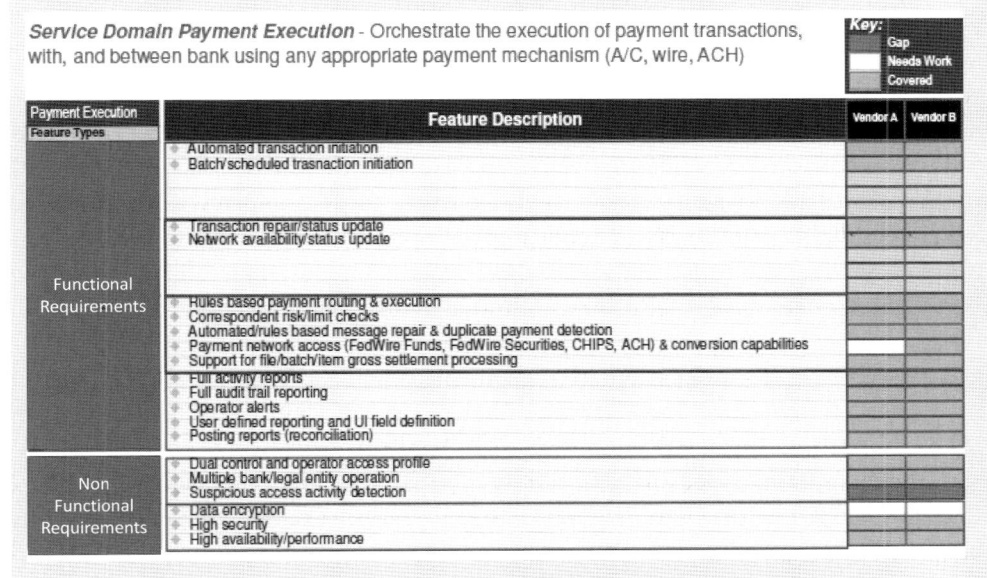

Service Domain Payment Execution - Orchestrate the execution of payment transactions, with, and between bank using any appropriate payment mechanism (A/C, wire, ACH)

Key:
- Gap
- Needs Work
- Covered

Payment Execution Feature Types	Feature Description	Vendor A	Vendor B
Functional Requirements	• Automated transaction initiation • Batch/scheduled transaction initiation		
	• Transaction repair/status update • Network availability/status update		
	• Rules based payment routing & execution • Correspondent risk/limit checks • Automated/rules based message repair & duplicate payment detection • Payment network access (FedWire Funds, FedWire Securities, CHIPS, ACH) & conversion capabilities • Support for file/batch/item gross settlement processing		
	• Full activity reports • Full audit trail reporting • Operator alerts • User defined reporting and UI field definition • Posting reports (reconciliation)		
Non Functional Requirements	• Dual control and operator access profile • Multiple bank/legal entity operation • Suspicious access activity detection		
	• Data encryption • High security • High availability/performance		

Figure 7-8 Requirement coverage comparison of candidate Group Payment systems for one Service Domain[83]

---

83   Ginsburgh 2015.

> A comparison of the coverage of the required Service Domains, reveals gaps in both systems, while the packages offered by the vendors on the shortlist both provide full coverage. Nevertheless, the Homeland International Payments system is selected. Both of the vendor packages lack the ability to "plug in" to the platform as required for the end-to-end solution. They are not able to use real-time current account position data nor ensure instant adaptation of the current account position. Opening up the packages' "raw" data would be a considerable (recurrent) cost. As both requirements are considered "essential" for the Group, the "Buy" option is discounted.

BUILD: system architecture

If the system is to be custom made, the next step is to detail its architecture. The BIAN-based reference architecture will facilitate the delimitation of the application components and their services.

Please note, it is not necessary to have a one-to-one relation between a Service Domain and an application component.

Service Domains represent "business service centers". Application components can also represent more fine-grained "utilities", such as interest calculation, currency exchange calculation etc. *Utilities are most certainly a valuable asset on an application platform. They should be treated on an equal base with Service Domain-based components in a reference application architecture.*

In theory and in certain technical environments, each Service Domain would be implemented as one application component, and all business activity would be supported by service orchestrations between these applications. In practice, applications will combine the capabilities of several Service Domains, for reasons such as performance and operational coherence. In an application component that realizes such a "Service Domain cluster", the functionalities should remain un-clustered (uncluttered). The application services must be delimited according to the uncluttered Service Operations.

Figure 7-9 illustrates the delimitation of a software product as an orchestration of three BIAN-based components. The software product offers BIAN-inspired services (Open APIs). Those three Service Domains are a cluster in the Business Scenarios and the Wireframe representing a "business story". Internally, each Service Domain remains a building block that provides its ("internal API") services as defined by the Business Scenarios and Wireframe.

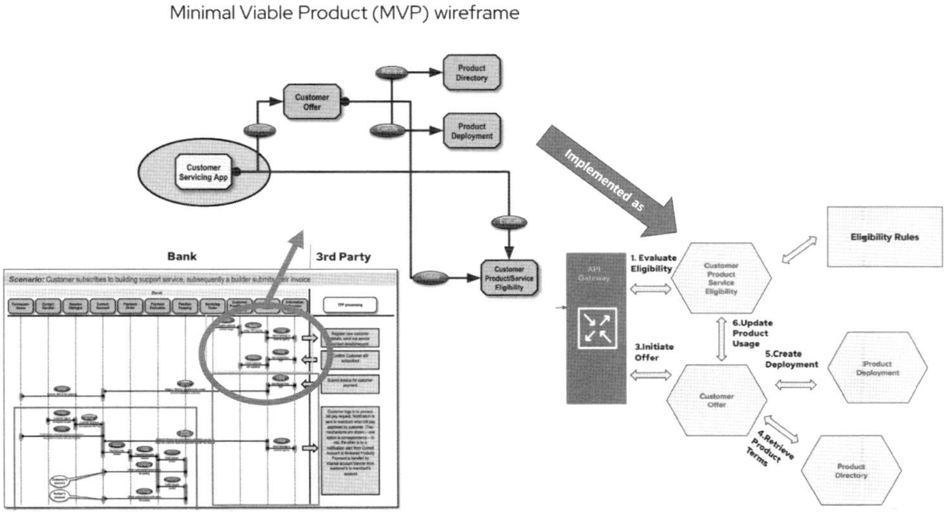

Figure 7-9 A software product, as a cluster of three Service Domains, internally remains "uncluttered"[84]

■ 7.5   BIAN AND APPLICATION ARCHITECTURE STYLES

The BIAN Reference Architecture is relevant for application architecture efforts from the 1970's to the 2020's. For all "architecture styles" from component-based design through service orientation and enterprise application integration (EAI) to containerized microservices, well-designed components (strong cohesion, encapsulated, substitutable, reusable) are important. Well-designed components and services facilitate the interoperability between styles and the migration to more sophisticated styles. Well-designed components and services become more important as the sophistication of the application architecture style and its ambition to function in an Open Finance ecosystem grows.

For inspirational purposes, BIAN distinguishes three "application architecture styles". These styles differ in the level of sophistication of the logical application architecture, concerning componentization and service orientation. They also differ in the level of sophistication of technology, connectivity, and security facilities. Obviously, many more combinations are possible.

The following levels are distinguished:
Level 1 ("direct to core"): Applications cooperate through services that are not always well delimited and use bank-specific language in their API. Service calls are addressed directly to the service-providing application. Access to services is only open to applications on the same technical platform. Access for end-users and partners is

---

84   Petroni, Nandakumar & Spadafora 2020.

possible through a "process logic application layer" for clearly defined, predictable and repeatable exchanges.

Level 2 ("wrapped host"): Access to services is facilitated by EAI facilities, such as an ESB[85]. This enables interoperability between platforms and makes interoperability more transparent for both service user and provider. The ESB's "translation" functionality enables the use of "canonical interfaces" (interfaces in a common language, both logically and technically). Its "integration" functionality can hide legacy application landscape issues by splitting application services into finer grained ones, concatenating them (e.g. gathering data available in different data stores). Its "addressing" functionality can hide the source of the service, whilst its "security" functionality can control access. Service sharing over technical platforms and multiple channels is enabled.

Level 3 ("distributed architecture"): Applications components are neatly delimited service centers. Application services are neatly delimited and provide "canonical interfaces" over sophisticated connectivity middleware. Level 3 connectivity provides an open, highly flexible access to application services aimed at orchestrating them flexibly and quickly into new interactions with, and functionality for, stakeholders in the Open API economy. Due to the unpredictability of the exchanges, a sophisticated security layer is required.

The application architecture styles correspond to different business needs, as illustrated Table 7-1.

Table 7-1 Architecture styles correspond to business drivers

	Direct to Core	**Wrapped Host**	**Distributed Architecture**
Business drivers	Provide access to established customer and partner exchanges.	Mask legacy limitations, enable cooperation between platforms and with different partners.	Support sophisticated interactions and new business models; third party integration.
Examples	Consult balance; retrieve account statements; initiate payment via customer access channel.	Sell consumer loans on partner platform; initiate payment from sales platform; provide PSD2 information.	Buy train and concert tickets; use best-of-breed business service providers; prospect onboarding, up/cross selling.

The efficiency and manoeuvrability of a "direct to core" platform is greatly enhanced by the use of the BIAN Framework in shaping the application architecture (as illustrated by Mfour Bank's excellent benchmark results in the footnote in Section 4.3).

85　Enterprise Service Bus.

A less well-architected legacy platform can be upgraded by the "wrapped host" style, using the BIAN Framework. Its flaws can be hidden by wrapping[86] techniques and externalization (as in Sub-section 7.1.6). The EAI infrastructure transforms the available application service portfolio into a BIAN-based service catalog. BIAN's Service Domains and Service Operations provide a "service directory" of discrete/non-overlapping elemental services. This extends the life of legacy applications (with a mitigating wrapper) and supports a migration strategy. A well-designed legacy platform also benefits from this style's techniques: its services can be opened up to other technical environments and translated in a canonical language, suitable for the Open API economy.

The "distributed architecture" requires open standards such as BIAN to delimit its service centers and specify its Open APIs.

The more basic business drivers, supported by the more basic styles, are not replaced but are supplemented by the needs that can be supported by the "distributed architecture" style.

The application architecture styles can coexist (actually, the same application can provide direct to core services while being wrapped to provide "wrapped host style" services and even "distributed architecture style" services).

To be successful, these styles share one necessary condition: the components and their services need to be well defined, elemental and MECE. The importance of the quality of the "semantic delimitation" grows with the level of technical sophistication.

BIAN's Service Domains and their Service Operations (detailed as Semantic API Endpoints) provide a stable, semantic high-level definition of such elemental, MECE components and services.

Using BIAN as the basis for component and service definition, ensures logical interoperability between architecture styles. It enables them to coexist. It facilitates a gradual migration, the evolution of one style to a more sophisticated style.

Using the elemental building blocks and service operations that BIAN proposes, ensures (functional) interoperability between styles and facilitates a gradual migration towards a more sophisticated style without major rework.

BIAN and microservices
"Microservices", as in the building blocks for a "microservice architecture", are the ultimate basic component, being cohesive, encapsulated, substitutable, reusable and

---

86 Applying a coding layer that transforms the interactions with an application to a desired format, without having to change the application itself.

organized around a business capability. They are highly maintainable and testable, and independently deployable.

Obviously, BIAN does not make any statement about the technology and middleware required to develop, deploy and run a microservice architecture.

A Service Domain performs a single, discrete, coherent function and handles all the instances of this business role. Its Control Record contains all the information required for and created by its functioning. It is functionally self-contained. As such, BIAN provides support for the high level, conceptual delimitation of a microservice [87].

■ 7.6 TEST YOURSELF QUESTIONS

1. Which of following statements correctly describe how BIAN can support application architecture and application design?
   A. Using BIAN Service Domains to delimit application components is only relevant if interactions with partners "in the cloud" is required.
   B. Business Scenarios and Wireframes can support the delimitation of application components, as they enable the detection of Service Domain clusters that work closely together.
   C. Service Domains provide a stable delimitation for application components, ensuring their replaceability.
   D. An application component needs to coincide with one and only one Service Domain.

2. Which of following statements does not describe a use of the Frame of Reference provided by BIAN?
   A. Overlaying an application on the BIAN-based Frame of Reference enables the identification of the functionality it provides.
   B. Overlaying applications on the BIAN-based Frame of Reference enables a like-for-like comparison of the functionality they provide.
   C. Overlaying a business organization and its application platform on the BIAN-based Frame of Reference facilitates the evaluation of the coverage the application platform provides.
   D. Overlaying a business organization and its application platform on the BIAN-based Frame of Reference is sufficient for the evaluation of the quality provided by the application platform.

---

87 As in "business micro (macro) service", not "utility nano-service". BIAN's Service Domains define elemental business roles. Microservices can also implement very fine-grained utilities such as check-digit calculation.

3. Which of following statements are not true?
   A. Optimizing the application portfolio requires the replacement of legacy applications by new ones that correspond with the BIAN architecture.
   B. Business Scenarios that are used to define the architecture for a new solution should be limited to the core functionality that needs to be introduced or changed.
   C. One of the elements in evaluating the quality of an application platform is the level to which the delimitation of its application components conforms to the BIAN architecture.
   D. Specifying requirements for a solution per Service Domain facilitates the comparison of possible solutions.

8 BIAN for information and data

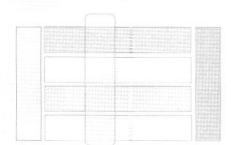

The importance of information[88] as an enterprise asset cannot be underestimated. The flexibly exploitable information provided by an agile data[89] architecture continues to remain a challenge.

Often, information has only been looked at from the point of view of one "business silo". Different business organizations do not share a common view on business concepts and lack the common language to share their information.

Data has been managed and stored only in view of the application that requires it – the application being designed to support a business silo. This results in a fragmented data landscape, with data duplicated endlessly[90], data conflicts and insufficient data quality. Data integration requires a huge effort, not least due to the lack of an unambiguous business meaning.

The BIAN Framework considers information an equal partner of "behavior". The BIAN BOM models all "Business Objects" that are relevant for a financial institution. Its Business Objects are elemental, MECE building blocks of the information needs of a financial institution.

The Information Profile of a Service Domain contains all the information required for, and describing the functioning of, the Service Domain. At this point in time, only the information, contained in the Control Record is described, in the Control Record Model.

The Service Domain BOM models this same information according to the Business Object Modeling approach (described in Section 2.6).

---

88 The term **"information"** is used for the business viewpoint. Information is what business needs/wants to know. It can be used by human beings.
89 The term **"data"** is used for the application viewpoint. Information is handled and stored on an ICT platform as data, that can be used by applications.
90 How many customer databases does your bank still have? Even though the concept of "party" as "master data" is usually one of the first to be remedied?

The BIAN BOM is built Service Domain by Service Domain, but is more than just the sum of Business Objects each Service Domain is interested in. Its completeness is ensured (*work in progress*) by the fact that it consolidates the Service Domain BOMs, but the structure of the BIAN BOM is not based on the usage by Service Domains. It is based on "information patterns" (the content and structure patterns, as described in Section 2.6). This approach ensures its consistence during a step-by-step elaboration. It ensures its extendibility, as the resulting model structure is not based on currently known usage of the information.

A Service Domain BOM (hence, a Control Record[91]) is a view on the BIAN BOM.

The BIAN BOM can be used in its base version, or can be tailored to a bank's specificities and detailed to represent its full information needs. Section 8.1 describes how the BIAN BOM can be tailored to a "Bank BOM".

This model can be used as a Frame of Reference, mapping the information landscape and the data landscape. This facilitates an overview of where and how the bank's information assets are managed and stored and how they flow through the enterprise (Sub-section 8.2.1). It provides the ability to evaluate and improve the landscape (Sub-section 8.2.2). It is especially useful in support of the "BI environment", that requires all the bank's information assets to be freely navigable (Sub-section 8.2.3). These information assets can be described by Business Objects and receive a strategic value and risk classification, a classification that is passed on the corresponding data stores (Sub-section 8.2.4).

Through configuration information, data technology can be mapped on the same Frame of Reference (Sub-section 8.2.5).

The business cases for integration of the information and data investment and change portfolio are improved by a clearer view on the impacted information assets and their value and risk (Section 8.3).

The Business Object Modeling approach and the BIAN BOM/Bank BOM, as a sum of Service Domain BOMs, support the specification of a system's information requirements and the embedding of an application system in the data architecture (Section 8.4).

---

91 The Control Record is described as a hierarchical model. It describes the information needs from the point of view of the Service Domain. The Service Domain BOM contains the same information, but there are two important differences. First, the Service Domain BOM is an entity relationship model. Secondly, the Service Domain BOM looks at things from the point of view of the BIAN BOM.

■ 8.1 TAILORING THE BIAN BOM

For use as an information Frame of Reference, a bank can decide to use the BIAN BOM in its base version, as delivered by BIAN. Or the bank can create a customized version. We will call this customized version the "Bank BOM".

Tailor the BOM
The bank can decide to tailor the Business Object Model to its own specificities. The steps in this effort are the same as described in Section 4.2 "Tailoring BIAN". In fact, tailoring the BOM should be part of the customization of the BIAN architecture as a whole.

As mentioned there, it is important to manage the relationship with the "base version" of the BIAN BOM, with a view to keeping up with BIAN updates and to communicating with partners who use the common BIAN language.

Changing the names of Business Objects and attributes to the terminology used in the bank may seem the simplest measure, but as there are probably many "speech communities" in the bank, why not remain with the BIAN terminology and provide a "dictionary" for each speech community? In any event, the link to the original names should be managed.

Tailoring the model consists of following steps:
– Select;
– Customize.

Select means that only those Business Objects that are relevant for the bank are retained (or those that are not, are eliminated).

This can be done from two "angles" – angles that are in fact complementary and should both be applied, as they serve as a consistency check for each other.

The first angle starts from the Service Landscape. By eliminating the Service Domains that are not relevant, the corresponding Service Domain BOMs are eliminated too, hence the corresponding Business Objects. The resulting BOM is checked for consistency and completeness.

The second angle is starting from the BIAN BOM and eliminating the Business Objects that are not relevant for the bank. Each remaining Business Object should be managed and used in at least one remaining Service Domain; the Service Domain BOM of each Service Domain should still be complete.

Customize can also be approached from these two angles.

It goes hand in hand with customizing the Service Domains. If these are merged or split, the corresponding Service Domain BOMs also need to be merged or split. This might require a "generalization" (merge), "specialization[92]" or "decomposition[93]" (split) of the involved Business Objects. New Service Domains require new Business Objects (see the example in Section 4.2, where a new Business Object "Standing Order" is created).

Starting from the information point of view, a Business Object can be added, generalized or specialized in the BIAN BOM. There also needs to be a Service Domain that manages and uses these Business Objects.

Augment the descriptions and detail the model
The definitions of Business Objects and attributes can be made more clear and precise, whilst the allowed values can be changed and/or extended.

Business Objects in the BIAN BOM can be rather abstract or more detailed. Attributes can be generic or specific, there can be a few attributes or a whole range. In view of its general applicability, the BIAN BOM will never be elaborated on the full level of detail of an individual bank's information needs.

The bank can specialize and/or decompose the Business Objects and add attributes as required. Sources for more detail can be other data models or message standards.

This is similar to detailing the Semantic API Endpoint descriptions (as in Sub-section 9.3.2). Or better: this precedes the detailing of the Semantic API Endpoint specification, as the Endpoint specification refers to the Control Record/Service Domain BOM.

It is not necessary to do all this upfront. The Bank BOM does not need to be fully tailored and attributed. Its structure already provides a major added value in terms of exploring and structuring the information and data landscape. The bank's BOM can be detailed step-by-step, as a particular area of the bank is analyzed in more detail (Section 8.4). The pattern-based structure of the BIAN BOM ensures stability: it can be elaborated in further detail, new domains can be added, without disturbing the structure.

The Control Record of a Service Domain is the source for the Service Domain BOM and as such the source for the BIAN BOM. As described in Section 2.5, the Control Record's Behavior Qualifiers can be broken down into Sub-qualifiers and even further detail. This is done by detailing the behavior of the Service Domain. This is also an approach to detailing the BOM, and to specifying the information requirements of a system (as in Section 8.4).

---

92 E.g. a Party is specialized as a Person or an Organization.
93 E.g. The Party Business Object is detailed by splitting off "Party Certificate", "Party Profile", "Party Location".

8.2 THE BIAN BOM FOR INFORMATION AND DATA ARCHITECTURE

8.2.1 Frame of Reference for the information and data landscape

The BIAN BOM (or the bank's tailored version) is a Frame of Reference to explore the information and data landscape. This facilitates an overview of the available information assets. It also facilitates the evaluation and remediation of the information and data landscape.

Information is generated and used in different processes, departments... Each one of these "business landscape elements" can be a separate "speech community", i.e. the same information can be addressed using different terminology.

The BOM can solve this speech confusion. All information that is managed and used in each process and organizational unit, can be labelled with the corresponding Business Objects. These labels are linked to the process or organizational unit. This provides a common language and a map to track information usage and detect possible duplication of information sources. Business landscape elements are thus labelled with both Business Objects and Service Domains (as described in Sub-section 6.1.3).

The labels can also be assigned to the data landscape. Each logical data store[94] is indexed with the Business Objects it realizes. As data stores are linked to application usage (through configuration information), the map of the data landscape, labelled with Business Objects, is linked to the map of the application landscape, labelled by the Service Domains.

An "information realization" view (Figure 8-1) can follow the trace of each Business Object through the business information landscape, to the data landscape and the technology landscape.

This mapping can (should) be done at different levels of abstraction. For overview purposes, an abstraction level should be chosen that results in a manageable number of business object (groups) comparable to the number of Service Domains. Where required, a more detailed mapping, even up to an attribute level, is possible.

The bank's BOM can be detailed to a level of "Canonical Information Model[95]", enabling the translation of that part of business terminology that is captured in the BOM. It

---

94 A data store is a more general concept than "database", any medium and any method for storing and retrieving can be used to store and retrieve the data. The expression "logical data store" stresses the fact that it is not the "physical database delimitation" that counts, but the "logical unit of storing and retrieving data".
95 An information model used to communicate between different speech communities. It is a "superset" of their views on information. Each view on reality can have its own model structure, own naming, definitions and notations. The Canonical Model is used to translate one view to another and spans all of the reality that is relevant for the organization.

becomes part of the business dictionary that enables different speech communities to communicate.

It can also be detailed in a "Canonical Data Model[96]", that can be used as "lingua franca" for communication between systems and for the integration of data.

The Frame of Reference provided by the BIAN BOM also enables the exploration and mapping of "data in motion".

Data is often copied between data stores. A bank can quickly lose the overview of what data comes from what source via what intermediate steps (data lineage). The data in motion, i.e. the data flows between data stores, can also be mapped on the BOM's Business Objects.

8.2.2 Evaluating and improving the data landscape

The overview of the information and data landscape that is facilitated by the "information and data Frame of Reference" provided by the BIAN or bank-specific Bank BOM, enables information and data architects to evaluate the landscape and find the root-cause of information-related problems. It allows them to delimit areas that need to be mitigated.

Figure 8-1 depicts a data landscape (icons with suffix "LDS" or Logical Data Stores) that is nicely structured according to the BOM (on top, with grey background). The information landscape (middle) corresponds completely with the BOM.

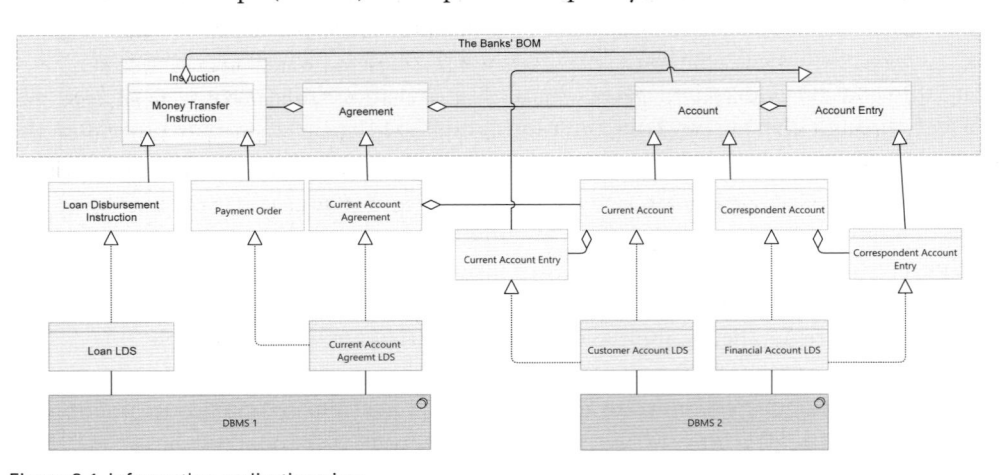

Figure 8-1 Information realization view

---

96 A data model used to communicate between different data models and to integrate them. It is a "superset", the data-equivalent of the Canonical Information Model.

Most likely, duplications and gaps[97] will be discovered. The architects will subsequently evaluate whether these are issues.

> At the point of introducing the enterprise architecture capability, the M5 Banking Group performs a high-level mapping of its data assets on the BIAN BOM.
>
> This reveals that each bank and a lot of lines of business have their own "currency" and "shares and bonds" data stores. Which is no surprise, as this "master data" is necessary for each application platform. What is also discovered, however, is that this information is purchased separately on the market for each data store. An improvement to the information landscape (how the business manages the information) could provide major cost savings: A small "market data" department is installed at Group level, and the contracts for currency and shares and bonds information are re-negotiated on a Group level. The information is bought once and stored in each bank's data stores. The cost savings provide a significant budget that can be invested in other architecture ventures.
>
> The same exercise reveals the existence of many employee-hiring processes, each resulting in employee agreements, stored in different data stores. This turns out to be no issue, as there is no overlap in employee agreement instances and hence no information inconsistency risks.
>
> However, the data landscape of one bank in the Group is something of a disaster. The uncoordinated generation of party information in many business processes, and its duplication in many data stores, is a continuous source of customers complaints and correction costs (dotted lines on the left, depicting the mapping on the BOM's Business Objects on Figure 8-2). It requires optimization on both an information and data landscape level. But the problems resulting from the presence of inconsistently duplicated and locally updated current account data in a series of software packages, is of another order of magnitude (dotted lines on the right, depicting the mapping on the BOM's Business Objects on Figure 8-2). The regulator deems this unacceptable, as this information is classified in the highest quality and risk category.

---

97 Information that is available on a business level, but for which no data store, capable of being exploited by applications, is found. Or a "data store" in a technology that is not sufficiently exploitable, nor safe, e.g. an Excel file.

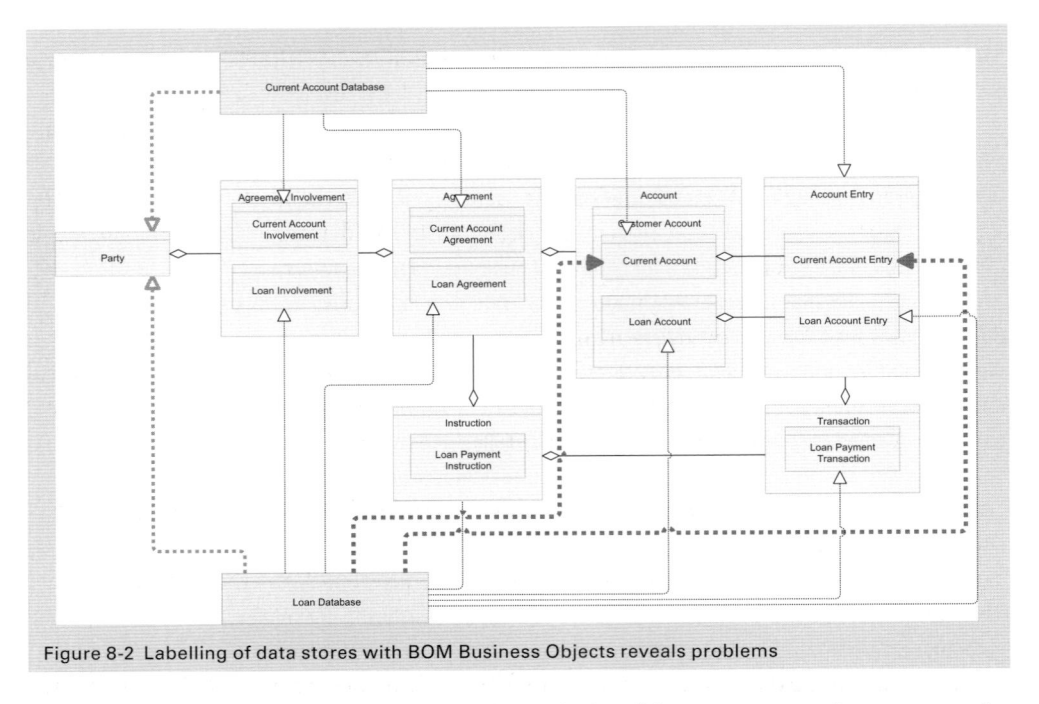

Figure 8-2 Labelling of data stores with BOM Business Objects reveals problems

A mapping of both the "data at rest" and the "data in motion" supports the disentanglement of the data landscape (what information is stored where and moved from where to where… to where. . .). It supports the elaboration of, and the migration towards, a managed data storage and data integration[98] architecture.

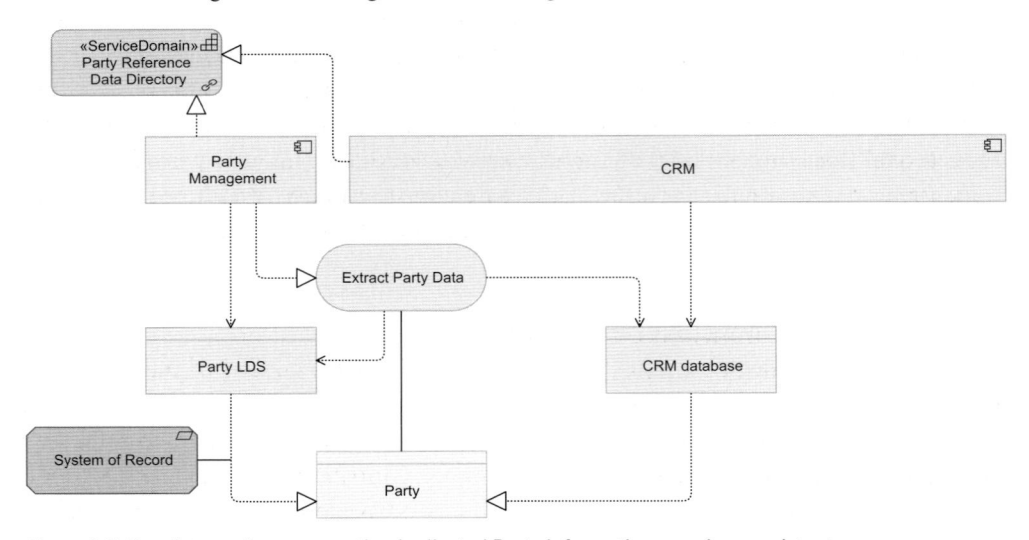

Figure 8-3 Data Integration ensures the duplicated Party information remains consistent

---

98 Data integration is the art of ensuring data is available in the application landscape where it is needed, with the required quality.

For example: for each Business Object instance, a System of Record (SoR[99]) data store can be assigned. This is the authoritative source of information. Other data stores need to be "slaves", receiving copies from the System of Record through an adequate data integration architecture. Figure 8-3 repeats the "data integration" mentioned in Figure 7-2. The "Party LDS" (Logical Data Store) is assigned as the System of Record. The "Extract Party Data" application service implements the dataflow that propagates this data to the CRM database.

8.2.3 In aid of the BI environment
A BI environment or "Business Intelligence" environment is a rather old-fashioned name for (a) data environment(s) that provide flexible, unpredictable access to all data available to the enterprise, including a historical overview.

The BIAN BOM – or the bank's tailored version can be detailed in a "Canonical Data Model" that supports the navigability of data originating from different sources, belonging to different speech communities and from sources that change in appearance and content over time.

The overview of the data landscape, provided by the "Business Object labels", enables the data architect to choose the appropriate data sources for the "BI purpose" (the Systems of Record, not the slaves) and facilitates the translation, aggregation and consolidation required for a BI environment.

The data for the BI environment is sourced from operational systems, that each have their own views on this data. Not just naming differences, but differences in formatting, value ranges, attribute collections and entity structures, quality levels etc. They are not always fully "translatable". Obviously, the BIAN BOM as a structure for the Canonical Data Model does not provide all the answers. Nevertheless, it does provide a stable structure and a common language that can be used to understand all sources and to mould them into a structure that supports navigability through the data from different sources.

8.2.4 BOM for information classification
The BIAN BOM provides a holistic view on the information assets of the bank. The mapping of the information landscape on the BOM provides an overview of what information is used and where. Information assets are assigned a strategic value and risk, based on their operational importance and their contribution to the bank's strategy. This classification is passed through to the data stores that contain this information[100].

---
99 Data store that is the authoritative source for the designated set of data.
100 Information classification is an aspect of enterprise information architecture governance.

8.2.5 Linking to data technology

The information and data landscape is mapped on the BIAN BOM or its tailored version, the Bank BOM. Configuration information links the data and communication technology to the data stores and data flows. This facilitates the creation of "information realization viewpoints", as shown in Figure 8-1.

Shortfalls can be identified, whilst opportunities for technology available on one platform can be linked to needs on other platforms more easily.

The positive impact of data technology investments and changes can be linked to the business functionality and information assets that will benefit from them. They "inherit" their strategic position, value, risk, quality and security requirements. This improves the integration of data technology investments in the enterprise investment and change portfolio.

8.3 BUSINESS CASES FOR THE INFORMATION AND DATA INVESTMENT AND CHANGE PORTFOLIO

The information and data landscape is overlaid on the BIAN-based Frame of Reference for information – i.e. the BIAN BOM or the bank's tailored BOM. The data flows can be traced through the application platform via the same mapping.

This facilitates the detection of issues (such as duplications and gaps). It facilitates a root cause analysis of information quality issues and clarifies other risks. The strategic value and risk of each information asset is established.

This input enables the information and data architect to define investment and change proposals (such as buying qualitative information, eliminating duplications, improving quality controls, opening up information etc.), in order to mitigate problems with the information and data landscape and make them future proof.

These proposals can be expressed according to this same BIAN-based Frame of Reference for information. Their business case is furnished by the value and risk of the information and by its positive impact on the business and application landscape.

8.4 BIAN FOR INFORMATION AND DATA ON SYSTEM LEVEL

The information model of a system expresses the information requirements of that system in a structured way.

If the system development approach fully leverages BIAN, two complementary angles ensure that the information requirements are of a high quality.

The system requirements are structured as a choreography of Service Domains (as in Sub-section 6.3.2). Its information model can be assembled by consolidating the Service Domain BOMs.

This approach creates a first draft, that should be challenged by the traditional approach to information requirements gathering such as interviewing users, looking at reports etc. The Business Object Modeling approach used by BIAN and the BIAN BOM/Bank BOM supports the creation of a qualitative information model, fitting nicely in the Bank BOM and contributing to the detail of the "Canonical Information Model".

In an environment that fully leverages BIAN for information and data, it is clear which information is already available as data. The application and data architect can "click" the new system "in" application services and data stores that already exist.

As a consequence of the new "Group Synergy" strategy of the M5 Banking Group, a Payment Group Service is created. The high-level delimitation of this Group Service is expressed as a choreography of Service Domains. The high-level information model for this system is put together based on the Service Domain BOMs (Figure 8-4). During the detailed information requirements analysis, this model is developed, based on a comparison with the preferred message standard for the Payment Execution Service Domain (ISO 20022). The model is detailed in accordance with the BOM content and structure pattern.

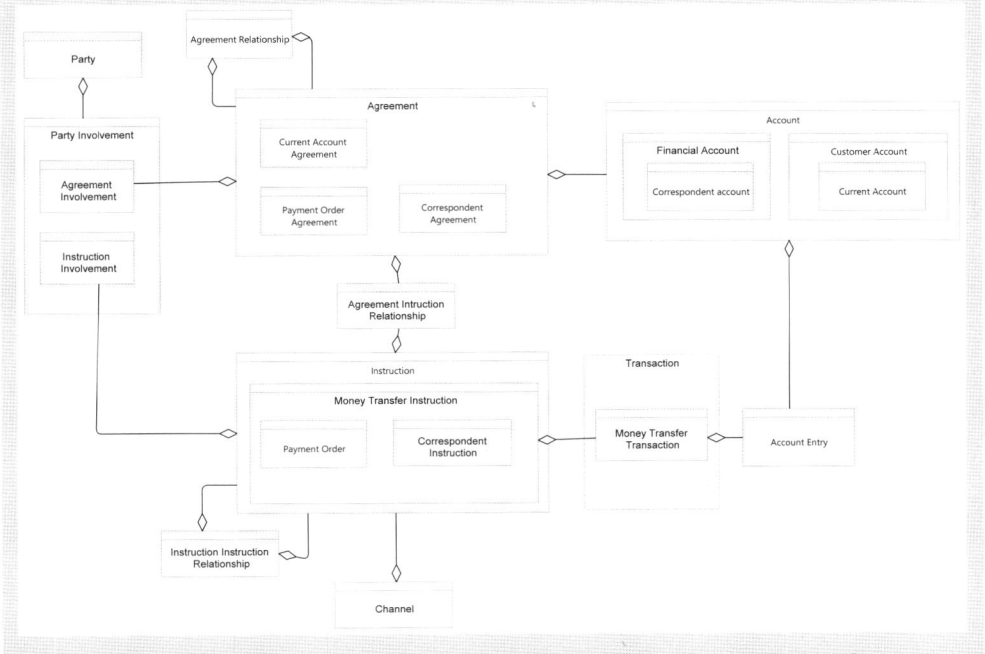

Figure 8-4 High level information model for the Payment Group Service of the M5 Banking Group

8.5 TEST YOURSELF QUESTIONS

1. **Which of these statements is not true?**
   A. A bank cannot customize the BIAN BOM, otherwise the BOM patterns could be violated and consistency with the Service Domains is lost.
   B. The BIAN BOM or Bank BOM can be detailed for use as a Canonical Data Model, as long as the BOM patterns are respected.
   C. If the scope of a system is expressed in Service Domains, the consolidation of the Service Domain BOMs can be used as a starting point for the gathering of the information requirements.
   D. The BIAN BOM can be used to obtain an overview of what information is used by which business entity.

2. **Which statements correctly describe the way in which the BIAN BOM can support data architecture?**
   A. The data landscape can be overlaid on the BIAN BOM. This results in the labelling of each data store with the Business Objects that are present in that data store.
   B. Each data flow can be overlaid on the BIAN BOM. This results in the labelling of each data flow with the Business Objects it carries.
   C. By overlaying the data landscape with the BIAN BOM, data duplications can be detected.
   D. By overlaying both the "data at rest" and the "data in motion" on the BIAN BOM, the elaboration of an adequate data integration architecture is facilitated.

3. **Which statement is true?**
   A. The Control Record model and the Service Domain BOM both depict the information requirements of the Service Domain.
   B. The Control Record model and the Service Domain BOM are one and the same.

9 BIAN for interoperability

Agility and the reduction of costs by reuse are no longer the sole drivers for an architecture based on interoperability between well designed components[101]. The interoperability challenges are no longer confined by the limits of the bank and its traditional partners (such as correspondents). The financial industry is embarking on a financial services revolution that will connect consumers, banks, their partners and third parties in ever-evolving ways. This is a revolution starting with Open APIs, driven by regulations (such as the EU's PSD2 directive, Plias 2020) and evolving naturally into banks participating in a broader Open Finance ecosystem.

The BIAN Framework is designed to support financial institutions in this paradigm change.

The role of BIAN as the organizing Frame of Reference for the service catalog is highlighted (Section 9.1).

In Section 9.2, we focus on the management of the application service landscape. This is facilitated when developers have a service catalog at their disposal. A catalog where they can easily find all application services, available for interoperability within the bank and with partners and other stakeholders in an Open API environment. Architects can use this application service catalog as an instrument to steer developers in the use of application services and their APIs.

The Application Service Landscape can be overlaid on the Frame of Reference, supporting the architects in the evaluation of this landscape and in defining and prioritizing improvements. The link with strategic goals and requirements and change portfolio management is facilitated by this common Frame of Reference.

---

101 From component-based to service-oriented to containerized microservices, from direct to core, to wrapped host to distributed architecture (see Section 4.6 "BIAN and application architecture styles").

BIAN also supports the delimitation of services and the design of (Open) APIs, as explained in Section 9.3.

This chapter addresses application services, not business services.

We cover application services and their APIs that provide "functionality building blocks" and "information building blocks". This is the type of application service that can be relevant for any financial institution, hence where BIAN comes in.

We do not discuss those that orchestrate these building blocks to provide user functionality. This is where every financial institution is able to develop its individual capabilities.

■ 9.1 BIAN AS ORGANIZING FRAME OF REFERENCE FOR THE APPLICATION SERVICE PORTFOLIO

9.1.1 The Service Domain / Service Operation Frame of Reference

A clear, complete and efficiently accessible overview of the available application services is indispensable for a system development organization that wants to combine speed with quality and future-proof flexibility. Even more so if APIs need to be made available to other organizations in an Open API environment. An application service catalog expressed in a common language, organized and accessible according to a common Frame of Reference is a must.

The BIAN Service Landscape offers a MECE collection of elemental service centers that can be relevant for any financial institution. Their delimitation and role in a bank are implementation-independent and stable over time. These service centers - the BIAN Service Domains- each have their specific Service Operations, delimiting stable, elemental services. As a result, the BIAN Service Landscape, as a sum of all Service Domains with all their Service Operations, provides an exhaustive overview of (very) elemental services that can support all required interactions within a financial institution and/or with its customers, partners and other actors in the Open API economy.

As described in Section 4.2, a bank can create its own view on the BIAN Service Landscape and its Service Domains. The link from this "tailored" version to the base BIAN version, should be managed consistently, to reinforce its value as a "common language" between stakeholders in the Open API economy.

Whether it is the base version or the tailored version, the BIAN-based Frame of Reference is well positioned to organize an application service catalog. Every existing application service can be expressed as a realization of one or more Service Operations of one or more Service Domains. Each application service can be indexed with the (first level) Service Domains and (second level) Service Operations it realizes.

As such, the "Service Domain" Frame of Reference, used to overlay the application landscape, is upgraded to a "Service Domain and Service Operation" Frame of Reference, to overlay the Application Service Landscape[102].

9.1.2 Organizing the application service catalog

To structure the application service catalog, the Service Domains are the first level of entry. The Service Domain description depicts its business role as a service center. An application architect or system designer looking for available application services, should understand the functionality of the system. As such, he/she should be able to pinpoint the Service Domains that can provide relevant services.

Within each Service Domain, the Service Operations provide the second search level.

Variations on this theme are possible. The "Service Operation Group" (or Action Term Group, see Sub-section 2.7.1) can be used as an intermediate or even lowest level of the index. Contrary to Action Terms (that define the Service Operations), they do not differ between Service Domains. They provide a more coarse-grained search, but are more intuitive.

Service Domains and Service Operations provide a universally valid structure to the application service catalog, that can be shared between organizations within the bank and with partners. But as an entry level for a search and as a "governance structure"[103], a bank will probably choose to group APIs belonging to a certain area of business. It will add higher organization levels to its catalog, such as a - possibly customized - Business Area/Business Domain access path.

In Sub-section 8.2.1, we explained how the BIAN BOM (or the bank's tailored BOM) can be used to label data flows. This index expresses the information content of services with the Action Term "notify" or "retrieve": application services that are classified as information services. The BOM Business Objects used as an "information index" are a useful addition to the application service catalog index.

Application services available in, and to, the bank can map on more than one Service Operation. They can map on Service Operations of different Service Domains. This can be a sound design decision. Or not. Whether or not, is an assessment that needs to be made by an architect.

---

102 The existing applications and the application services they provide, and the "nesting" relationships between application services.
103 As in Section 7.1.4, governance of the application service portfolio will probably require a "divide and conquer" approach. This can also be organized according to the (customized) Business Area-Business Domain structure.

The M5 Banking Group created an application service catalog on a Group level as one of the first initiatives of the enterprise architecture capability. Since the Group adopted BIAN as an industry reference architecture (and customized it to the Group's needs) they did not have to think twice about an organizing Frame of Reference for this catalog.

The architecture repository, that is used as tool to exploit this catalog, provides indexes on Service Domain, Service Group and Service Operation, as well as (level +1) Business Object.

The party reference data available on the Homeland platform is provided by (among other) the "Consult Party Data" and the "Extract Party Data" application services (Figure 9-1).

The interactive "Consult Party Data" application service provides information on individual parties, or limited groups. (Which parties depends on the access rights of the service user e.g. a customer can only request information about him/herself and parties he/she has power of attorney over.) The "Extract Party Data" application service provides a file with a wide range of parties. It can be used in a "notify" mode – a file is "pushed" to the subscribers periodically, or in "retrieve" mode. (The selected parties are limited by privacy constraints and the interests of the subscriber/requester.)

As these services are "information services", they are also indexed by Business Objects.

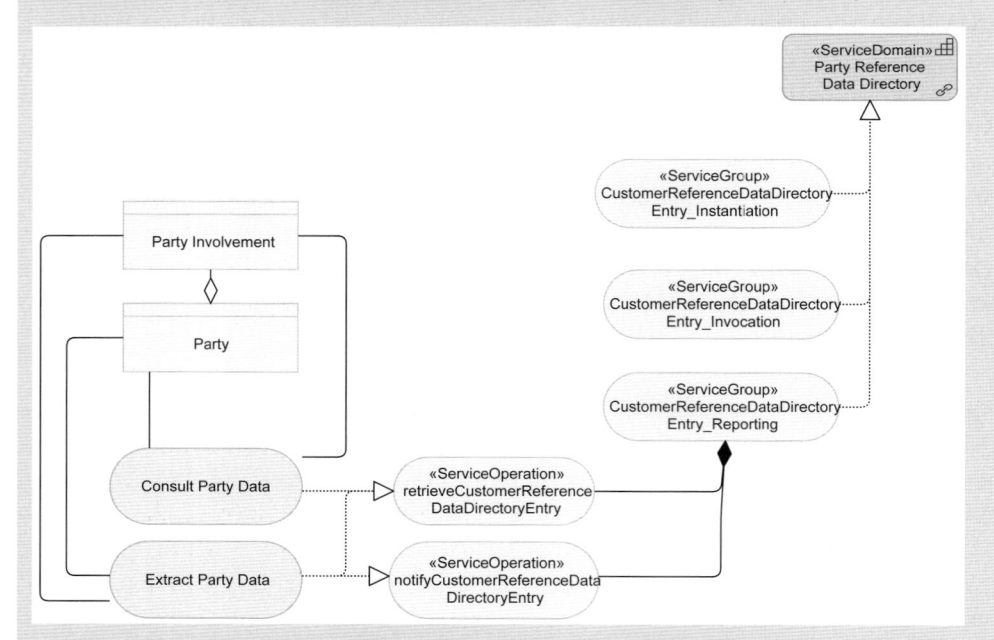

Figure 9-1 The Service Domain / Service Operation Frame of Reference facilitates the search in M5 Banking Group's application service catalog

■ 9.2 BIAN SUPPORTING APPLICATION SERVICE LANDSCAPE MANAGEMENT

The "application service landscape" is not only the collection of application services available for developers. It also contains their "service providers" (the application components providing the services) and their interrelationships (application services are usually "nested": one service uses another that uses another. . .).

Application service landscape is not to be confused with the BIAN Service Landscape that is the representation of the collection of the BIAN Service Domains.

A bank's application service landscape is concerned with the application services and their APIs that the bank itself developed for internal use and as public APIs, as well as those that are provided by other parties that the bank interacts with. It should contain available Open APIs from third parties, approved by the bank's architects.

A well elaborated application service landscape provides the bank with a much needed "box of building blocks" for digitalization and digital transformation initiatives.

9.2.1 Steering the use of application services

For architects, responsible for the management of the bank's application service landscape, a well-organized application service catalog is an important instrument.

It facilitates the follow-up and evaluation of the API portfolio. Architects can recognise candidates for critical comparison and evaluation (such as strangely delimited services or possible duplicates) more easily if every service is mapped on the same Frame of Reference.

Architects can add their evaluation and recommendations for use of services to the catalog, such as "standard", "for use on platform xyz only", "to deprecate".

Service Domains that map on application components but for whom no application services are available, may indicate gaps in the application service portfolio. Architects may look into the possibility to externalize such services (as in Sub-section 7.1.6).

The catalog supports and steers application designers and developers in the re-use of available building blocks. The BIAN index[104] efficiently leads them to identify candidate application services. The functionality, as described by the "Service Domain /Service Operation index" on each service, enables a first elimination of these candidates. The instructions and comments added by the architects further narrow down the choice.

---

104 Service Domain, Service Operation, possibly Business Object.

Obviously, this is a necessary but it is not a sufficient condition to select a suitable application service. To select the best match, supported "non-functional requirements", such as the type of interaction, the available security measures etc. need to be documented too, as well as the technology that will be used to implement the application service.

BIAN does not make any statements on what information, apart from the "semantics" of the service, should be available in the application service catalog.

9.2.2 Evaluating and improving the application service landscape

Overlaying the bank's application service landscape on BIAN's Service Domains and Service Operations, provides a management instrument for its evaluation and for defining and prioritizing changes to the bank's application service landscape. As mentioned in Section 5.3, the common Frame of Reference provided by BIAN can be used for documenting strategic positioning, requirements and assessments. These requirements and assessments can relate to functionality, as well as "non-functional" considerations such as security, openness, scalability, interactivity...

The strategic positioning of, and requirements for, Service Domains are input as priorities in the elaboration and improvement of the application service landscape. For example, if the enterprise strategy requires the bank to interact with partners in the Open API economy, then attention should be turned to the interaction area. The available service stack may need to be upgraded (such as refining the granularity or enhancing the security) for a better fit with the requirements of digitalization. Open APIs will need to be provided and a search for the best way to plug into services provided by partners should be launched.

Figure 9-2 represents a heatmap of the API coverage, as it could have been made by a BIAN member. Colors represent the level of availability of APIs, whilst another heatmap could represent the urgency and importance of the availability of APIs. This will send a clear message to management, in respect of the priority of project proposals.

The Service Domain/Service Operation Frame of Reference provides future-proof delimitations for elemental application services. As such, this Frame of Reference is at the same time a *Reference Architecture* that steers the delimitation of elemental application services. This is discussed further in Section 9.3.

The BIAN-inspired APIs are an important "lubricant", providing stability and agility to an application landscape.

9 BIAN for interoperability

Figure 9-2 API coverage heatmap on the BIAN-Service Landscape[105],[106]

---

105 Freely after Plias 2020.
106 We apologize for the fact that the names of the Service Domains are not readable. The purpose of this figure is to illustrate the power of the Service Landscape to manage and communicate the quality of the application service landscape. For online version of this figure see free download at https://www.vanharen.store/bian-2nd-edition-a-framework-for-the-financial-services-industry

They provide a common communication language between systems within the bank and with partners. As such, they can be used to specify the "ESB[107] service catalog".

They can "wrap" legacy systems, as well as vendor software, prolonging the lifespan of these investments. They can also ensure replaceability. BIAN Service Operation (as detailed in the Semantic API Endpoints) can be considered a high-level specification for an application service and its API. Two software implementations corresponding to these specifications will most probably differ in their detail, but it should be possible to map the information exchanges and main functionality consistently on the BIAN Service Operations. If a service user wanted to switch between service providers, any disruption would be confined to the immediate vicinity of the service exchange.

9.2.3 Changing and migrating the application (service) landscape

The "renovation" of the application service portfolio according to the BIAN-based reference architecture can be done service-by-service, according to priorities and need not create a major disturbance of the application portfolio. Services can coexist. The "legacy" service can continue to function, alongside the new "elementary services". This allows the service users to gradually migrate to the new portfolio.

The testimonial in Figure 9-3 illustrates the power of the BIAN Architecture in architecting and prioritizing changes to the application service landscape.

Currently, there is a monolithic "card account data service", that contains far too much information, gathered from far too many applications. This does not provide the manoeuvrability required for a digital environment.

To ensure a qualitative decomposition of the monolith into elementary application services, this monolith is overlaid over the BIAN Service Domains. The implementation of the elementary services is prioritized according to the API priorities of the bank.

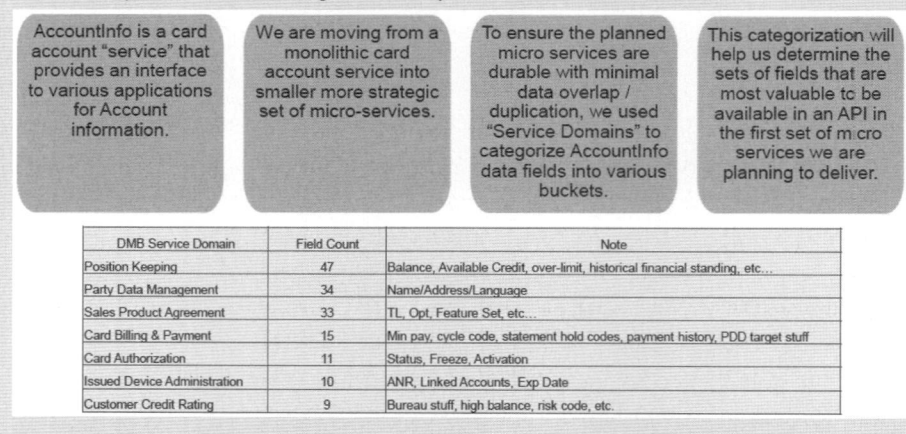

- AccountInfo is a card account "service" that provides an interface to various applications for Account information.
- We are moving from a monolithic card account service into smaller more strategic set of micro-services.
- To ensure the planned micro services are durable with minimal data overlap / duplication, we used "Service Domains" to categorize AccountInfo data fields into various buckets.
- This categorization will help us determine the sets of fields that are most valuable to be available in an API in the first set of micro services we are planning to deliver.

DMB Service Domain	Field Count	Note
Position Keeping	47	Balance, Available Credit, over-limit, historical financial standing, etc...
Party Data Management	34	Name/Address/Language
Sales Product Agreement	33	TL, Opt, Feature Set, etc...
Card Billing & Payment	15	Min pay, cycle code, statement hold codes, payment history, PDD target stuff
Card Authorization	11	Status, Freeze, Activation
Issued Device Administration	10	ANR, Linked Accounts, Exp Date
Customer Credit Rating	9	Bureau stuff, high balance, risk code, etc.

Figure 9-3 Testimonial: delimiting and prioritizing the development of future-proof APIs[108]

---

107 A system that ensures a transparent exchange of services between applications.
108 BIAN Architecture Working Group 2017b.

The impact analysis of any change initiatives is facilitated through the shared use of the "Service Domain /Service Operation" Frame of Refence by change portfolio management (as mentioned in Sub-section 5.3.4) and the bank's application service landscape management. As both the scope of projects and programs and the changes to the application service landscape refer to the Service Domains, communication in both directions is made easier. Change initiatives can be projected on to the application service landscape and any required changes to the bank's application service landscape can be assigned to projects/programmes.

Services are well suited as a "lubricant" in an application migration strategy. Well-designed services can hide changes to the systems that provide (the information for) the service. Upgrading systems or a switch to an entirely new service providing system is possible with limited impact. The BIAN Service Domain specification provides a blueprint to wrap and repurpose legacy capabilities behind a stable service boundary. This allows the bank to rationalize the access to functionality and information by providing a standard set of services, while the legacy applications are being replaced or repaired behind the wrapper. This isolates the bank from disruption during the migration.

> The Mfour Bank, the "founding member" of the M5 Group, has a long history of sound application architecture practices. They were among the first to adopt a component-based architecture. Every database was in fact a "corporate" database ("one attribute managed only once" was the principle).
> In the beginning, all applications had direct "read" access to these databases. Soon, application services were developed, "encapsulating" the systems and databases. As the application service catalog on a M5 Group level is introduced, the Service Domain/Service Operation Frame of Reference is used to organize it. The majority of Mfour Bank's application services turn out to match perfectly on this Frame of Reference (see Figure 9-1 and Figure 9-5).
>
> The Party Reference Data system is one of the most solicited service providers. As the bank grew its product offerings and began to target corporate parties, its functionality was lagging. A major upgrade was undertaken, on both the functional and technical levels. To avoid a big bang, the changes to the system and database were hidden from the service users. A new set of application services was developed, that included the new functionality, but still made use of the old database. New service users could already start using this "final version" of the application services. Those applications that were still relying on direct access could start their migration by using these new services. Once the new system was finished, the old and new service stacks converted to the new database. During a limited migration period, the old service users converted to the new service stack. This was not for free, but the effort was mainly technical, with the impact on business logic being practically nil.

9.3 BIAN FOR FUTURE-PROOF APIS

Delimiting components and defining their services in respect of "loose coupling" and "encapsulation", for a manoeuvrable application architecture, has always been the first and certainly not the least challenge for an application architect. From the first "direct to core[109]" component-based architectures, to "loosely coupled, cloud-based, containerized microservice architectures", investments in technology only turn out to be beneficial if the components and services are adequately defined and delimited on a semantic business level. Supporting financial institutions in this challenge is BIAN's primary calling.

In this section, we discuss application services and their APIs that expose functionality and data from an application component. We do not cover those APIs that expose orchestrated functionality to a partner or end- user. It is the first type of APIs that provides the agility required by the second type.

BIAN's Semantic API initiative supports a bank's application service architecture from architecture over design to even development.

BIAN can be used as a *"reference architecture"*, steering a bank's application service landscape. (Clusters of) Service Domains define the delimitation of the components that provide the application services. (Groups of) Service Operations delimit the functionality of the application services.

BIAN's Semantic APIs extend the detail of Service Operation specifications, to a level that can be considered high level *design* for an application service and API.

The BIAN API Portal provides access to a BIAN API Sandbox Platform. This platform contains the Semantic API catalog. It provides an overview of the available Semantic API descriptions: for each Service Domain, a series of "Semantic API Endpoints" is provided, expressed as RESTful API specifications.

The Swagger Files, generated from these specifications, provide a "JSON *code Stub*" that can be used by developers as starting point for an actual JSON specification.

The Semantic API initiative developed an approach to delimit APIs, that can be used by a bank to refine the APIs provided on the BIAN API Portal and/or to define its own API catalog.

The approach consists of the following steps. The steps in brackets are not required if there are BIAN-supplied Semantic APIs. If not yet, the bank can apply these steps itself.

---

109 See Section 7.5.

- Delimit service centers and services, prioritize (Open) APIs:
  o Use Wireframes to scope service centers and find enterprise boundaries;
  o Use Business Scenarios to define the business context for Service Operations and their APIs.
- Elaborate API specifications:
  o (Transform Action Terms to http "verbs" and into "nouns");
  o (Refine Service Operation functionality and API content based on Information Profile and Control Record decomposition);
  o Detail information exchange based on the Business Object Model;
  o Enrich information exchange based on message standards.

9.3.1 Delimit service centers and services

A Wireframe shows the available Service Connections between a related collection of Service Domains[110]. A Wireframe is derived from a collection of Business Scenarios that navigate comparable collections of Service Domains. A Wireframe is rather like a city map that shows the possible Service Connection pathways between the Service Domains. A Business Scenario is then one possible journey that traverses this map. A Business Scenario will use its particular Service Connections path and provides a specific business use for each Service Connection. The route of each Business Scenario through the "urban district" described by the Wireframe will be different, but several Business Scenarios will share the same business use of individual Service Connections.

As such, the BIAN Wireframe is an excellent instrument to delimit service centers and define services. The collection of Business Scenarios will probably never be complete, as not all activities of a bank will be documented and new Business Scenarios will become relevant. Nevertheless, a Wireframe, if based on a representative sample[111], will be a reliable base for service center and service delimitation.

Examples of how Wireframes and Business Scenarios support the delimitation of applications and the definition of services are given in Chapter 7.

The Business Scenarios provide business context to the service exchanges detected on the Wireframe. The key business information that is exchanged between the "calling" Service Domain and the "service providing" Service Domain is described in each Business Scenario. The exchanges are linked to the Service Operation of the providing

---

110 A Service Domain may make use of more than one of the services offered by another Service Domain, for example requesting a specific action be performed or simply retrieving information.
111 To define application services, the Wireframe needs to be based on Business Scenarios with as many different purposes as possible. This will provide an overview of the different kinds of services a Service Domain needs to provide. Different kinds are based on content, but also on "non-functional requirements" such as interactivity and volume. An application service should be "one to many" and not "custom sized" to individual service users, but it should provide several "confection sizes" based on functional and non-functional considerations.

Service Domain. This sheds light on the semantic business information content that would need to be exchanged through the API (Figure 9-4).

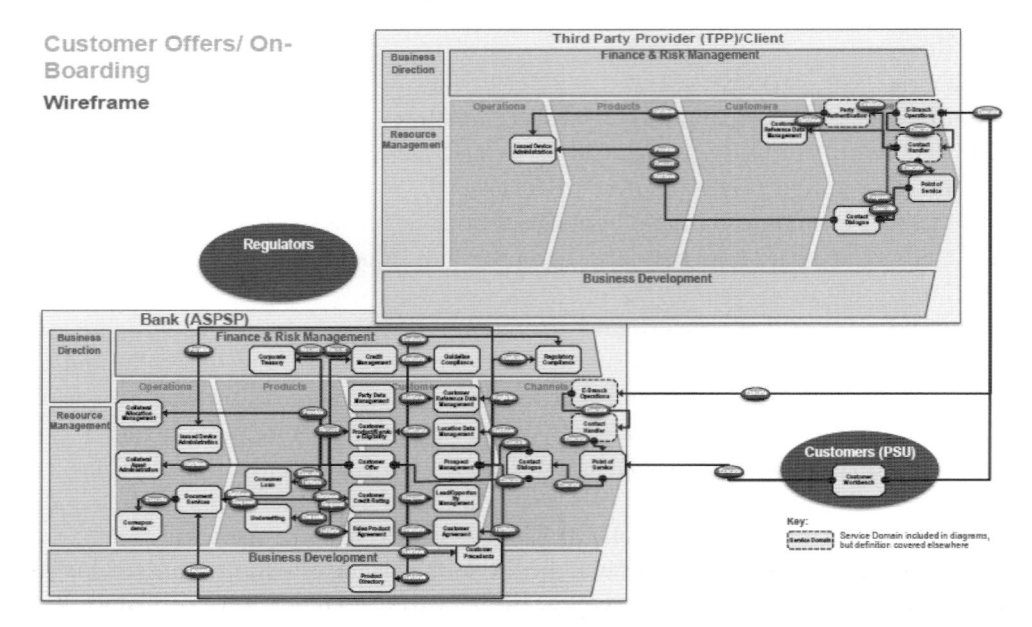

Figure 9-4 Business Scenarios provide business context and information content to the service exchanges

As BIAN is strictly semantic, non-functional requirements for the interactions between Service Domains are not defined. Moreover, non-functional requirements such as interaction style and security, will in most cases depend on the specific circumstances and choices of an individual bank.

Differences in non-functional requirements may require different API implementations, so it is important that a bank elaborates them. The bank can use the Wireframes and Business Scenarios to do this.

9.3.2 Elaborate API specifications
Based on the Wireframe and its Business Scenarios, the Service Connections that are candidates for implementation as application services are highlighted. These Service Connections are linked to the Service Operations that realize them.

BIAN's API Portal provides Semantic API Endpoints for a growing number of Service Operations.

The bank can use these as a starting point for its own application service and API specifications. The Swagger File, generated from the Semantic API, can be used as a "code stub".

A bank's APIs do not need to be as granular as the Semantic API Endpoints. What level of granularity the lowest "API nesting level[112]" refers to, is a choice made by the bank's architects.

If there are no Semantic API Endpoints available yet, the bank can specify its own, based on the Service Operation's Action Term and the Service Domain's Information Profile and Control Record model, as described in Section 2.7. This involves transforming Action Terms into noun-form and http verbs, and refining Service Operation functionality and API content based on Information Profile and Control Record decomposition.

The information exchange, as described in the Endpoint's message, will always need to be detailed, as BIAN only provides generally applicable attributes.

The BIAN BOM (or the tailored Bank BOM) can be used to enrich this information payload. As the bank's BOM will be enriched with detailed information requirements (as in Section 8.4), it is a particularly useful source for extra detail in a "common language".

The information content can also be enriched based on message standards such as IFX or ISO 20022. BIAN is assigning a reference standard to Service Domains, i.e. a standard the Service Domain is maximally aligned to.

> The fit of the Homeland Party Reference data services to the BIAN Frame of Reference is not limited to the level of Service Domain and Service Operation.
>
> M 5
>
> The "Consult Party Data" service can be invoked with parameters that define what entities of the party data-model are requested. Although there is no complete mapping, there is a great similarity between the business functionality of these subservices and the Semantic API Endpoint specifications (Figure 9-5). The "Extract Party Data" application service delivers on a Control Record level, the "Consult" service allows the service user to choose Behavior Qualifiers.

---

112 As stated before, application services and their APIs are "nested" in that they can use other application services as functionality/data providing building blocks and are themselves potential functionality/data providing building blocks.

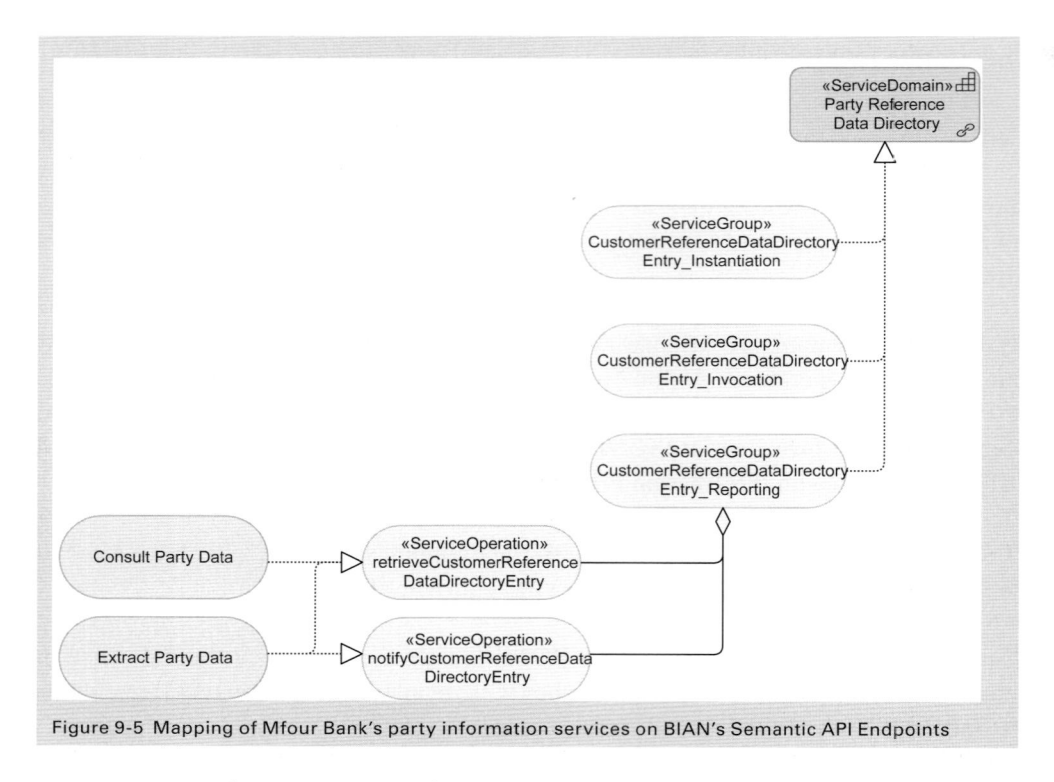

Figure 9-5 Mapping of Mfour Bank's party information services on BIAN's Semantic API Endpoints

Figure 9-6 provides an overview of how a member-bank uses the BIAN Framework to support the development of APIs and govern its API portfolio. The "inner APIs" are BIAN-inspired and provide a stable "common language" layer wrapping the bank's legacy systems. The API Toolkit uses the bank's BOM – a canonical data model based on the BIAN BOM- to populate the information exchanges.

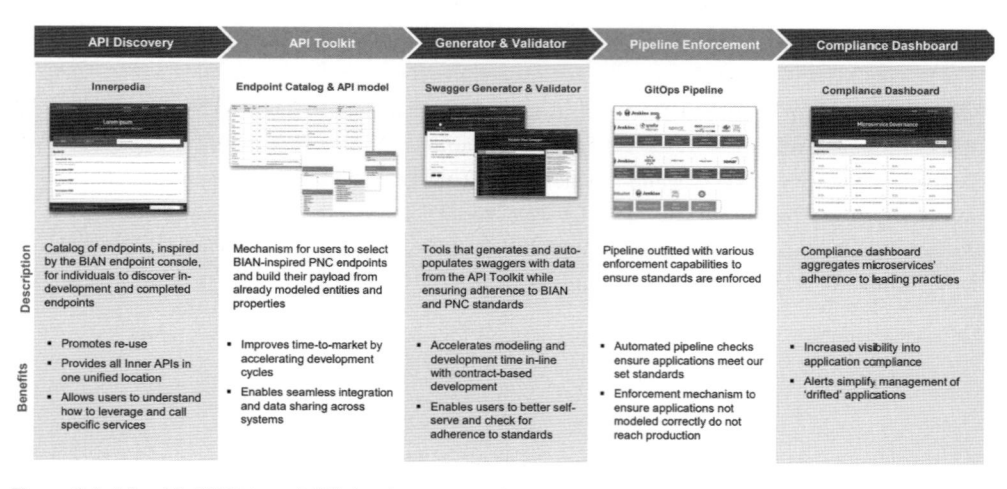

Figure 9-6 A bank's BIAN-based API development and governance toolbox[113]

---

113 PNC Bank 2020.

■ 9.4 TESTIMONIAL

Aleksandar Milosevic, Chief Software Architect at banking software provider Asseco SEE, explained the business benefits of working with BIAN to define standardized APIs in the first edition of this book:

Using standard interfaces to consolidate and modernize a portfolio
As a vendor that grew through acquisitions, we inherited a rich collection of applications that have their application-specific interfaces. Applications that had similar scope ended up having their specific interfaces for essentially the same responsibilities. One of our strategic goals was to cut integration time and cost and, over time, achieve plug-and play interoperability between different applications in our portfolio. Another goal was to hide any application or platform specifics behind the interfaces, so we can gradually modernize individual applications without disturbing the others. Finally, our goal was to enable easier consumption of our interfaces from customers and partners. As we were already using BIAN as a map for application portfolio tracking and optimization, we decided to go a step further with BIAN – to define standard A2A interfaces aligned with BIAN and retire legacy application-specific interfaces.

Asseco reference REST APIs
We formed working groups made up of domain experts and gave them the charter to standardize REST APIs for Asseco SEE banking applications. One of the biggest challenges when defining a large set of consistent APIs is the alignment of their responsibilities and boundaries. Through our experience with BIAN we learned that we could utilize the landscape for functional decomposition of APIs in which each Service Domain becomes a candidate boundary for an API definition. Having clear rules for establishing Service Domains reduced the risk of unclear boundaries and increased the productivity of our working groups.

Since the beginning of 2016, our working groups were able to define an increasing number of APIs and our many product teams implemented those APIs as both consumers and providers. Working on standard APIs had an integral impact on our development organization and helped broaden the perspectives outside organizational and application siloes. APIs and their alignment with BIAN is a hot topic in almost any discussion that we have with banks today.

9.5 TEST YOURSELF QUESTIONS

1. **Which statements are not true?**
   A. Application service centers can be delimited based on Wireframes and Business Scenarios.
   B. Business Scenarios provide the business context for application service interactions.
   C. Non-functional requirements such as security and interaction type are part of the Semantic API specifications.
   D. Non-functional requirements such as security and interaction type need to be taken into account when elaborating the Semantic API specifications into detailed designs for application services.

2. **Which statements do not correctly describe how BIAN can support interoperability within a bank and between banks and partners?**
   A. The information exchange described in the Semantic API specifications is archetypical but needs to be elaborated in more detail by the bank.
   B. Service users that switch between BIAN aligned physical implementations will not need to make any changes to their programming logic.
   C. Working RESTful API implementations can be generated directly from the Semantic API specifications.
   D. BIAN-based application services make sense regardless of the technology architecture style, as they provide stable component and service delimitations.

3. **Which statements are correct?**
   A. An application service catalog should contain all application services approved by the application architects.
   B. An application service catalog should include Open APIs provided by other stakeholders in the Open API economy, as far as they are approved by the architects.
   C. The application service landscape can be overlaid on the Service Domain Frame of Reference to reveal gaps in the application service portfolio.
   D. BIAN-based application services only make sense in an open, web-based environment, not when service exchanges are limited to the bank's own application platform.

PART III

BIAN AND OTHER STANDARDS

What to expect

This part of the book addresses two topics:

It seeks to create awareness with management and architects of the synergy between a framework such as BIAN, that provides enterprise-wide architecture content, and a framework such as TOGAF, that provides a methodology for developing and maintaining the enterprise architecture.

The second topic illustrates how BIAN seeks cooperation with other standards, to benefit from available experience, competence and content.

10 BIAN and TOGAF

This chapter describes the relationship between the BIAN Architecture framework and the TOGAF® Architecture Development Methodology (ADM[114]) and framework.

Both frameworks are complementary. The BIAN Architecture framework provides the common Frame of Reference and the building blocks for a reference architecture, that support the iterative development of a consistent enterprise-wide architecture, as envisioned in the TOGAF Methodology. Applying the TOGAF ADM can enrich the BIAN Architecture, as its results can be fed back to the BIAN community to extend and enrich the BIAN Framework.

This chapter describes how the BIAN deliverables can be used in the different phases of the ADM and how they relate to TOGAF's Architecture Content Framework[115] and Extended Guidance[116].

The figures in this chapter are taken from/based on The Open Group (2018).

■ 10.1   A SHORT INTRODUCTION TO TOGAF

This section focuses on those TOGAF concepts that are discussed in relation to BIAN. It is based on the TOGAF® website (The Open Group (2018)).

The **TOGAF ADM** describes a method for developing and managing the lifecycle of an enterprise architecture. It consists of a series of phases (Figure 10-1).

---

114 An iterative sequence of steps to develop an enterprise-wide architecture.
115 A model of architectural work products intended to drive greater consistency in the outputs that are created when following the Architecture Development Method (The Open Group (2018)).
116 A set of concepts and guidelines to support the establishment of an integrated hierarchy of architectures being developed by teams within larger organizations that operate within an overarching architectural governance model (The Open Group (2018)).

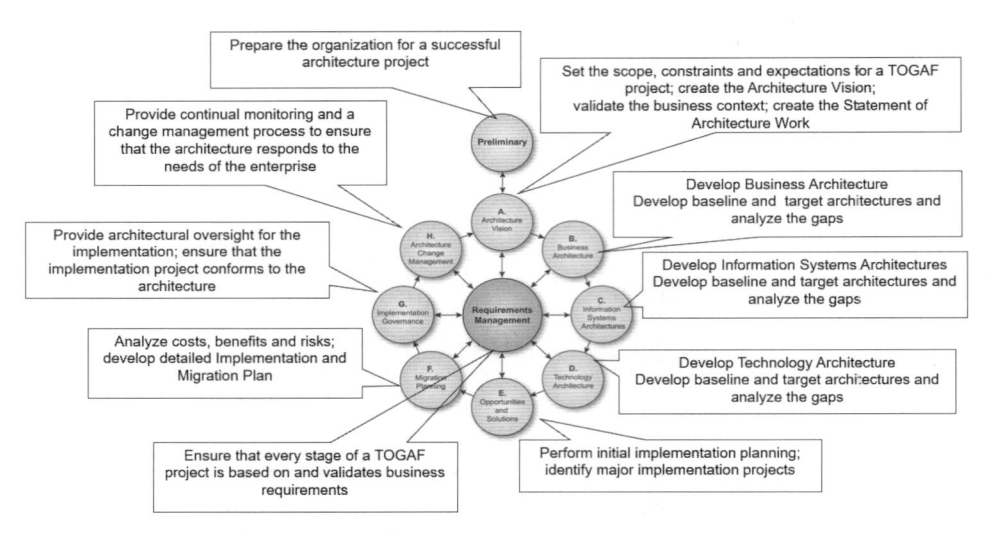

Figure 10-1 The phases of the TOGAF ADM

The **Preliminary Phase** pertains to "the preparation and initiation activities required to meet the business directive for a new enterprise architecture". This includes, amongst other things, the definition of the (enterprise) architecture organization, including the relationships with other frameworks, such as portfolio management, system development... It includes the selection and installation of an (enterprise) architecture toolbox, with instruments such as reference architectures and standards, and documentation tools and guidelines.

Phase A, Architecture Vision, sets the expectations for the architecture project, including defining its scope and sketching the architecture vision, i.e. a high-level view of the expected architecture.

This vision is elaborated further in the three next phases. **Phase B, Business Architecture, Phase C, Information Systems Architecture** and **Phase D, Technology Architecture**. These phases describe the baseline architecture and elaborate the target architecture on a business, application and data, and technology level. For each architecture layer, the gaps between the current landscape (baseline) and the target situation are described.

In **Phase E, Opportunities and Solutions**, the solutions that will implement the target architecture are selected. An architecture roadmap is elaborated, which delivers the target architecture. This typically includes deriving a series of transition architectures that deliver continuous business value. **Phase F, Migration Planning**, elaborates on the implementation projects conceived in Phase E and produces actual project plans. **Phase G, Implementation Governance**, represents the architecture oversight on design and implementation during these projects.

Requirements management is at the heart of the ADM cycle, ensuring all architecture projects are fully informed about all valid(ated) requirements.

Phase H, Architecture Change Management, ensures that the enterprise architecture stays consistent and in tune with the changing demands of the enterprise and the challenges of the environment.

TOGAF elaborates on the use of **architecture patterns**, "a way of putting building blocks into context; for example, to describe a re-usable solution to a problem". Building blocks are what you use: patterns can tell you how you use them, when, why, and what trade-offs you have to make in doing so. Patterns are relevant to steer and support all ADM phases in which the architecture is elaborated (i.e. phases A, B, C and D).

The TOGAF ADM is iterative by principle. Iterations are expected within a phase and between phases. The enterprise architecture is developed and maintained though consecutive ADM cycles.

In a typical enterprise, many architecture descriptions will exist at any point in time. Some architectures will address very specific needs; others will be more general. Some will address detail; some will provide a big picture. To address this complexity, the TOGAF standard uses the concepts of **levels** and the **Enterprise Continuum.** These concepts are tightly linked with organizing actual content in the **Architecture Repository.**

Figure 10-2 depicts the **levels,** as they are named by TOGAF. The enterprise, segment and capability levels are equivalent to the enterprise, domain and system levels as described in Appendix A2.2. Zooming in on architecture from a more coarse-grained to a more detailed level, involves a new ADM cycle. This is another dimension of the iterative approach built into the TOGAF methodology.

While TOGAF's levels depict abstraction in the sense of "coarse grained" versus "detailed", the TOGAF **Enterprise Continuum** (Figure 10-3) depicts abstraction in the sense of "generally applicable" versus "organization specific" and "conceptual" versus "concrete". It provides a mechanism for classifying architecture and solution artefacts on these axes.

The Enterprise Continuum (Figure 10-3) consists of the **Architecture Continuum**, situated on the conceptual level, and the **Solution Continuum**, that is concerned with existing solutions. The Architecture Continuum guides the development and selection of the building blocks for the Solution Continuum. The Organization- Specific Architectures/Solutions can be based on, or make use of, Industry Architectures/Solutions, relevant for the entire industry that the organization belongs to. These in turn can be based on/make use of Common Systems Architectures/Solutions, relevant for all industries. Foundation Architectures/Solutions underpin all of these.

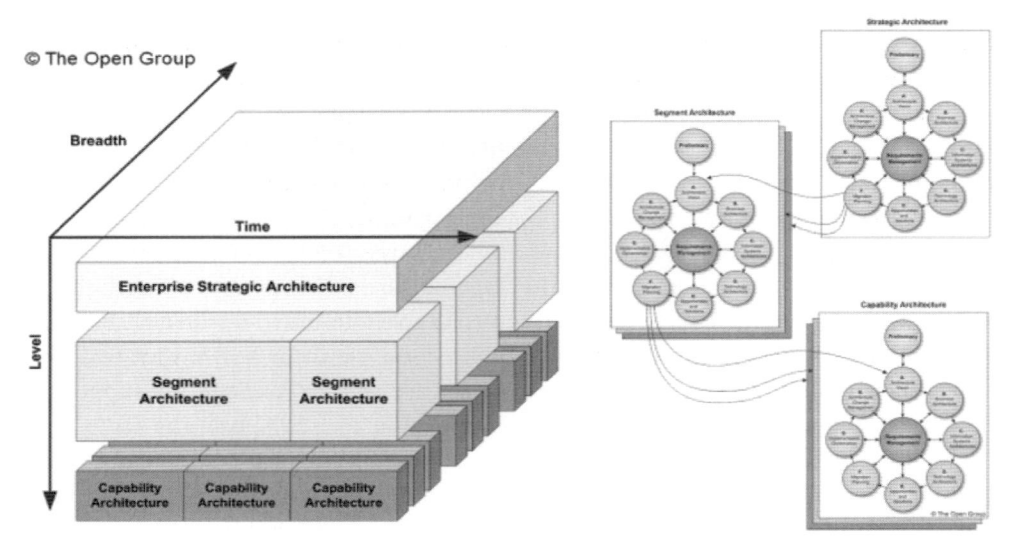

Figure 10-2 TOGAF's "zooming" levels imply an iterative approach to elaborating architectures

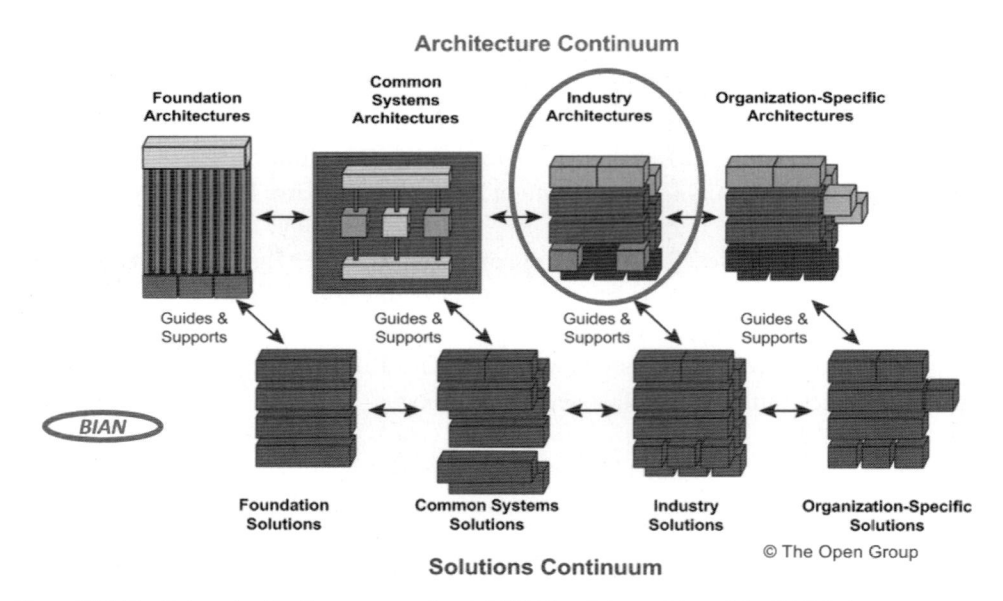

Figure 10-3 The Enterprise Continuum according to TOGAF and the position of the BIAN Reference Architecture for the financial industry

The TOGAF ADM describes the process of developing an enterprise-specific architecture and an enterprise-specific solution(s) which conform to that architecture, by adopting and adapting (where appropriate) generic architectures and solutions (left to right in the continuum classification). In a similar fashion, specific architectures and solutions that prove to be credible and effective will be generalized for re-use (right to left in the continuum classification).

For example: BIAN provides a Financial *Industry* Reference *Architecture* that can be tailored to an Organization-Specific Architecture. It contains building blocks pertaining to security, which is a *"common system"* relevant for all industries.

BIAN guides the development of financial *industry solutions* that can be acquired by financial institutions and implemented as part of the organization-specific solutions landscape. *Common solutions* for security are generally available on the market.

The **Enterprise Repository** contains the information relevant for the architecture capability. Figure 10-4 represents the structure of an Enterprise Repository. It overarches the Solution Repository, the Requirements Repository and the Architecture Repository.

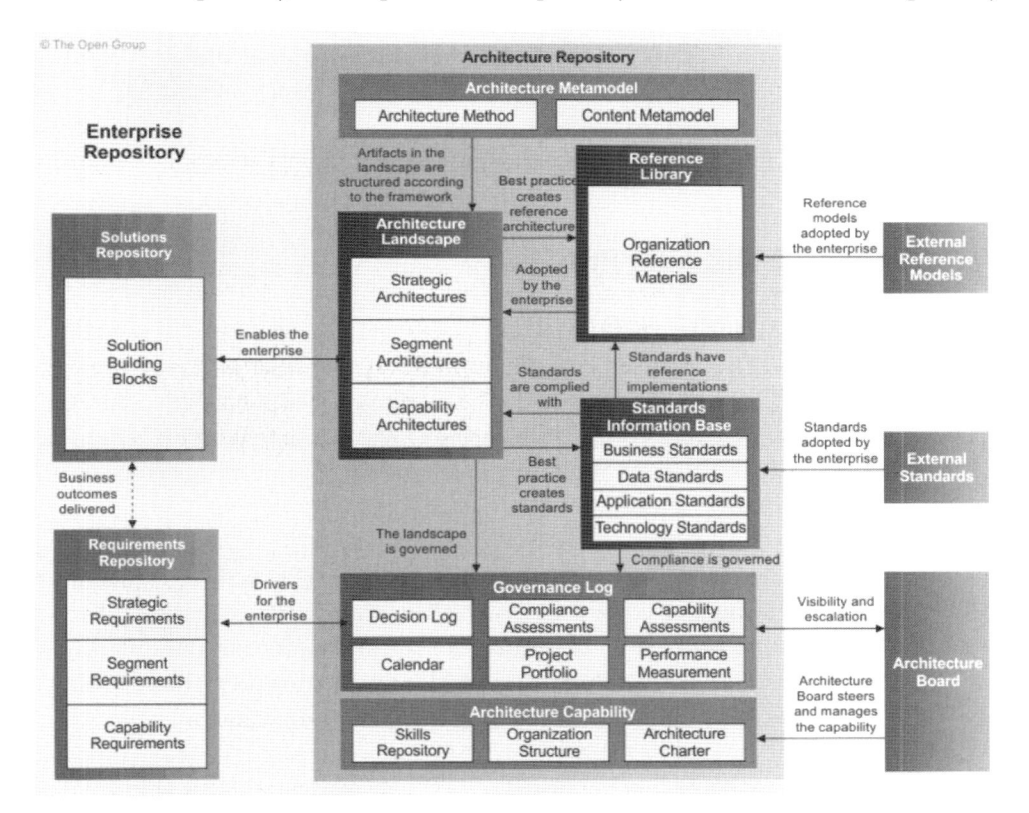

Figure 10-4 The Enterprise Repository according to TOGAF

The **Requirements Repository** is used by the Requirements Management Phase of the Architecture Development Method (ADM) to record and manage all information relevant to the architecture requirements.

The **Solutions Repository** holds the (documentation of) the existing solution building blocks.

At a high level, six classes of architectural information are expected to be held within an **Architecture Repository**:
- The "Architecture Metamodel" describes the organizationally-tailored application of an architecture framework, including a method for architecture development and a metamodel for architecture content.
- The "Architecture Capability" defines the parameters, structures and processes that support governance of the Architecture Repository.
- The "Architecture Landscape" presents an architectural representation of assets in use, or planned, by the enterprise at particular points in time.
- The "Standards Information Base" captures the standards with which new architectures must comply, which may include industry standards, selected products and services from suppliers, or shared services already deployed within the organization.
- The "Reference Library" provides guidelines, templates, patterns and other forms of reference material that can be leveraged in order to accelerate the creation of new architectures for the enterprise.
- The "Governance Log" provides a record of governance activity across the enterprise.

10.2 BIAN AND THE ADM PHASES

10.2.1 Preliminary phase

The existence of the BIAN network contributes to the awareness and acceptance of an architectural approach and, in that sense, can be used to create sponsorship. The BIAN Framework can contribute to Preliminary phase by providing content for the "enterprise architecture toolbox", as well as by providing an organizing Frame of Reference for the Enterprise Repository (Figure 10-5).

BIAN provides a **Financial Industry Reference Architecture**. Its Service Domains are the architecture building blocks for any financial institution. By exchanging Service Operations (made more concrete in the Semantic API Endpoints and their messages), orchestrations of these Service Domains can provide any functionality. The BIAN BOM provides a Reference Information Architecture model for the financial industry.

BIAN brings along architecture **principles** (such as service orientation and information guardianship) and generic **patterns** (documented as Business Scenarios).

Each financial institution can either use BIAN as such, or tailor it into an organization-specific **Frame of Reference.** Service Domains as elemental conceptual functionality building blocks, Service Operations as elemental services and Business Objects as elemental information building blocks, can be used as a uniform conceptual overlay for architecture or solution artefacts, in baseline as well as target architecture.

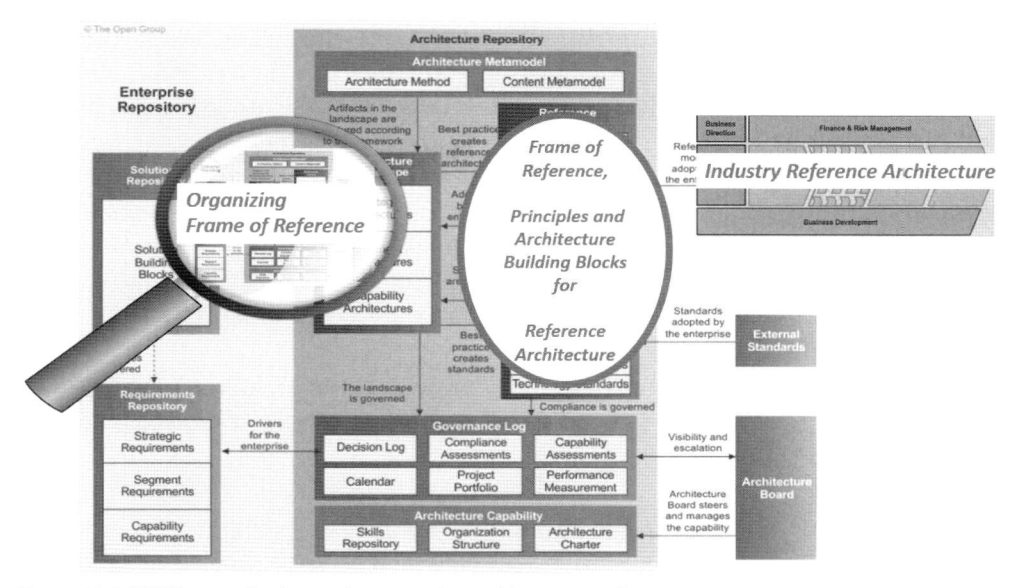

Figure 10-5 BIAN's contribution to the enterprise architecture toolbox

These conceptual **architecture building blocks** can be combined in organization-specific conceptual **architecture patterns** for business and information system architecture.

This BIAN(-based) Frame of Reference can be exploited to **organize** the **Architecture Repository** and optimize the accessibility of the **Requirement** and **Solution Repository**.

The conceptual building blocks of the BIAN-based Frame of Reference can be used to create the conceptual layer of the organization's **Reference Architecture**, describing business and application patterns.

The BIAN Framework can provide a contribution to the enterprise architecture organization. The **interaction with "other frameworks"**, such as strategy, portfolio management and performance management, is facilitated by the common Frame of Reference which BIAN provides. It facilitates information exchange and cooperation by providing a common language and common documentation anchor points. (See also Chapter 5.)

The BIAN Service Landscape, or a tailored version thereof, can support **enterprise architecture governance** by suggesting the delimitation of responsibility areas (Segments/Domains).

10.2.2 Phase A: Architecture vision
The **scope** of the architecture project can be described in terms of the involved Service Domains and Business Scenarios.

The common Frame of Reference provided by the Service Domains and Business Objects, facilitates the identification of **stakeholders** of the architecture project. It facilitates the detection of **related** architecture **project**s.

The Service Domains and Business Objects can be used as building blocks to express the target **architecture vision** on a business and application level. The common Frame of Reference facilitates the detection of available **solutions** within and without the organization, both on a business level and an application level.

10.2.3 Phase B: Business architecture
The **target business architecture** can be expressed as an orchestration of Service Domains. The Business Scenarios provided by BIAN can serve as a starting point and be adapted based on the organization's rules and practices.

The **business requirements** will be documented per business component, i.e. Service Domain. The Requirement Repository will be consulted to detect requirements waiting for realization. The access is facilitated by the common BIAN-based Frame of Reference.

The **baseline business architecture** can be overlaid by the BIAN-based Frame of Reference. This facilitates the detection of available **solutions** as well as the detection of gaps. These **gaps** will be documented per business component – i.e. Service Domain.

The information architecture model and the information quality requirements can be gathered as a sum of the involved Service Domain's Control Record Models and expressed as a view on the BIAN BOM (or its tailored equivalent).

This exercise can result in the detection of new business components and Business Objects. These should be fed into the organization's reference framework. This might require the execution of "Phase H, Architecture change Management".

10.2.4 Phase C: Information systems srchitecture
The **target application architecture** will be an orchestration of application components, exchanging application services. The Service Domains, used as business components in the target business architecture, provide a stable delimitation for application components. Service Operations (especially decomposed to an elemental level as in the API Endpoints) provide stable, elemental building blocks for application services.

The **Requirement Repository** will be completed according to the Service Domain structure. Its consultation to detect requirements awaiting realization will be facilitated by the common BIAN-based Frame of Reference.

The **baseline application architecture** can be overlaid by the BIAN-based Frame of Reference. This facilitates the detection of available **solution**s as well as the detection of gaps. These **gaps** will be documented per Service Domain.

The BIAN-based structure of the target architecture, with stable, elemental and standardized Service Connections between components, facilitates solutions involving the bank, business partners and software vendors.

The Control Record provides the Service Domain's "CUD[117]" relationship with the information requirements. This supports the elaboration of the **target data architecture**. The **baseline data architecture** will be overlaid on the BIAN BOM (or Bank BOM). This facilitates the detection of available solutions as well as the detection of gaps. These gaps will be documented according to the BIAN-based Frame of Reference for information.

10.2.5 Phase D: Technology architecture
BIAN has no deliverables that support the "technology architecture" directly. The (indirect) mapping of Service Domains on the technology resources, can help in detecting available technology for the target architecture.

10.2.6 Phase E: Opportunities and solutions
BIAN has no deliverables that support "opportunities and solutions" as such. The common Frame of Reference BIAN offers does, however, have an added value for this phase.

The structuring of the target architecture and requirements according to the Frame of Reference provided by BIAN, facilitates the selection of solutions offered by service providers or software vendors – or available inhouse. The BIAN architecture is created in cooperation with software vendors serving the financial industry. The compliance of products with the BIAN Service Landscape and Business Scenarios using BIAN building blocks, will increase the seamless integration of the software products in an existing BIAN-compliant target business and application architecture, and thus reduce integration costs.

The structuring of the existing architecture landscape according to the BIAN-based Frame of Reference facilitates the search for reusable elements.

The BIAN-based Frame of Reference, used to structure all architecture viewpoints as well as project scope, facilitates impact analysis. The elaboration of a consistent project portfolio and migration plan is facilitated.

---
117 Create, Update, Delete.

10.2.7 Phase F: Migration planning

BIAN has no deliverables that support "migration planning" as such. The advantages of the common Frame of Reference provided by BIAN for the project portfolio, as described for Phase E, also apply to the elaboration of the migration scenario and project plans in this phase.

10.2.8 Phase G: Implementation governance

BIAN has no deliverables that support "implementation governance" as such. However, the Swagger Files that can be generated from the Semantic APIs can speed-up the development of application services, which is an incentive for compliance with the BIAN-based enterprise reference architecture.

10.2.9 Phase H: Architecture change management

BIAN has no deliverables that support "architecture change management" as such.

The tracking of changes to the BIAN Framework should be incorporated in architecture change management.

10.2.10 Requirements management

BIAN has no deliverables that support "requirements management" as such, but does suggest to structure the documentation of requirements according to the elemental, stable building block structure offered by its Service Domains, Service Operations and Business Objects.

■ 10.3 TEST YOURSELF QUESTIONS

1. Which of these statements do not describe how BIAN can contribute to the organization and exploitation of the Enterprise Repository?
    A. The Service Landscape and its Service Domains can be used as a Frame of Reference to organize the Enterprise Repository.
    B. The BIAN BOM and its Business Objects can be used as a Frame of Reference to organize the Architecture Repository.
    C. The Business Scenarios can be used as a Frame of Reference to organize the Architecture Repository.
    D. The Service Landscape and its Service Domains can be used as a Frame of Reference to organize the Requirements Repository.

2. Which of these statements correctly describe the role that BIAN can play in the TOGAF framework?
    A. The BIAN Architecture is a reference architecture for the financial industry.
    B. The BIAN Architecture is an organization-specific architecture.

C. The BIAN Architecture is a common systems architecture aimed at security for financial institutions.
D. The BIAN Architecture contains elements of a common system architecture for security.

3. **Which of these statements do not describe how BIAN can be used in the TOGAF ADM?**
   A. The BIAN Service Landscape and its Service Domains can be used to define the target technology architecture.
   B. The BIAN Service Landscape and its Service Domains can be used to define the target business architecture.
   C. The BIAN Business Scenarios can be used to define the scope of an architecture project.
   D. The BIAN Service Landscape and its Service Domains can be used to define the scope of an architecture project.

11 Alignment with other standard bodies

In developing the BIAN standard, alignment with other industry standards is optimized. BIAN cooperates with other standard bodies.

■ 11.1 ISO 20022

The ISO 20022 Business Model is a part of the ISO 20022 standard, an ISO standard for electronic data interchange between financial institutions. The ISO 20022 Business Model is used to derive the data elements used in ISO 20022 message definitions (the ISO 20022 Message Concepts), thereby ensuring a common understanding across all messages used to support the various business domains.

The BIAN Metamodel has been based on the ISO messaging standards from the onset. The BIAN Association continues to work closely with the relevant ISO working groups to ensure that the standards remain aligned and that any content developed by the BIAN Association builds on ISO content and similarly that any new content the BIAN Association develops is provided for consideration by the ISO operation when appropriate.

BIAN has developed a mapping between the Business Objects and attributes of the BIAN BOM and the business components and elements of the ISO 20022 Business Model. This is called the "ISO 20022 Light Mapping". These mappings are published as tables in Excel files on the BIAN Wiki page.

The BIAN Association documents potential additions to the ISO model for their consideration in future versions of ISO 20022.

The information exchange between BIAN and ISO 20022 is an important factor in view of the newest phase of the ISO 20022 project. This involves the major standardization bodies in the financial services sector working on mapping their standards to the ISO 20022 Business Model. When the mappings of the major standards ISO 20022 are in place, they will be mapping to a model that is well aligned with the BIAN Architecture. This will make it easier for the BIAN Association members (and other BIAN users) when they work on projects that use BIAN in combination with other financial services standards.

■ 11.2   OMG & EDM COUNCIL

The Financial Industry Business Ontology (FIBO) is a joint effort between the EDM Council[118] and the Object Management Group. It can be seen as an industry thesaurus. It defines financial services concepts and allows for these definitions to be specific to a particular business context, maintaining synonyms and homonyms in addition to the conceptual definitions. As BIAN builds out its own Business Object Model, reference is made to the content of FIBO and the terms are used where possible. The content development of FIBO is at an early stage and so the precise mechanics of this collaboration are likely to evolve.

■ 11.3   THE BUSINESS ARCHITECTURE GUILD®

The Business Architecture Guild® is a community of business architects who have come together to build and expand their profession. The Guild is an international, diverse community of business architecture practitioners, beneficiaries and interested parties. The Guild is also a collaborative collective where individuals can learn with and from their peers, explore and develop new ideas and further the practice and discipline of business architecture.

Whilst developing BIAN's Business Capability model, the Guild discovered that there was an overlap in participation of the BIAN Working Group members and the Architecture Guild membership. Based on this knowledge, both organizations granted each other access to their deliverables so that best practices can be shared.

■ 11.4   TEST YOURSELF QUESTIONS

1. Is the following statement concerning the BIAN standards right or wrong?

BIAN wants to provide standards for the financial industry that are fully independent of existing standards.

---

118 The EDM Council is the Global Association created to elevate the practice of Data Management as a business and operational priority.

APPENDICES

Appendix 1: BIAN adoption journey

BIAN provides a typical adoption roadmap that can be used as a guidance in the adoption journey of BIAN in a financial institution. This journey is animated on the BIAN website.

BIAN defines six adoption stages. In stage 1, BIAN is evaluated and compared with other frameworks. As interest grows, stage 2 commences: a BIAN pilot is prepared. When the pilot's scope and goals are well defined and key stakeholders are committed and involved, the pilot can be executed (stage 3). During the pilot, expectations are validated. A decision to rollout BIAN (or not) concludes this stage. Stage 4 introduces BIAN in the organization. From now on (stage 5) BIAN will be used as a means to support the creation and evolution of an organization-specific banking architecture and architecture practice. The new architecture is monitored by assessing the key indicators that enable the follow-up of the realization of the BIAN value proposition. A continuous improvement cycle keeps the process running (stage 6).

Stage 1: Evaluate BIAN
Banking professionals and/or ICT professionals feel a need for guidance in getting a grip on the rapidly evolving and complex environment of the financial industry. Banking Reference Architecture models can help. So, is BIAN fit for this purpose?

During the evaluation process a number of industry models have been assessed. Maybe it is your first impression that your organization needs BIAN. How will BIAN strengthen your value proposition? For example, will it provide standards-based integration, low vendor lock-in, application portfolio rationalization and monitoring across country entities, compatibility with other standards etc.?

Typical steps in this first stage of the adoption process are:
- Assess your needs. Why does your organization need a banking model?
- Conduct a GAP analysis. Review industry models and perform a GAP evaluation against the use of each of the candidates.

- Determine the value proposition. What is BIAN's value proposition to your organization?

If BIAN is the reference architecture of your choice, then take the next step and build a pilot case to test the value it could potentially deliver.

If there is no BIAN interest, the journey stops here.

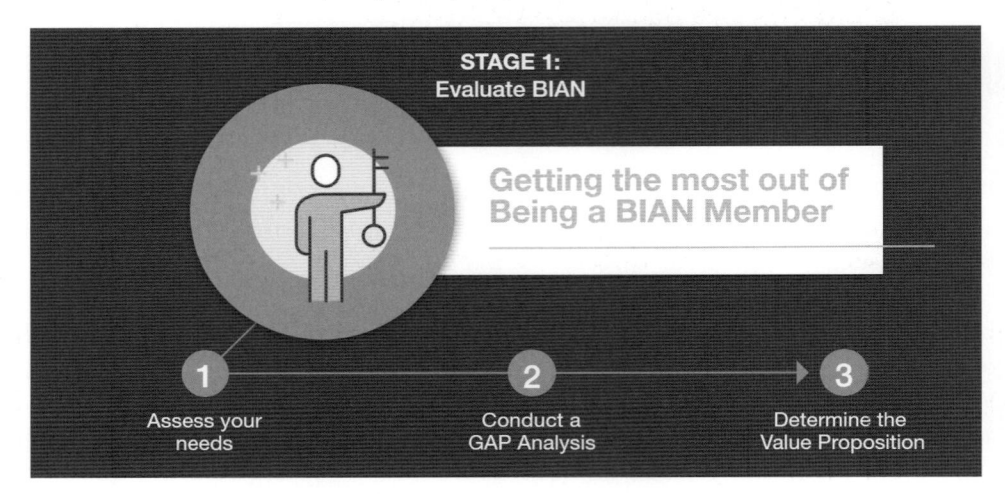

Figure A1-1 Stage 1 of a BIAN adoption roadmap: Evaluate BIAN

Stage 2: Build a business case for a BIAN pilot
When your organization has an interest in BIAN, then build a pilot case first.

Typical activities performed in this second step of the adoption process are:
- Train/educate a key-team in BIAN;
- Identify the key opportunities for the introduction of BIAN;
- Create a proof of concept;
- Get a go/no-go for the proof of concept.

This stage in the journey answers the basic questions such as:
- How will BIAN support your goals?
- Have you educated your key-team on BIAN's concepts?
- What part of the organization will you target with BIAN? Who are the key people to involve?
- Have you identified your main opportunities?
- Have you identified your pilot candidates?
- Have you received the go/no-go for your chosen pilot?

This second stage will result in a go/no-go decision for a BIAN pilot. In case of a "go" for the BIAN pilot, the journey continues; in case of a "no-go" the journey ends.

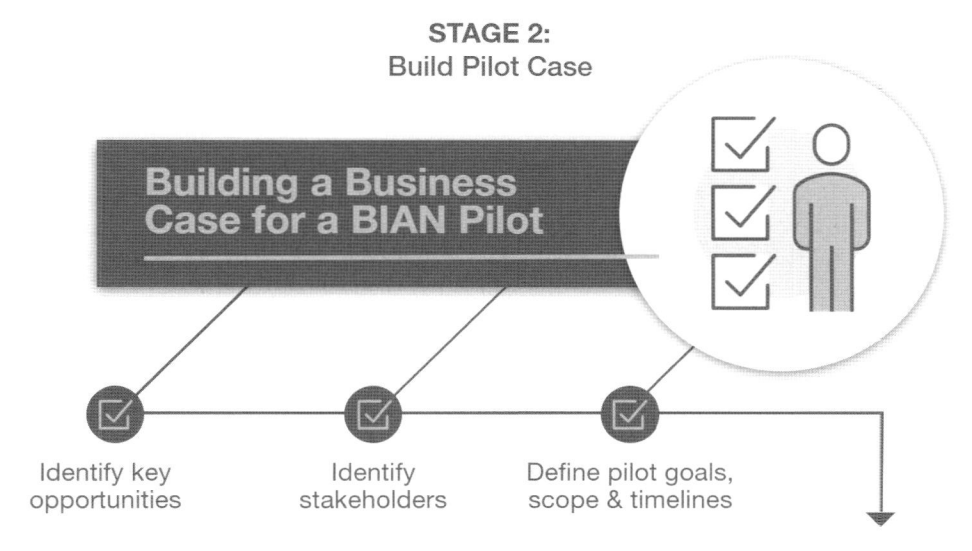

Figure A1-2 Stage 2 of a BIAN adoption roadmap: Build pilot case

Stage 3: Pilot BIAN
When a "go" for the BIAN pilot is received, stage 3 in the BIAN adoption journey can start. Develop and execute the BIAN pilot by:
- Preparing the pilot project and kick-off;
- Executing the pilot project by applying the BIAN concepts to the scoped areas of the business;
- Making recommendations in the light of a go/no-go for a BIAN roll-out;
- Receiving a go/no-go decision for a BIAN rollout.

This stage in the journey answers basic questions such as:
- Have you identified your pilot goals (SMART[119])?
- Have you identified your resources and training requirements?
- Have you selected the projects to be included in your pilot?
- Have you executed your pilot?
- Have you summarized your findings and recommendations in view of a go/no-go decision?

This third stage will result in a go/no-go for a BIAN rollout. In case of a "go" for the BIAN rollout, the journey continues; in case of a "-go", the journey ends.

---
119 Specific, Measurable, Achievable, Relevant, Time-bounded.

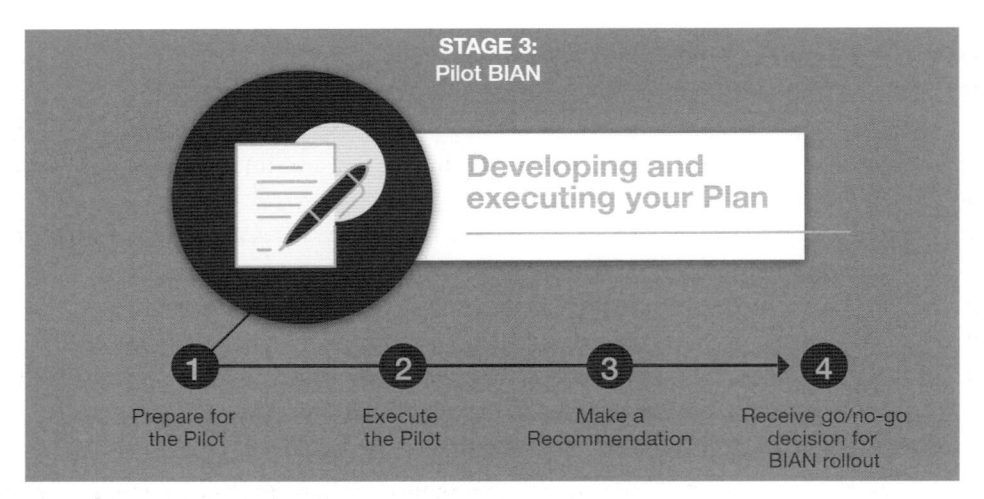

Figure A1-3 Stage 3 of a BIAN adoption roadmap: Pilot BIAN

Stage 4: Adopt BIAN

When a "go" for the BIAN rollout is received, stage 4 in the BIAN adoption journey can commence. BIAN can be adopted across the organization by:

- Defining guiding principles for the use of BIAN across the organization (e.g. aligning BIAN with BIAN's annual release schedule, the operating model for BIAN usage, defining metrics etc.).
- Promoting the usage of BIAN to ensure a successful adoption. This can be done by ongoing training, participation in BIAN working groups, communicating success stories etc.
- Training the BIAN workforce. Establish your BIAN champions by training key-stakeholders.
- Evaluating the adoption approach. For instance, roll-out BIAN for the enterprise versus roll-out by line of business, for all products versus specific products, globally versus regionally.

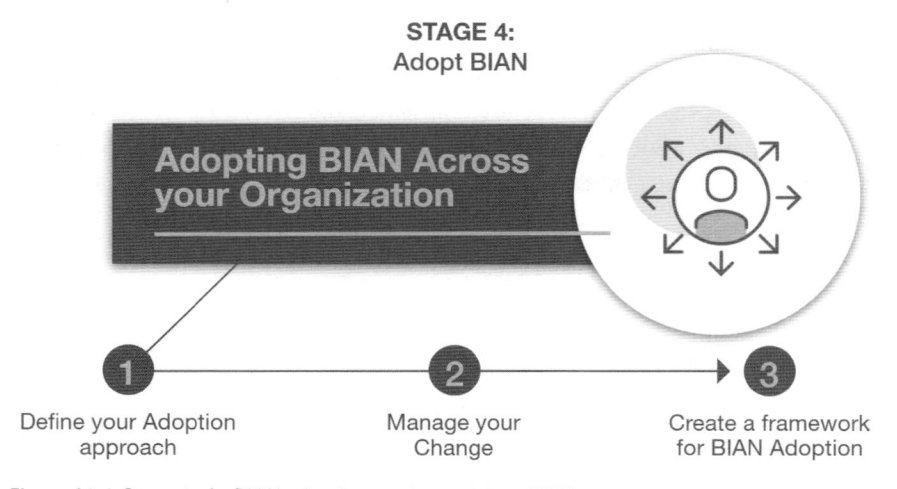

Figure A1-4 Stage 4 of a BIAN adoption roadmap: Adopt BIAN

Stage 5: Evolve your architecture practice using BIAN

In this stage of the adoption process it is time to start realizing the benefits. Your organization has moved to the level of adoption where an organization-specific architecture according to BIAN can gradually be defined and improved. Key activities here are:

- Design principles are defined, using BIAN as a reference is mandatory and designs are created conformingly;
- Define and introduce typical design patterns;
- Identify and prioritize domains for implementation;
- By continuously measuring and evaluating the value added by BIAN, a continuous improvement cycle of BIAN usage in the bank's architecture and architecture practice is made possible.

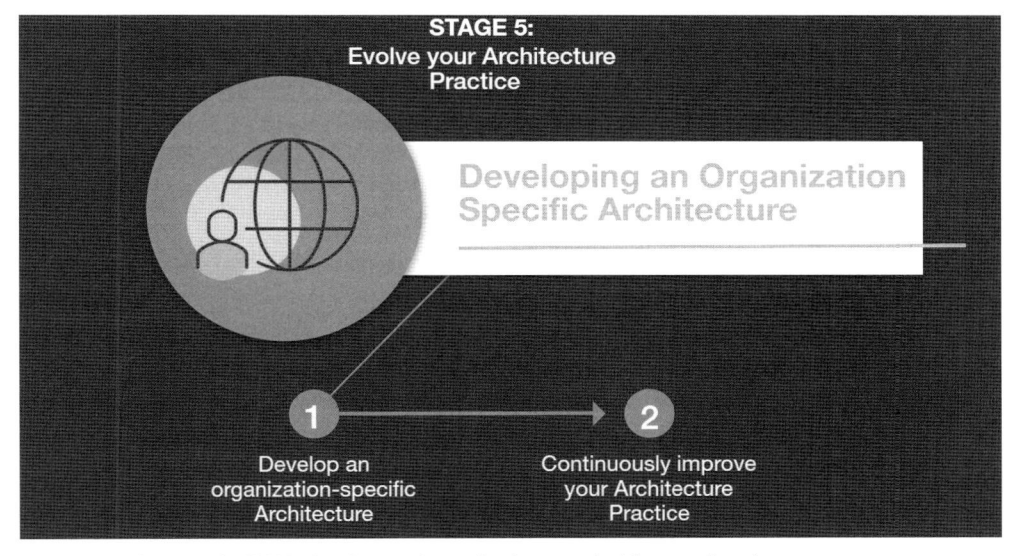

Figure A1-5 Stage 5 of a BIAN adoption roadmap: Evolve your Architecture Practice

Stage 6: Realize the benefits of using BIAN

As implementation progresses, a continuous monitoring of the anticipated benefits will inform the change process with a view to extending and improving the usage of BIAN across the organization. A new cycle can start by selecting another key-opportunity or by identifying an improvement initiative.

Appendix 2: Terminology and concepts

■ A2.1 ARCHITECTURE LAYERS AND ASPECTS[120]

A bank can be seen as an ecosystem consisting of three different layers (Figure A2-1). The value to customers and other stakeholders is delivered by the "**business layer**", based on the support by the "**application layer**", that functions thanks to the "**technology layer**".

Business Layer
Grasps the business direction and the business capabilities, including people, business concepts, processes, and business technology.

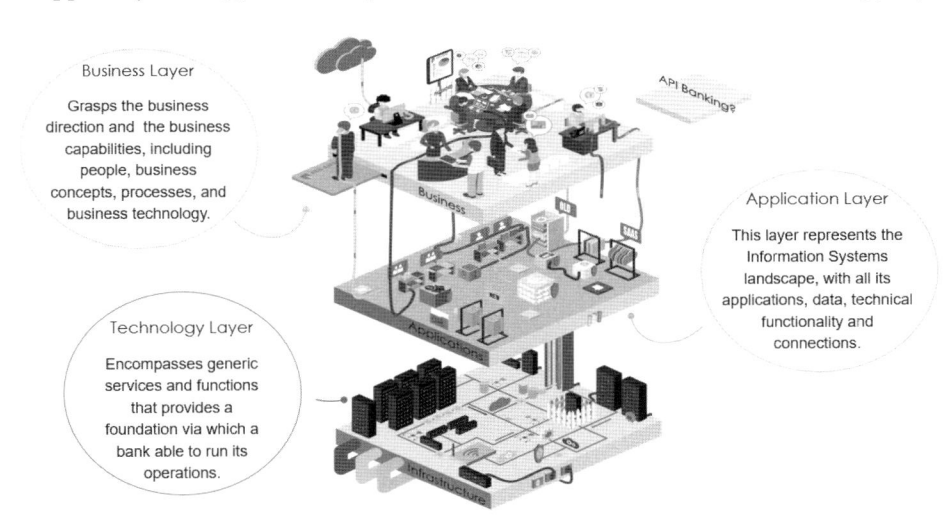

Application Layer
This layer represents the Information Systems landscape, with all its applications, data, technical functionality and connections.

Technology Layer
Encompasses generic services and functions that provides a foundation via which a bank able to run its operations.

Figure A2-1 A bank consists of three different layers

The "business architecture landscape" depicts how the business layer works, by modeling the structure and-relationships between "business landscape elements" (such as business functions, processes, services, business objects and actors. . .).

The "application architecture landscape" depicts how the application layer works through a model of "application landscape elements" (such as application components and their functions, application services, data stores…).

---
120 Inspired by ArchiMate®

The "technology architecture landscape" depicts the structure and-relationships of "technology landscape elements" (such as devices, networks, middleware and the actual programming code and physical data storage).

The enterprise strategy, as expressed in the **"strategy layer"**, defines the way a bank seeks to meet its stakeholders concerns. It defines the business capabilities through which the bank looks to create its value and corresponding strategic *goals* and *requirements*.

The operations of the bank need to be "architected" accordingly. The architecture landscapes on the different layers should be organized according to business, application and technology requirements that trickle down from the strategic level to an ever more detailed level.

To evaluate and ensure the fit of the operations to the goals and requirements, they are monitored by *assessments*.

Goals, requirements and assessments represent the **"motivation aspect"** of a bank. This can relate to any layer.

As goals and requirements evolve and assessments reveal possible shortcomings, *change* may be required. A bank's investment and change portfolio ensures the desired, planned and ongoing "**implementation and migration**", organized through change initiatives, such as projects and programs. The "implementation and migration aspect" can also relate to any layer.

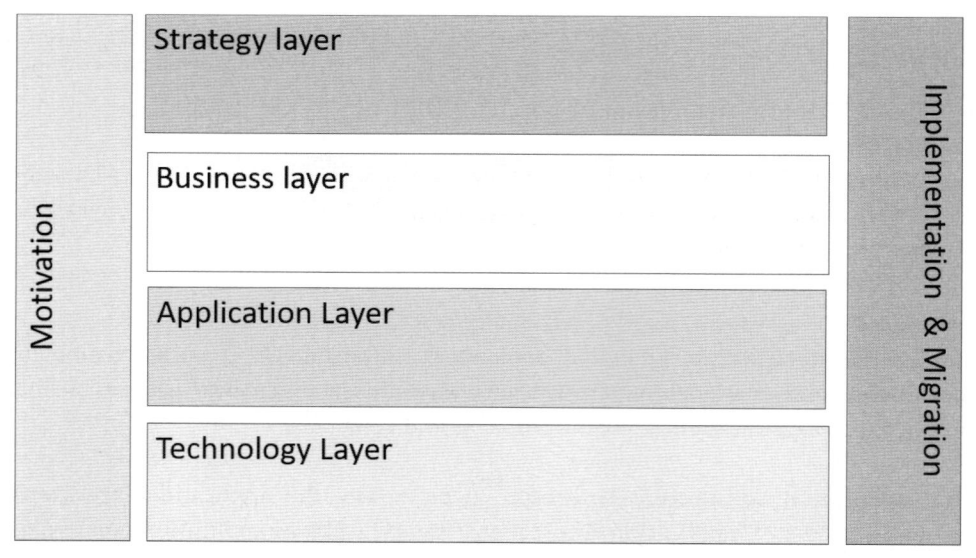

Figure A2-2 Viewpoints on a bank: Architecture layers and aspects

A2.2 ZOOMING LEVELS FOR ARCHITECTURE

Architecture with a broad scope, overarching all (the core-activities of) an organization, becomes more and more relevant. Architects, however, are faced with the dilemma of scope versus time. The wider the scope, the higher the reliability of the results and the stronger the impact on the implemented solutions. But also, the wider the scope, the higher the effort and throughput time[121] and the later the benefit is delivered. The answer to this dilemma is to zoom.

The highest level of abstraction/lowest level of detail, but the widest scope, is the **enterprise** level. A comprehensive, but extremely high-level enterprise[122] architecture spans the entire area deemed relevant for the architecture.

The overarching nature of an enterprise architecture should guarantee cohesion, interoperability and manoeuvrability on an enterprise scale.

The prefix "enterprise" can be used for business, application and technology architecture, but also for any other discipline such as performance management and change portfolio management.

The enterprise architecture scope is than divided – based on architectural considerations - into architecture **domains**[123]. Each domain architecture zooms in on a certain part of the enterprise architecture and elaborates it further, on a more detailed scale. This can be done piece by piece, depending on urgency or opportunity.

Finally, "**systems**" architectures can be elaborated on a scale that is sufficiently detailed to steer and support the design and implementation of the system[124]. This is obviously also driven by urgency or opportunity.

The levels of enterprise, domain and system are used as an indication of the need to zoom in when architecting – or indeed managing in general. It is by no means mandatory to distinguish three levels.

---

121 Paralysis by analysis can lead to the phenomenon where by the time the architecture is ready the business circumstances have changed, the opportunity has long gone, and the temporary solutions have become final.
122 Given the term "enterprise", one would expect this to be the entire organization (bank or banking group). This is not necessarily so. It is not necessary to deploy an enterprise architecture, together with the BIAN Framework that supports it, for an entire bank or banking group in order to benefit from its advantages. However, the wider the scope of an enterprise architecture, the greater the benefits in terms of (for example) synergy and reuse, information quality, manoeuvrability...
123 A domain is a logical grouping of systems. Its architecture needs to be sufficiently detailed to structure and steer the systems architecture within the domain.
124 A "system" is an organized collection of parts (or subsystems) that are highly integrated to accomplish an overall goal.

The "zoom levels" are relevant for business, application or technology architecture and can be used as a prefix for any of these architecture layers. They are also relevant for management processes related to the "motivation" view and to the "implementation and migration" view.

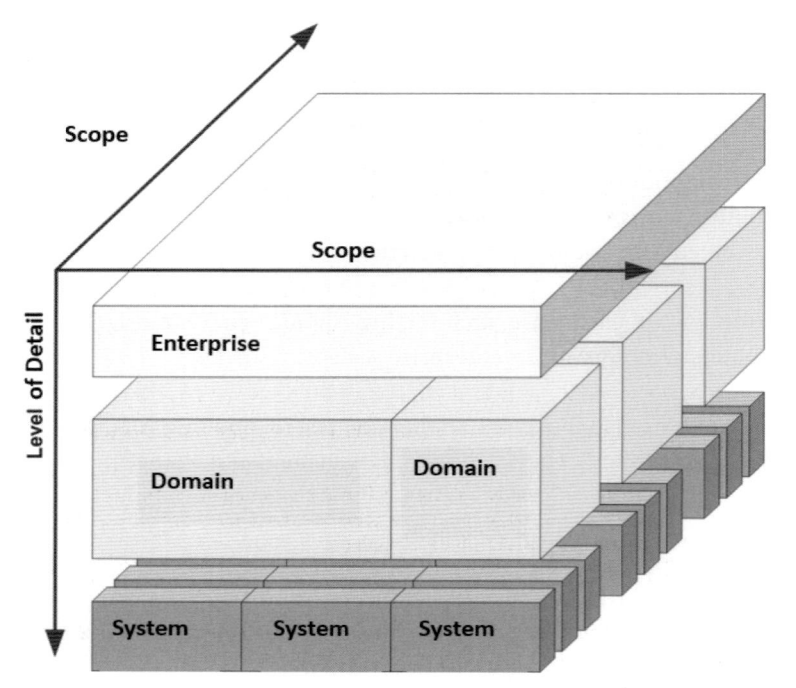

Figure A2-3 Zooming levels: divide and conquer a wide scope and a great complexity[125]

■ A2.3 TERMS AND ABBREVIATIONS

Term/abbreviation	Explanation
API	Application Programming Interface.
	A series of definitions that allow applications to communicate (freely after Wikipedia). An API provides access to an application service.
Application architecture	Architecture of the application layer.
Application (architecture) landscape	The structure and relationships of the components, part of the application layer, that are implemented (as-is) or required to be implemented (to-be).
Application layer	Application point of view on a bank's ecosystem.
	The application layer supports the business layer with application services which are realized by (software) application components.

---

125 Inspired by BIAN Architecture Working Group 2017b.

Term/abbreviation	Explanation
Application platform	A group of applications, able to cooperate technically and managed as a whole.
Application service landscape	The applications and the application services they provide, and the "nesting" relationships between application services.
Architectural artefact	A part of an architecture description. Architectural artefacts are made from model elements of an architecture model and are created in order to describe a system, domain or state of the enterprise for stakeholders.
Architecture	The structure of the components of a system, their inter-relationships, and the principles and guidelines governing their design and evolution over time. The structure of components and their inter-relationships is described in an architecture model (The Open Group (2019)).
Architecture repository	A system in which architecture documentation is stored and made available.
Assessment	Analysis of the state of affairs with respect to certain criteria.
"Bank on a page"	Representation of the enterprise blueprint for one entity, presented on one page.
BIAN Framework	The entire "toolbox" offered by BIAN, consisting of, amongst other things, the BIAN Architecture, tools to exploit it, best practices and approaches, books, guides, trainings…
Blueprint	The collection of activities required to achieve the goals of an entity. In our context, the activities are expressed in Service Domains. The enumeration and its representation as "bank on a page" are both called "blueprints".
Building block	A building block represents a (potentially re-usable) component of business or ICT, that can be combined with other building blocks to deliver architectures and solutions.
Business (architecture) landscape	The structure-and-relationships of the components part of the business layer, that are implemented (as-is) or required to be implemented (to-be).
Business capability	A capability that represents the abilities and capacities of an organization to create the outcomes it requires to create value in its ecosystem.
Business layer	Business point of view on a bank's ecosystem. The *Business* layer offers products and services to external customers, which are realized in the organization by business processes performed by business actors and roles.
Canonical Data Model	A data model used to communicate between different data models and to integrate them. It is a "superset", the data equivalent of the Canonical Information Model.

Term/abbreviation	Explanation
Canonical Information Model	An information model used to communicate between different speech communities. It is a "superset" of their views on information. Each view on reality can have its own model structure, own naming, definitions and notations. The Canonical Model is used to translate the one to the other.
Change initiative	Initiative to change something from an "as-is" state into a "desired to-be" state. Change initiatives can be small and informally organized, they can be organized as a project or combined in a program.
Configuration information	Information describing how application level and technology level elements are interrelated.
CRM	Customer Relationship Management.
CRUD	Create Read Update Delete (actions on information and data).
Data	Facts that are used and stored on an ICT platform, that can be used by applications. Information, used by a business, is stored on and handled by a logical application platform as data. When presented to a business, it becomes information.
Data integration	The art of ensuring data is available in the application landscape where it is needed, with the required quality.
Data store	A logical unit for storing and retrieving data, accessible for applications. Any medium and any method for storing and retrieving can be used to "store" and "retrieve" the data.
Diagram	A graphical representation of a (part of a) model. Diagrams are created to highlight points of view.
Domain architecture	An architecture on an intermediate level, overarching a logical grouping of systems.
Enterprise	A collection of organizations that have a common set of goals. In the context of this book, it can be a banking group, a bank or a business line, and can include partners. The enterprise defines the scope for what is deemed relevant for the highest, overarching level of architecture.
(BIAN-based) Frame of Reference	The set of reference or anchor points offered by BIAN, that enable a unique identification, understanding and positioning of the elements of a bank. We discern three viewpoints that provide a Frame of Reference: Service Domains, Business Objects and Service Operations.
Functional requirements	Requirements relating to business functionality.
Heatmap	A visual representation of information, using colors. Each color represents a different value.

Appendix 2:   Terminology and concepts

Term/abbreviation	Explanation
ICT	Information and Communication Technology. Relates to the organization responsible for, and the elements of, the application and technology layers.
Industry reference architecture	An architecture that is generic for an entire industry.
Information	What business needs/wants to know. Information is exploitable by people.
JSON	JavaScript Object Notation is a programming language independent format to describe and store attribute-value pairs. It is used for transferring content from server provider to service user in a web-service context.
Logical application architecture	Architecture based on the business functionality provided by applications.
MECE	Mutually Exclusive, Collectively Exhaustive.
Microservice	A microservice is a tightly scoped, strongly encapsulated, loosely coupled, independently deployable and independently scalable application component (Gartner Glossary).
Model	An abstract representation of reality. The concepts that are used to model the reality are: – Model elements: "something that plays a role in the modeled reality"; – Relationships between the model elements.
Non-functional requirements	Requirements relating to the way functionality is delivered and guaranteed over time, e.g. response times, availability, recoverability.
Pattern	A combination of building blocks (types) that provide a solution to a recurring (type of) problem.
Reference architecture	An architecture that steers the design of solutions and their end-to-end embedding in the enterprise architecture, by providing reference models, patterns, principles and guidelines, and by prescribing standards. A reference architecture is not implemented as such; it steers the landscape architectures that are actually implemented and ensures their consistency and quality.
Requirement	A statement of need that must be met.
REST	Representational State Transfer, a software architectural style that defines a set of rules to be used for creating webservices.
Service	A valuable functionality, corresponding to a need.
SoR System of Record	System of Record, a data store (and the application that manages it) that is the authoritative source for the designated set of data.
Standard	An imperative guideline.
System	An organized collection of parts (possibly organized in subsystems) that are highly integrated to accomplish an overall goal. A system can be on a business, application or technology level. It delivers results to other systems or people.

Term/abbreviation	Explanation
System architecture	Architecture of a system. A system's architecture coincides with the high-level design for that system, a system's design is the pattern for its development.
Technology architecture	Architecture of the technology layer.
Technology layer	Technology point of view on a bank's ecosystem. The technology layer offers infrastructural services (e.g., processing, storage and communication services) needed to run applications, realized by hardware and system software.
TOGAF	The TOGAF® Standard, a standard of The Open Group, is a proven enterprise architecture methodology and framework used by the world's leading organizations to improve business efficiency (The Open Group (2018)).
TOGAF ADM	Architecture Development Method. An iterative sequence of steps to develop an enterprise-wide architecture.
Wrapping	Applying a coding layer that enables the interactions with an application and transforms them to a desired format, without having to change the application.

Appendix 3 Feedback to the Test yourself questions

■ FEEDBACK SECTION 1.5

1. **What is not part of the BIAN Framework?**

   Answer: B

   BIAN does not prescribe architecture methodology, tooling or modeling language. The BIAN Framework can enrich the existing architecture practices of the bank.

2. **The goal of the BIAN Association is to develop the most important content, concepts and methods in interoperability, supporting the aim of lower integration costs in the financial services industry and facilitating business innovation and agility.**
   Which statement does not express how BIAN seeks to achieve this?

   Answer: D

   BIAN aims at acceptance by the members of the BIAN Association and the industry of the way the requirements will be implemented by both financial institutions and solution suppliers, resulting in the defined services becoming the de-facto-standard in the financial services industry.

3. **What statements describe the BIAN approach?**

   Answer: C, D

   BIAN promotes a component- and service-based approach, not a process-driven one. Components, providing each other services, are the "ingredients" that can flexibly support any "behavior" (process) when provided according to a well-elaborated "enterprise plan" (enterprise architecture). Process-based architectures lead to duplications, point-to-point connections and uncontrollable complexity.

BIAN is technology agnostic.

■ FEEDBACK SECTION 2.11

1. **Which statements are not true?**

   Answer: B, C, D

   The Service Landscape is not meant as a design blueprint, actually BIAN has used several representations over the years.

   Business Scenarios are archetypical examples of Service Domain orchestrations, they depict how BIAN Service Domains might work together through Service Operations in response to an event. They are not meant as standards for the financial industry and the collection BIAN offers is not meant to be exhaustive.

   Service Domains are mutually-exclusive and collectively-exhaustive. There is no functional redundancy between the Service Domains and, together, they cover all functionality required by a bank.

2. **Which statements are true?**

   Answer: all

3. **Which statements express how the BIAN BOM can be trusted to provide the financial sector with a reference model for information architecture?**

   Answer: C, D

   A Control Record can indeed be decomposed into Behavior Qualifiers, but this results in a hierarchical Control Record Model. This is "remodeled" by applying the Business Object Modeling approach (with its BOM content and structure patterns) into the Service Domain Business Object Model.

   These patterns ensure the consistency of the Service Domain BOMs.

4. **Which statements illustrate how BIAN seeks to provide standards for service interchanges?**

Answer: B, C

A Service Operation is characterized by its Action Term. For each Functional Pattern, a set of Actions Terms is defined. A Service Domain with a certain Functional Pattern will have Service Operations corresponding to these Action Terms.

BIAN Semantic Endpoint descriptions are far from implementation specifications. The BIAN Service Domain Service Operation descriptions that can be found on the BIAN Semantic API Portal are formatted to look like a REST endpoint specification simply as means of easing their adoption by developers familiar with the REST architecture style. It is important for developers to recognize early on that these semantic descriptions are some way from implementation level specifications. The Swagger File can only be considered as a code stub.

■ FEEDBACK SECTION 4.4

1. **Which of these statements express valid reasons for customizing the BIAN Architecture?**

Answer: A, B, C

2. **How can the BIAN standards be used, which statements are correct?**

Answer A, B, C

3. **Right or wrong: The use of BIAN only makes sense if it is done systematically, for the entire enterprise and in all change initiatives.**

Answer: B, wrong

The fact that it is not a "give or take", but can be a one-off, can be introduced gradually, can be used in only parts of a bank... is an advantage of BIAN. It is correct that the more it is used, the greater the benefits will be.

■ FEEDBACK SECTION 5.5

1. Which statements correctly express the role of the Service Domain Frame of Reference?

   Answer: all

2. Which statements correctly express why the Service Landscape (especially the Value Chain representation) is well suited as a quick start for an enterprise blueprint?

   Answer: A, C

   Business Areas in any Service Landscape representation BIAN provides, are not meant to represent organizational units. They are not part of the "BIAN Standard" and are not expected to be mirrored in an bank's blueprint. They are meant as a visual aid in the Service Landscape representation and to make the great number of Service Domains better accessible.

   Service Domains are stable, elemental and MECE, hence they are suitable for describing the functionality of any bank or organizational or legal entity but they are not mandatorily present.

3. Which of these statements do not represent the possible use of an enterprise blueprint as a Frame of Reference for analysis?

   Answer: A

   Business Capabilities are composed of Service Domains and their value and risk can be passed on to the Service Domains. Business Capabilities however are no building blocks for the Frame of Reference.

■ FEEDBACK SECTION 6.4

1. Which statements do not correctly describe why BIAN can provide support for business architecture?

   Answer: B

   Business Scenarios provided by BIAN are archetypical examples but not standards.

Appendix 3 Feedback to the Test yourself questions   235

2. **Which statements correctly describe what overlaying the business landscape on the Service Domain-based Frame of Reference facilitates?**

Answer: all

3. **Which statements express why BIAN can provide support for business architecture?**

Answer: B, C

A is not correct because Wireframes support the specification of business requirements but are not functionality building blocks, hence they are not suitable as anchor points for organization-independent requirements specification. The requirements related to Service Domains (and Service exchanges) from different business scenarios should be consolidated on a Service Domain level.

D is not correct because Business Areas and Business Domains are only groupings of Service Domains, not instruments for delimiting projects. Projects are delimited based on, amongst other things, impact analysis and migration scenarios. Service Domains are instruments that support these activities.

■ FEEDBACK SECTION 7.6

1. **Which of following statements correctly describe how BIAN can support application architecture and application design?**

Answer: B, C

Well-designed application components are relevant, regardless of the architecture style. They do not need to coincide with one and only one Service Domain, they can cover Service Domain clusters, or they can cover reusable functionality on a finer grain than Service Domains.

2. **Which of following statements does not describe a use of the Frame of Reference provided by BIAN?**

Answer: D

The coverage of an application platform is only one element in the evaluation of its quality. Its conformance to requirements is another and so is how future-proof it is (factors might include componentization and service enablement).

3. Which of following statements are not true?

Answer: A, B

Legacy applications can be optimized by externalizing functionality that needs to be entrusted to other applications (calling services and eliminating the corresponding code) and by using wrapping techniques to externalize services they are expected to provide. Business Scenarios and the corresponding Wireframe need to cover the end-to-end embedding of a system in the bank. This enables an optimal delimitation of the new system(s) and their embedding in the application platform.

■ FEEDBACK SECTION 8.5

1. Which of these statements is not true?

Answer: A

A bank can tailor the BIAN BOM to its own specificities as long as the BOM patterns are respected. Tailoring the Service Landscape should go hand-in-hand with tailoring the BOM and vice versa, as conformance with the BIAN principles is a prerequisite for any tailoring.

2. Which statements correctly describe the way in which the BIAN BOM can support data architecture?

Answer: all

3. Which statement is true?

Answer: A

Both depict the same information needs, but with different modeling conventions and from another point of view.

■ FEEDBACK SECTION 9.5

1. Which statements are not true?

Answer: C

BIAN is strictly semantic.

Appendix 3 Feedback to the Test yourself questions

2. **Which statements do not correctly describe how BIAN can support interoperability within a bank and between banks and partners?**

   Answer: B, C

   Service users that switch between BIAN-aligned physical implementations can expect to have to make changes to the implemented field-level mappings and local processing logic, but the overall business logic should remain stable.

   Swagger files, generated from the Semantic API specifications, can be used as code stub, but this is no working application service.

3. **Which statements are correct?**

   Answer: A, B, C

   Well-designed services are relevant in all environments and for all application architecture styles.

■ FEEDBACK SECTION 10.3

1. **Which of these statements do not describe how BIAN can contribute to the organization and exploitation of the Enterprise Repository?**

   Answer: C

   Business Scenarios are a) not BIAN standards and b) not elemental stable building blocks. Hence they are not suitable to "overlay" or act as an "index" to organize documentation.

2. **Which of these statements correctly describe the role that BIAN can play in the TOGAF framework?**

   Answer: A, D

   BIAN offers an architecture that is relevant for all financial institutions. It offers building blocks that a bank can use to compose an organization-specific architecture. It covers all of the functionality a bank requires on a high, semantic level.

3. **Which of these statements do not describe how BIAN can be used in the TOGAF ADM?**

   Answer: A

   BIAN is semantic and does not make statements about technology.

■ FEEDBACK SECTION 11.4

1. **Is the following statement concerning the BIAN standards right or wrong?**

   Answer: Wrong

   BIAN wants to provide an exhaustive reference architecture for the financial industry while aligning with other standards where relevant.

Appendix 4   Literature and sources

BIAN Architecture Working Group (2017a). Banking Use Cases supported by BIAN. Unpublished discussion document.
BIAN Architecture Working Group (2017b). *Driving Value with BIAN*. Unpublished discussion document.
Blair, A., & Marshall, S. (2016). *Open Group Guide: Business Capabilities*. The Open Group.
Derde, P. & Alaerts, M. (2019). Archi Banking Group: Combining the BIAN Reference Model, ArchiMate® Modeling Notation, and the TOGAF® Framework [White paper]. The Open Group.
Gartner Glossary. Retrieved January 2021 from www.gartner.com/en/information-technology/glossary/microservice
Ginsburgh, H. (2015). Using BIAN in vendor selection [Case study]. BIAN Association.
Homann, U. (2006). A business-oriented foundation for service orientation. Microsoft Developer Network.
Knaepen, K., & Brooms, D. (2013). *A complete and consistent business: Introduction to the COSTA model for business architects*. Lannoo Meulenhoff.
Petroni, A., Nandakumar, S., Spadafora P (2020). A cloud-native approach to accelerate BIAN implementation, in the open source way [Webinar]. BIAN Association.
Plais, A. (2020). Global Open Banking Initiatives and the added value of the BIAN Open Standards [webinar]. BIAN Association.
PNC Bank (2020). Adoption of BIAN APIs in Day-to-Day Development [Webinar]. BIAN Association.
Qumer, A., & Henderson-Sellers, B. (2008). A framework to support the evaluation, adoption and improvement of agile methods in practice. Journal of Systems and Software 81(11): 1899-1919.
Rackham, G. (2020). BIAN Semantic API Practitioner's Guide. BIAN Association.
Rettig C. (2007). The trouble with enterprise software Has enterprise software become too complex to be effective?. MIT Sloan Management Review fall 2007.
The BIAN Association, Rackham, G. Tesselaar, H. & de Groot, K. (2018). *BIAN Edition 2019 - A framework for the financial services industry*. Van Haren Publishing.
The Open Group (2018). *The TOGAF® Standard - Version 9.2*. Van Haren Publishing
The Open Group (2019). *ArchiMate® 3.1 Specification*. Van Haren Publishing.
Wikipedia, de vrije encyclopedie. Retrieved January 2021 from https://nl.wikipedia.org/wiki/Application_programming_interface

Index

A
Action Term   32, 34, 41, 61, 62, 67, 195
Action Term Group   185
API Portal   23, 69, 192
API Swagger File. See: Swagger File
Asset Type   32, 34, 40, 44, 46, 47, 53

B
Behavior Qualifier   33, 34, 46, 48, 53, 64, 92, 94, 95, 174, 195
Behavior Qualifier Type   33, 34, 46, 49, 94
BIAN API Portal. See: API Portal
BIAN-based reference architecture. See: Enterprise reference architecture
BIAN BOM   IX, 12, 13, 19, 22, 52, 61, 86, 92, 171, 173, 175, 176, 179, 180, 181, 193, 195, 196, 206, 213, 214
BIAN Business Object Model. See: BIAN BOM
BIAN digital repository   23
BIAN Framework   21, 206
BIAN Metamodel   23, 31
BIAN Reference Architecture. See: Reference Architecture for the Financial Industry
BIAN Service Landscape. See: Service Landscape
BOM content pattern   55, 94
BOM structure pattern   56, 94
Business Area   32, 34, 36, 39, 93, 125, 146, 185
Business Capability   33, 34, 73, 102, 214

C
Business Domain   32, 34, 36, 39, 93, 125, 146, 185
Business Object   12, 33, 35, 52, 61, 86, 171, 173, 175, 179, 185, 186, 206, 208, 213, 228
Business Scenario   33, 35, 70, 129, 133, 135, 164, 193, 194, 206

C
Control Record   33, 35, 46, 47, 53, 63, 67, 92, 94, 149, 172, 174, 195, 208
Control Record Diagram   51, 69
Control Record pattern   46, 94

E
Enterprise architecture governance   125, 146, 179, 185, 207
Enterprise reference architecture   90, 129, 132, 136, 148, 152, 158, 160, 164, 188, 190, 192, 201, 207
Externalization   154

F
First Order Connection   70
Frame of Reference   13, 81, 85, 92, 99, 105, 108, 122, 129, 131, 133, 135, 143, 147, 149, 151, 155, 157, 158, 159, 173, 175, 176, 180, 184, 187, 188, 201, 206

Functional Pattern   32, 35, 40, 41, 46, 47, 49, 62, 94

G

Generic Artifact   33, 35, 41, 47, 49, 53, 94

I

Information Profile   46, 61, 64, 134, 149, 171, 195
Investment and change portfolio management   113, 131, 158, 180, 191
ISO20022   IX, 10, 59, 213

P

Performance management   89, 112, 123

R

Reference Architecture for the Financial Industry   5, 6, 17, 21, 23, 31, 146, 148, 152, 165, 190, 205, 206
Requirement management   89, 109, 126, 135, 159, 180

S

Semantic API   11, 22, 23, 33, 35, 61, 65, 192
Semantic API Endpoint   33, 35, 61, 65, 86, 167, 174, 190, 192, 194, 195, 206, 208
Semantic API Endpoint Message   33, 35, 61, 206

Semantic API Swagger. See: Swagger File
Service Connection   36, 70, 72, 159, 193, 194
Service Domain   5, 11, 32, 35, 36, 40, 68, 86, 91, 92, 103, 105, 108, 122, 123, 125, 126, 129, 132, 133, 136, 143, 147, 149, 152, 155, 157, 158, 159, 160, 167, 171, 173, 174, 175, 184, 187, 188, 206, 228
Service Domain BOM   53, 94, 171, 173, 181
Service Domain BOM Diagram   59, 69
Service Domain Business Object Model. See: Service Domain BOM
Service Domain Overview Diagram   68
Service Domain pattern   40, 94
Service Domain Semantic API. See: Semantic API
Service Landscape   5, 13, 16, 21, 32, 36, 86, 92, 95, 105, 125, 129, 146, 173, 184, 207, 209
Service Operation   36, 61, 62, 64, 65, 70, 71, 72, 86, 91, 135, 149, 155, 167, 184, 185, 188, 190, 192, 194, 206, 228
Service Operation Group   62, 69, 185
Service Operation pattern   61
Swagger File   33, 34, 62, 68, 192, 195

W

Wireframe   33, 36, 70, 72, 133, 135, 160, 193, 194